COMPREHENSIVE TRAVEL GUIDE

LOS ANGELES '93-'94

by Dan Levine

PRENTICE HALL TRAVEL

NEW YORK • LONDON • TORONTO • SYDNEY • TOKYO • SINGAPORE

FROMMER BOOKS

Published by Prentice Hall General Reference
A division of Simon & Schuster Inc.
15 Columbus Circle
New York, NY 10023

ISBN 0-671-84702-3
ISSN 0899-3238

Design by Robert Bull Design
Maps by Geografix Inc.

Frommer's Editorial Staff
Editorial Director: Marilyn Wood
Editorial Manager/Senior Editor: Alice Fellows
Senior Editor: Lisa Renaud
Editors: Charlotte Allstrom, Thomas F. Hirsch, Peter Katucki, Sara Hinsey Raveret, Theodore Stavrou
Assistant Editors: Margaret Bowen, Lee Gray, Christopher Hollander, Ian Wilker
Editorial Assistant: Gretchen Henderson
Managing Editor: Leanne Coupe

Special Sales
Bulk purchases of Frommer's Travel Guides are available at special discounts. The publishers are happy to custom-make publications for corporate clients who wish to use them as premiums or sales promotions. We can excerpt the contents, provide covers with corporate imprints, or create books to meet specific needs. For more information write to Special Sales, Prentice Hall Travel, Paramount Communications Building, 15 Columbus Circle, New York, NY 10023

Manufactured in the United States of America

CONTENTS

LIST OF MAPS

INVITATION TO THE READERS

In researching this book, I have come across many wonderful establishments, the best of which I have included here. I am sure that many of you will also come across appealing hotels, inns, restaurants, guesthouses, shops, and attractions. Please don't keep them to yourself. Share your experiences, especially if you want to comment on places that have been included in this edition that have changed for the worse. You can address your letters to:

Dan Levine
Los Angeles '93–'94
c/o Prentice Hall Travel
15 Columbus Circle
New York, NY 10023

A DISCLAIMER

Readers are advised that prices fluctuate in the course of time and travel information changes under the impact of the varied and volatile factors that affect the travel industry. Neither the authors nor the publisher can be held responsible for the experiences of readers while traveling. Readers are invited to write to the publisher with ideas, comments, and suggestions for future editions.

SAFETY ADVISORY

Whenever you're traveling in an unfamiliar city or country, stay alert. Be aware of your immediate surroundings. Wear a moneybelt and keep a close eye on your possessions. Be particularly careful with cameras, purses, and wallets, all favorite targets of thieves and pickpockets.

CHAPTER 1

INTRODUCING LOS ANGELES

Bustling Los Angeles is not just a microcosm of the United States, it is a magnification of America, and all that's good and bad about this country. Los Angeles is the personification of American fulfillment, revealing both the country's shadow and its strength. Nowhere in the world are dreams more likely to be realized than in Los Angeles, a city that embraces the new and different to an almost disturbing extreme.

Los Angeles has always been a fantasyland of dreams and ambition, a sunny pleasure ground of movie and TV studios and Disneyland extravaganzas, a place where inhibitions are released and imagination given full rein—an entranceway to the real-life magic of southern California. The city is, and always has been, a haven for the offbeat and eccentric, somehow coexisting with what has been called "the most seriously dedicated conservative constituency in America."

Whether you agree with the direction it's headed or not, Los Angeles continues to be a trend-setter, leading the nation toward a lifestyle that includes shopping malls, sprawling suburbs, jogging, holistic medicine, and roller skating. It's also one of the most fashion-conscious cities in the world (albeit, mostly tasteless), trailing only New York, Paris, and Milan.

Much of the unofficial capital of southern California sprawls across endless miles of flat, uneventful terrain, marked by monotonous housing developments and unending strip malls. Yet the city is also packed with arresting sights and tremendous variety. In both quality and quantity, L.A. has some of the best restaurants in the world, yet for many status-conscious Angelenos, food often takes a back seat to seeing and being seen. Since Los Angeles is home of the world's most important film industry, it may be difficult for people to distinguish art from reality on the streets of Santa Monica or Hollywood. And yet this smoggy suburbia, crisscrossed by an astonishing number of freeways, is somehow intensely magnetic. A colossal technicolor ode to pop culture, Los Angeles is a scene like no other. The variety of lifestyles, activities, and places to see can be

WHAT'S SPECIAL ABOUT LOS ANGELES

Film and TV Studios

- ☐ Universal Studios Hollywood—more an amusement park than a backstage tour, but fun!
- ☐ The Burbank Studios, an intimate look into the world of television production.
- ☐ Tapings at NBC of any number of game shows—fun to watch, even more fun to participate in as a contestant.

Museums

- ☐ The J. Paul Getty Museum, reputedly the most heavily endowed museum in the world.
- ☐ The Rancho La Brea Tar Pits, a prehistoric find in the center of one of the world's most contemporary cities.

Hollywood Sights

- ☐ The Walk of Fame, where you can see your favorite stars honored on the world's most famous sidewalk.
- ☐ Mann's Chinese Theatre, fantastic for its unusual architecture but best known for the stars' hand- and footprints (and occasionally noses) pressed in cement in the theater's forecourt.
- ☐ The "Hollywood" sign, internationally recognized symbol of the city of film.

Shopping

- ☐ Rodeo Drive, the poshest street in Beverly Hills, contains the city's most chic shops.
- ☐ Santa Monica, fun shopping by the sea.
- ☐ Melrose Avenue, the place to go for youth-oriented, cutting-edge street fashions.
- ☐ Malls, where Los Angeles really shops.

Beaches

- ☐ Zuma Beach, Malibu's famous seafront stretch is one of the largest and most popular in Los Angeles.
- ☐ Santa Monica, easy to reach and jam-packed on hot summer weekends.
- ☐ Southern beaches, great for swimming and sunning.

Theme Parks

- ☐ Disneyland, the most famous of them all, is the state's largest single tourist attraction.
- ☐ Knott's Berry Farm, close to Disneyland, was really a farm that almost accidentally became a theme park.

mind-boggling. Forget your preconceptions and discover L.A. for what it is—a glitzy, grimy, glittery, and gritty study in contemporary Americana. Whether you love it or hate it, no life can be called complete without having had at least one good look at L.A.

1. CULTURE, HISTORY & BACKGROUND

CULTURAL & SOCIAL LIFE

When most first-time visitors think of L.A., they think of Beverly Hills and Bel Air, and are awed not only by the beauty of these residential areas, but primarily by the apparent endless wealth of their residents. What most visitors don't imagine is the cultural, social, and economic mix that typifies most of the city. In general, hilltops and oceanfronts are the city's highest priced parcels, often topped with spectacular homes. But for every rich landlord there are countless struggling tenants, whose work-a-day lifestyles are Los Angeles' real bread and butter. Mexican immigrants, who often occupy blue-collar jobs, make up the largest segment of the city's non-native population. Large communities of Mexican-Americans can be found in almost every section of L.A.

HISTORY

EUROPEAN DISCOVERY & COLONIZATION

Although very little remains to mark the existence of West Coast Native Americans, anthropologists estimate that as many as half a million aboriginals flourished on this naturally abundant land for thousands of years before the arrival of Europeans in the mid-16th century. Sailing from a small colony, established 10 years before, on the southern tip of the Baja (Lower) California, Portuguese explorer Juan Rodríguez Cabrilho (in the service of Spain) is credited with being the first European to "discover" California, in 1542. Over the next 200 years, dozens of sailors mapped the coast, including British explorer Sir Francis Drake, who sailed his *Golden Hind* into what is now called Drake's Bay, north of San Francisco, in 1579; and Spanish explorer Sebastian Vizcano, who, in 1602, bestowed most of the place-names that survive today.

THE FOUNDATION OF LOS ANGELES

European colonial competition and Catholic missionary zeal prompted Spain to establish settlements along the Alta (Upper) California coast and claim the lands as its own. In 1769, Father Junípero Serra, accompanied by 300 soldiers and clergy, began

DATELINE

- **1542** Juan Cabrilho enters San Diego Bay and sails up the California coast in the first documented visit by a European.
- **1579** Sir Francis Drake drops anchor in the area of San Francisco Bay and claims the land for England's Queen Elizabeth I.
- **1602** Spanish explorer and merchant Sebastian Vizcano sails up the coast and names many areas.
- **1769–76** Spanish missions are founded along the so-called Royal Road (Camino Real) from San Diego to Sonoma.
- **1775** Juan Manu-

(continues)

forging a path from Mexico to Monterey. A small mission and presidio (fort) were established early that year at San Diego, and a few months later, in August 1769, Los Angeles came into being.

Los Angeles was "discovered" by Gaspar de Portola and Father Crespi. What their expedition really found was a small Indian village, which they named "Pueblo del Rio de Nuestra Señora la Reina de los Angeles."

By 1804, the Spanish missionaries had erected a chain of 21 missions, each a day's walk from the next along a dirt road called Camino Real (Royal Road), stretching all the way from San Diego to Sonoma.

During that time, thousands of Native Americans were converted to Christianity and coerced into labor. Many others died from imported diseases. Because not all the natives welcomed their conquerors with open arms, many missions and pueblos (small towns) suffered from repeated attacks, leading to the construction of California's now ubiquitous, fireproof red-tile roofs.

No settlement had more than 100 inhabitants when Spain's sovereignty was compromised by an 1812 Russian outpost called Fort Ross, 60 miles north of San Francisco. But the biggest threat came from the British—who had strengthened their own claims to America with the Hudson's Bay Company trading firm—and their short-lived, last-ditch effort to win back their territories in the War of 1812.

Embattled at home as well as abroad, the Spanish finally relinquished their claim to Mexico and to Spain's California possessions in 1821. Under Mexican rule, Alta California's Spanish missionaries fell out of favor and lost much of their land to the increasingly wealthy Californios—Mexican immigrants who'd been granted vast tracts of land.

AMERICAN EXPANSION Beginning in the late 1820s, Americans from the East began to make their way to California, via a three-month sail around Cape Horn. Most of them settled in the territorial capital of Monterey and in northern California.

From the 1830s on, motivated in part by the doctrine of Manifest Destiny—an almost religious belief that the United States was destined to cover the continent from coast to coast—more and more settlers headed West. Among them were daring explorers. In 1843, Marcus Whitman, a missionary, seeking to prove that settlers could travel overland through the Oregon Territory's Blue Mountains, helped blaze the Oregon Trail; the first covered-wagon train made the four-month transcontinental trip in 1844. Over the next few years, several hundred Americans traveled to California over the Sierra Nevada range via Truckee Pass, just north of Lake Tahoe.

As increasing numbers of people moved West, the U.S. government sought to extend its control over Mexican territory north of the Rio Grande, the river that now separates the United States from Mexico. In 1846, President James Polk offered Mexico $40 million for California and New Mexico. The offer might have been accepted, but America's simultaneous annexation of Texas, to which Mexico still laid claim, resulted in a war between the two countries. Within months, the United States overcame Mexico and took possession of the entire West Coast.

In January 1847, Los Angeles was claimed for the United States by Commodore Stockton and General Stephen Kearny.

GOLD & STATEHOOD   In 1848, California's non-Native American population numbered about 7,000. That same year, flakes of gold were discovered by workers who were building a sawmill along the American River. Word of the discovery spread quickly. By 1850 the state's population approached 93,000, although very few settlers found significant gold. Within 15 years interest in gold had waned, but the new residents intended to stay.

In 1850, California was admitted to the Union as the 31st state. The state constitution on which California applied for admission included several noteworthy provisions. In order to protect the miners, slavery was prohibited. To attract women from the East Coast, legal recognition was given to a married woman's own property. (California was the first state to offer such recognition.) By 1870, almost 90% of the state's Native American population had been wiped out,

DATELINE

called Bear Flag Republic is proclaimed; California is drawn into the Mexican-American War; the U.S. flag is raised in Yerba Buena (San Francisco) and Los Angeles.
- **1847** Yerba Buena is renamed San Francisco.
- **1848** James Wilson Marshall discovers gold at Coloma, on the south fork of the American River.
- **1849** The Gold Rush is in full swing. A constitutional convention meets in Monterey; San Jose becomes the state capital.
- **1850** California, with a population of nearly 93,000, becomes the 31st state.
- **1854** Sacramento becomes the permanent state capital.
- **1862** The first telegraph line is established between San Francisco and New York.
- **1864** A state parks system is created. Samuel Clemens arrives in California and signs himself "Mark Twain."
- **1867** Anti-Chinese demonstrations erupt in San Francisco in the wake of rising immigration.

(continues)

and most of the rest were removed to undesirable inland reservations.

Mexican and Chinese laborers were brought in to help local farmers as well as to work on the transcontinental railroad, which was completed in 1869. The new rail line, which could transport Easterners to California in just five days, marked a turning point in the settlement of the West. In 1875, when the Santa Fe Railroad reached Los Angeles, southern California's population of just 10,000 was divided equally between Los Angeles and San Diego.

In 1885 the Southern Pacific and the Santa Fe rail companies—fierce competitors—reduced their fares to only $1 from cities on the Mississippi River to Los Angeles. Another "rush" was on. Of course, not everybody came by rail. It is said that Charles F. Lummis (1859–1928), later to become a well-known writer, editor, and historian of the Southwest, walked from Cincinnati! Obviously, he was a man to take his own advice: He originated the slogan "See America First."

GROWTH AND THE FILM INDUSTRY

Los Angeles really began to grow in the second decade of the 20th century, when the film industry moved there from the East Coast to take advantage of cheap land and a warm climate that allowed movies to be shot outdoors year round. By 1912, 16 motion picture companies were operating out of Hollywood. Films such as *Birth of a Nation* (1915), established Hollywood in the eyes of the world and earned for its director, D. W. Griffith, the moniker "father of American cinema."

By World War I the Hollywood studio system was firmly entrenched, led by the young trio of Charles Chaplin, Douglas Fairbanks, Sr., and Mary Pickford. William S. Hart rode into the hearts of Saturday-afternoon moviegoers as the first prototype of the American Western hero, while Theodosia Goodman, daughter of an Ohio haberdasher, vamped across the screen as Theda Bara.

In the '20s, salaries and box office receipts multiplied fantastically. An opulent spending spree was launched as each star or producer tried to outdo the other. Newly rich stars created a mystique of luxury and glamour. Valentino, as *The Sheik*, electrified women around the world. Mae Murray, the eternal *Merry Widow* with "bee-stung" lips, was "self-enchanted." Clara Bow, with her red chow dogs to match her flaming hair, was the "It" girl. And Cecil B. DeMille saw to it that Gloria Swanson took a lot of on-screen baths!

On August 6, 1926, the Manhattan Opera House in New York screened Vitaphone's *Don Juan,* with John Barrymore. Although the great actor didn't speak, there was background music. Warner Brothers released *The Jazz Singer,* with Al Jolson, in October of the following year, and the Talkie Revolution was on. Garbo could speak, albeit with a Swedish accent, but her romantic leading man, John Gilbert, couldn't—at least not very well. The invasion of voice-trained Broadway stage stars began, including the likes of Tallulah Bankhead, who made a number of films but later said, "I'd rather forget about them."

Perhaps no invader was as formidable as Mae West, who wondered if she could "show my stuff" in a "land of palm trees, restaurants shaped like derby hats, goose-fleshed bathing beauties, and far-flung custard pies." She could and did! Her invitation to "Come up 'n' see me sometime" was accepted around the world, and she became a phenomenal success at the box office. Or, to use her own modest summation: "More people had seen me than saw Napoleon, Lincoln, and Cleopatra. I was better known than Einstein, Shaw, or Picasso."

The '30s marked the rise of some of Hollywood's greatest stars: Bette Davis, Joan Crawford, Humphrey Bogart, Cary Grant, Jean Harlow, Clark Gable, James Cagney, Marlene Dietrich, Gary Cooper, Shirley Temple, James Stewart, Katharine Hepburn, Spencer Tracy, and Claudette Colbert. The decade was climaxed by the release of the Civil War classic *Gone with the Wind.*

The movies' glamorous, idyllic portrayal of California boosted the region's popularity and population, especially during the Great Depression of the 1930s, when thousands of

DATELINE

- **1919** William Randolph Hearst breaks ground on San Simeon castle.
- **1921** Oil is discovered at Signal Hill.
- **1922** The Hollywood Bowl amphitheater opens.
- **1924** The first transcontinental airmail flight takes place from San Francisco to New York.
- **1925** An earthquake hits Santa Barbara.
- **1927** The first "talkie" is released—*The Jazz Singer,* with Al Jolson.
- **1929** The Academy of Motion Pictures Arts and Sciences bestows its first Oscar.
- **1930s** Hollywood's heyday. Great stars like Bette Davis, Joan Crawford, Humphrey Bogart, Cary Grant, Jean Harlow, Clark Gable, James Cagney, and Shirley Temple become household names.
- **1936** The San Francisco–Oakland Bay Bridge opens.
- **1937** The Golden Gate Bridge opens.
- **1939** John Steinbeck writes *Grapes of Wrath,* about migrants to California.
- **1942** California's Japanese-American

(continues)

DATELINE

residents are forcibly relocated to inland camps because of World War II security concerns.

- **1945** The United Nations is founded in San Francisco.

- **1950** California's population swells to more than 10½ million; San Francisco has more than 674,000 residents but is surpassed by Los Angeles, with nearly 2 million.

- **1955** Disneyland opens.

- **1960** San Francisco's Candlestick Park opens.

- **1962** California overtakes New York as the nation's most populous state.

- **1967** The "Summer of Love" is centered in San Francisco's Haight-Ashbury.

- **1968** Robert F. Kennedy is fatally shot in Los Angeles after winning California's Democratic Party presidential primary.

- **1972** The BART system opens in San Francisco.

- **1974** The Oakland Athletics defeat the Los Angeles Dodgers in the World Series.

- **1975** Jerry Brown becomes governor.

- **1980** Since 1950, the population of

(continues)

families packed up their belongings and headed West in search of a better life.

In 1940 Dudley C. Gordon wrote: "Having survived a long, leisurely pioneering infancy, and an uncouth adolescence characterized by intensive exploitation, Los Angeles has now blossomed into one of the major cities of the nation." It was at the dawn of great change.

World War II brought heavy industry to southern California, in the form of munitions factories, shipyards, and airplane manufacturing. Freeways were built, military bases were opened, and suburbs were developed.

After the war, the threat of television loomed over Hollywood, but instead of being destroyed by the "tube," Los Angeles was strengthened by it, as the television industry headquartered itself in the region.

In the 1950s, California became popular with artists and intellectuals. The so-called beat generation appeared and inspired later alternative-culture groups, notably the "flower children" of the 1960s. During the "Summer of Love" in 1967, as the war in Vietnam escalated, student protests increased at Berkeley and elsewhere in California, as they did across the country. A year later, amid rising racial tensions, Martin Luther King, Jr., was killed, setting off riots in the Watts section of Los Angeles and in other cities; and Robert F. Kennedy was fatally shot in Los Angeles after winning the California Democratic Party presidential primary.

Indeed, as Los Angeles entered the 1970s, it appeared to some that the dream factory had become a near nightmare. One large studio reported a loss of $67 million; another announced that its 52-acre main lot was for sale. In the months that followed, MGM, which once boasted that it had "more stars than there are in heaven," auctioned off Clark Gable's trench coat. The days of film glory were over, but few doubted that a more stable cinema would emerge and remain as one of Los Angeles' chief attractions and employers.

Perhaps in response to an increasingly violent society, the 1970s also gave rise to several exotic religions and cults, which found eager adherents in California. The spiritual "New Age" continued into the 1980s, along with a growing population, environmental pollution, and escalating social ills. California also became very rich. Real estate values soared; the computer industry, centered in "Silicon Valley," south of San Francisco, boomed; and banks and businesses prospered.

In the early 1990s, southern Californians still like to think of themselves as being on the cutting edge of American society. Whatever happens in the country, they say proudly, takes place here first. But Angelenos, going deeper than their characteristic superficiality, have become keenly concerned about the nation's problems—economic competition from abroad, the environment, drugs, the blight of homelessness, and racial tensions that afflict both large and small cities. The long-range effects of the 1992 Los Angeles riots are not yet clear, but it would seem that the violence has raised society's consciousness about many problems that confront America's inner cities. Los Angeles has become a complex city of

DATELINE

California more than doubles, to nearly 24 million; San Francisco now has some 775,000 inhabitants, while Los Angeles has nearly 3 million.

● **1984** Los Angeles hosts the Summer Olympic Games.

● **1991** The presidential library of Richard Nixon opens in Yorba Linda, his birthplace (1913).

● **1992** Los Angeles experiences the worst race riots in modern American history; more than 40 dead, hundreds injured.

fantasy and reality. Sure, it's a cultural melting pot with major concerns and problems, but it also remains a sunny land of plenty, with dreams and visions that are somehow just as real.

POLITICS

After Democrat Jerry Brown, an avowed liberal, succeeded conservative Republican Governor Ronald Reagan in the 1970s, California gained a reputation for progressive leadership. The state enacted some of the most stringent antipollution measures in the world, actively encouraged the development of renewable forms of energy, and protected the coastline from development and despoliation. At the same time, California emerged at the forefront of the gay-rights movement, and there was a general resurgence of interest among Californians in alternative lifestyles and the exploration of foreign cultures.

Southern California's reputation as a liberal mecca, however, is largely mistaken, for the state, as a whole, has traditionally leaned to the right; Governor Brown's tenure almost seems an aberration. In 1990, Republican Pete Wilson was elected governor, succeeding Republican George Deukmejian, whose conservative fiscal and social policies, consonant with the swing to the right that occurred nationally during the 1980s, he promised to continue.

Wealthy Orange County and, to a lesser extent, Los Angeles (surprisingly) have always been more conservative than the rest of the state. Residents of Orange County, who have consistently voted for right-wing candidates since they firmly supported Barry Goldwater in

1964, are mocked by other Californians as living in splendid isolation behind the "Orange Curtain." San Diego, with a large military presence, is also predominantly Republican, supporting those administrations in Washington that promise to serve its economic interests.

ARCHITECTURE

Los Angeles' buildings reflect several historical styles of architecture. The first, dating from the late 18th century, during the Mexican era, consists of Spanish-style adobe structures, often topped with red-tile roofs. Several structures, primarily missions, exemplify that style. The missions also tended to employ distinctive Native American construction methods.

The second major style, popularized about a century later, reflects a Victorian tendency in design and ornateness. Although this style is more obvious in San Francisco, Victorian homes and offices can be found along the entire California coast.

The city's most interesting and varied buildings are the art deco structures from the 1930s. Kitsch diners and buildings constructed to look like objects were popular in the 1950s, and there are still many examples around Los Angeles.

Concrete was the preferred building material in the late 1960s and in the 1970s; as a consequence, a plethora of rather uniform ugly concrete structures mar almost every urban center. Glass-and-steel office buildings—a trend that took hold in the 1980s—dominate much of downtown Los Angeles, giving it a sleek, futuristic look.

2. FOOD & DRINK

California cuisine is one of the newest and most important genres in regional American cooking. The style stresses local ingredients and light preparations that are both calorie- and health-conscious. "Designer" vegetables are often used, as are fresh local spices and locally produced wines.

A strong Mexican influence is apparent; avocados are everywhere, and salsa is served with almost every meal. Mexican restaurants are the most popular ethnic eateries; you're never very far from a taco or a burrito. Yet nearly every other ethnic cuisine is also represented here. Sushi is fresh and popular; Chinese food, especially in Los Angeles and San Francisco, is excellent; and superior French cuisine can be found in the state's major cities.

The growing emphasis on health food has inspired a debate about whether California's water is safe to drink. Opinions vary, according to various studies. The state consumes more bottled water per capita than any other region in America, but many more locals drink water straight from the tap. Suffice it to say that if you do decide to order bottled water at a restaurant, there are usually plenty of brands, both domestic and foreign, to choose from.

Few will argue, however, with the assertion that California is wine country. You will find that what supremely enhances a good California meal is a bottle of wine from a local growing region. Many state restaurants offer excellent selections, which usually include several good buys. Try some new wines from a vineyard you've never heard of, and enjoy further exploration of a region you may have thought you knew well.

3. RECOMMENDED BOOKS, FILMS & RECORDINGS

BOOKS Almost from the beginning, novelists and poets were an essential part of the mélange that settled in California. Although their personal stays were often in the nature of passing-through, their works have left lasting records of the history of America's fastest changing region. From Mark Twain, who created vivid tales of the Comstock Lode silver mines and 1860s frontier, to Joan Didion and Amy Tan, contemporary novelists who write about the California of their childhoods, there has been no lack of talent here. Writing in between we find Aldous Huxley, who lived in and wrote about California and Hollywood; and Jack Kerouac, who was one of the most influential of the "beat" writers.

John Steinbeck, one of the state's best-known authors, would have earned his reputation with just one of the many books he wrote about life in the center of the state. His *Grapes of Wrath* (which Hollywood turned into a compelling movie) remains the classic account of Midwest migrants coming to California during the Great Depression. *Cannery Row* (also filmed) has forever made the Monterey waterfront famous, and *East of Eden* (one of James Dean's three films) brings deep insight into the way of life in the Salinas Valley.

FILMS Los Angeles' beautiful sites and year-round good weather have always made it a natural for directors searching for captivating, yet relatively inexpensive, film locations. Tens of thousands of movies have been shot here; too many to mention. *California Suite* (1978), Neal Simon's sentimental slapstick script, is set in the Beverly Hills Hotel. *Beverly Hills Cop* (1984), a runaway hit, stars Eddie Murphy in the role of a Detroit police officer in Los Angeles. *Pretty Woman* (1989), starring Richard Gere and Julia Roberts, was filmed in and around Hollywood and the Beverly Wilshire Hotel.

RECORDINGS California has made a major contribution to the American musical scene, from the classical to the popular. Composer Arnold Schoenberg, violinist Jascha Heifetz, and conductor Zubin Mehta are just a few who attracted world attention to Los Angeles and gave the city a fittingly prominent place in classical music. Popular composers from George Gershwin and Jerome Kern to Henry Mancini have enriched America's musical heritage with the songs and scores they wrote for movies, a medium that helped spread American culture abroad and made it as likely you would hear those songs hummed in Paris and Buenos Aires as in New York and St. Louis.

In the past 25 years, the influence of rock music has thrust

California into the forefront of a different musical tradition that has outlasted its critics and been felt as far away as Moscow and Beijing. That tradition derives from the various groups that emerged in the mid-1960s and changed American music. Of those groups, The Grateful Dead, formed in 1965, are the only surviving psychedelic band. Santana, a local band known for their innovative blending of Latin rhythms and low-key jazz vocals, made their debut in California. Soon after, they landed a deal with Los Angeles-based Columbia Records.

In the '60s and '70s, the Beach Boys and the Eagles perfected the "California sound," a blend of sweet harmonies and fun, if somewhat sentimental, lyrics. Of course, The Doors, were one of the most famous bands to come out of Los Angeles. More recent L.A. rockers include Warrent, Guns 'N' Roses, Van Halen, and Motley Crue.

PLANNING A TRIP TO LOS ANGELES

How you get to Los Angeles and how you get around it obviously depend on where you're coming from, how much you want to spend, and how much time you have. It is possible to arrive in L.A. without an itinerary or reservations, but your trip will be much more rewarding with a little bit of advance planning. This chapter will help you discover your options and plan the trip that's best suited to your needs and interests.

1. INFORMATION & MONEY

INFORMATION Tourism is big in Los Angeles, and the city is rich with information on what to see and do. For general information on the city, contact the Los Angeles Convention and Visitors Bureau, 515 S. Figueroa St., 11th Floor, Los Angeles, CA 90071 (tel. 213/689-8822). They will mail you a free information packet.

You should know that almost every city and town in California has a dedicated tourist bureau or chamber of commerce that will be happy to send you information on its particular site. Contact the California Office of Tourism, 1121 L St., Suite 103, Sacramento, CA 95814 (tel. toll free 800/862-2543) for a list of local tourist boards.

Foreign travelers should also check Chapter 3, "For Foreign Visitors," for entry requirements and other pertinent information.

MONEY Soaring real estate prices have made Los Angeles one of America's most expensive cities. U.S. dollar traveler's checks are the safest, most negotiable way to carry currency. They are accepted by most restaurants, hotels, and shops and can be exchanged for cash at banks and check-issuing offices. American Express offices are open weekdays from 9am to 5pm and Saturdays from 9am until noon. See "Fast Facts: Los Angeles" in Chapter 4 for Los Angeles office locations.

Most banks offer Automated Teller Machines (ATMs), which accept cards connected to a particular network. The ubiquitous Security Pacific Bank accepts Plus, Star, and Interlink cards, while First Interstate Bank is on-line with the Cirrus system. Each bank has dozens of branches all around the city. For additional locations, dial toll free 800/424-7787 for the Cirrus network and 800/843-7587 for the Plus system.

Credit cards are widely accepted in Los Angeles. MasterCard and VISA are most common, followed by American Express, Carte Blanche, Diner's Club, and Discover. ATMs at the above-listed banks will make cash advances against MasterCard and VISA cards. American Express cardholders can write a personal check, guaranteed against the card, for up to $1,000 in cash at an American Express office.

Foreign travelers should also see Chapter 3, "For Foreign Visitors," for monetary descriptions and currency exchange information.

WHAT THINGS COST IN LOS ANGELES	U.S. $
Taxi from the airport to downtown	30.00
Bus fare to any destination within the city	1.10
Double at the Beverly Hills Hotel (very expensive)	250.00
Double at the Radisson-Huntley Hotel (expensive)	145.00
Double at the Royal Palace Westwood Hotel (inexpensive)	66.00
Lunch for one at Tom Bergin's Tavern (moderate)	12.00
Lunch for one at Roscoe's House of Chicken (inexpensive)	6.00
Dinner for one, without wine, at L'Ermitage (expensive)	50.00
Dinner for one, without wine, at Antonio's (moderate)	30.00
Dinner for one, without wine, at the Source (inexpensive)	12.00
Glass of beer	2.75
Coca-Cola	1.25
Cup of coffee	.80
Admission to the J. Paul Getty Museum	Free
Movie ticket	7.50
Theater ticket	20.00

2. WHEN TO GO — CLIMATE

Summer is Los Angeles' primary tourist season, but moderate temperatures and year-round visitor services make it a pleasure to travel there during less busy seasons as well. The city is particularly delightful from early autumn to late spring, when skies are bluest; theater, opera, and ballet seasons are in full swing; and restaurants and stores are less crowded.

It's possible to sunbathe throughout the year, but only die-hard enthusiasts and surfers in wet suits venture into the water in winter. You can swim in spring, summer, and fall, though the Pacific is still quite chilly.

CLIMATE

Los Angeles is usually much warmer than the Bay Area, and it gets significantly more sun. L.A.'s beaches are the golden sands that have given the entire state a worldwide reputation for tropical temperatures and the laid-back lifestyle they encourage. Even in winter, daytime thermometer readings regularly reach into the 60s and warmer. Summers can be stifling inland, but this city's beach communities are always comfortable. Don't pack an umbrella. When it rains, southern Californians go outside to look at the novelty.

As you can see from the temperature chart below, Los Angeles remains relatively temperate year round.

Los Angeles' Average Temperatures

	Jan	Feb	Mar	Apr	May	June	July	Aug	Sept	Oct	Nov	Dec
Avg High (°F)	65	66	67	69	72	75	81	81	81	77	73	69
Avg Low (°F)	46	48	49	52	54	57	60	60	59	55	51	49

LOS ANGELES CALENDAR OF EVENTS

JANUARY

✪ **TOURNAMENT OF ROSES** An annual celebration of the first day of the new year. Festivities include the spectacular parade down Colorado Boulevard, famous for its lavish floats, music, and extraordinary equestrian entries; followed by the Rose Bowl Game.
  Where: Pasadena. **When:** January 1. **How:** Contact the Pasadena Tournament of Roses office at 391 S. Orange Grove Blvd., Pasadena, CA 91105 (tel. 818/449-4100) for more details.

☐ **Oshogatsu.** The Japanese New Year is celebrated annually at the Japanese American Cultural and Community Center in Little

Tokyo. Participate in traditional Japanese ceremonies and enjoy ethnic foods and crafts. It takes place during the first weekend in January. For more information, call 213/628-2725.

☐ **Martin Luther King Parade.** Long Beach's annual parade down Alameda and 7th Streets, ending with a festival in Martin Luther King Park. For more information, contact the Council of Special Events (tel. 310/436-7703).

FEBRUARY

☐ **Chinese New Year.** Colorful dragon dancers parade through the streets of downtown's New Chinatown. An event not to be missed. Contact the Chinese Chamber of Commerce, 978 N. Broadway, Suite 206, Los Angeles 90012 (tel. 213/617-0396) for this year's schedule.

MARCH

✪ *LOS ANGELES MARATHON* *It might seem counterproductive healthwise, but this 26.2-mile run through the streets of Los Angeles attracts thousands of participants.*

Where: Downtown Los Angeles. When: Early March. How: Call 213/444-5544 for registration or spectator information.

✪ *AMERICAN INDIAN FESTIVAL AND MARKET* *Showcase and Festival of Native American arts and culture. The fun includes traditional dances, storytelling, and a display of arts and crafts as well as a chance to sample ethnic foods.*

Where: Los Angeles Natural History Museum. When: Late March. How: Admission to museum includes festival tickets. Call 213/744-3314.

APRIL

✪ *RENAISSANCE PLEASURE FAIR* *One of America's largest Renaissance festivals, this annual happening, set in L.A.'s relatively remote countryside, looks very much like an authentic, albeit somewhat touristy, old English village. The fair provides an entire day's activities, shows and festivities, food and crafts. Participants are encouraged to come in costume.*

Where: Glen Ellen Regional Park, San Bernardino. When: Weekends from April through June. How: For ticket information, phone toll free 800/523-2473.

✪ *TOYOTA GRAND PRIX* *An exciting weekend of Indy-class auto racing and entertainment in and around the streets of downtown Long Beach.*

Where: Long Beach. When: Mid-April. How: Contact

Grand Prix Association, 100 W. Broadway, Suite 670, Long Beach, CA 90802 (tel. 310/436-9953).

MAY

✪ ***CINCO DE MAYO*** *A week-long celebration of one of Mexico's most jubilant holidays takes place throughout the city of Los Angeles. The fiesta's carnival-like atmosphere is created by large crowds, live music, dances, and food.*
   Where: *Main festivities held in El Pueblo de Los Angeles State Historic Park, downtown. Other events around the city.* ***When:*** *One week surrounding May 5th.* ***How:*** *Phone 213/628-1274 for information.*

☐ **Redondo Beach Wine Festival.** The largest outdoor wine-tasting event in southern California is held in early May in Redondo Beach. For exact dates of this year's locations, contact the Redondo Chamber of Commerce, 1215 N. Catalina Ave., Redondo Beach, CA 90277 (tel. 310/376-6912).

☐ **National Orange Show.** This 11-day county fair includes various stadium events, celebrity entertainment, livestock shows, and carnival rides. It's held in San Bernardino in mid-May. Phone 714/383-5554 for information.

JUNE

☐ **Greek Festival.** The city salutes its Greek community with a cultural celebration that includes dancers, foods, and crafts. The festival is held in Riverside in early June. Phone 714/787-7950 for information.

☐ **Playboy Jazz Festival.** Usually held in the Hollywood Bowl, this mid-June event is widely recognized for the great artists it attracts. Phone 213/850-2222 for details.

✪ ***ANNUAL GRAND NATIONAL IRISH FAIR AND MUSIC FESTIVAL*** *Bagpipes, Gaelic music, song, and dance ring in this traditional event. You may even see a leprechaun, if you're lucky.*
   Where: *Griffith Park.* ***When:*** *June.* ***How:*** *Phone 213/395-8322 for dates and more information.*

JULY

✪ ***FOURTH OF JULY CELEBRATION*** *Southern California's most spectacular display of fireworks follow an evening of live entertainment.*
   Where: *The Rose Bowl, 1001 Rose Bowl Dr., Pasadena.* ***When:*** *July 4th.* ***How:*** *Phone 818/577-3100 for further information.*

☐ **Fireworks Display at the Marina.** Burton Chase Park in Marina del Rey is a favorite place to view traditional Fourth of

July fireworks. Arrive in the afternoon for best parking and viewing sites.

✪ *HOLLYWOOD BOWL SUMMER FESTIVAL* Summer season at the Hollywood Bowl brings the world's best sounds of jazz, pop, and classical music to an open-air setting. The season includes an annual Fourth of July concert.

    Where: 2301 N. Highland Blvd., Hollywood. *When:* July through mid-September. *How:* Phone the Bowl's box office (tel. 213/850-2000) for information.

✪ *INTERNATIONAL SURF FESTIVAL* Four beachside cities collaborate in the oldest international surf festival in California. Competitions include surfing, boogie boarding, sand-castle building, and other beach-related categories.

    Where: Hermosa Beach/Manhattan Beach/Redondo Beach/Torrance. *When:* The end of July. *How:* Contact the International Surf Festival Committee, 2600 Strand, Manhattan Beach, CA 90266 (tel. 310/546-8843) for information.

AUGUST

☐ **Nisei Week Japanese Festival.** A week-long celebration of Japanese culture and heritage is held in mid-August in the Japanese-American Cultural and Community Center Plaza, in Little Tokyo. Festivities include parades, food, music, arts, and crafts. Phone 213/687-7193 for details.

☐ **African Marketplace & Cultural Fair.** African arts, crafts, food, and music are featured during this mid-August cultural awareness event held in Rancho Cienega Park. Phone 213/734-1164 for more information.

☐ **Long Beach Sea Festival.** The last two weeks of August are dedicated to a variety of water-related events, including a sailboat regatta and jet ski and swimming competitions. Contact the Long Beach Department of Parks and Recreation, 2760 Studebaker Rd., Long Beach, CA 90804 (tel. 310/421-9431) for specific scheduling information.

SEPTEMBER

✪ *LOS ANGELES COUNTY FAIR* Horse racing, arts, agricultural displays, celebrity entertainment, and carnival rides are among the attractions of the largest county fair in the world.

    Where: Los Angeles County Fair and Exposition Center in Pomona. *When:* September. *How:* Call 714/623-3111 for information.

☐ **Long Beach Blues Festival.** An annual outdoor festival featuring top names in blues music, usually held toward the end of September. Call 310/985-5566 for information.

☐ **Annual Bob Hope Celebrity Golf Tournament.** Bob Hope is the honorary chairman of this annual golf tournament in Riverside. For ticket and other information, contact the Riverside Visitors and Convention Bureau, 3443 Orange St., Riverside, CA 92501 (tel. 714/787-7950).

☐ **Bandfest.** Bands participating in the Hollywood Christmas Parade compete in various categories in a battle of the marching bands. Call 213/469-8311 for details.

✪ *HOLLYWOOD CHRISTMAS PARADE This spectacular star-studded parade marches through the heart of Hollywood just after Thanksgiving.*
    ***Where:** Hollywood Boulevard.* ***When:** End of November.* ***How:** For information, phone 213/469-2337.*

3. HEALTH, INSURANCE & OTHER CONCERNS

Health and safety are serious issues. Take a little time before your trip to make sure these concerns don't ruin it. Foreign travelers should see Chapter 3, "For Foreign Visitors," for entry information and other related matters.

INSURANCE Most travel agents sell low-cost health, loss, and trip-cancellation insurance to their vacationing clients. Compare these rates and services with those offered by local banks, as well as your personal insurance carrier.

Most American travelers are covered by their hometown health insurance policies in the event of an accident or sudden illness while away on vacation. Make sure your Health Maintenance Organization (HMO) or insurance carrier can provide services for you in California. If there is any doubt, a health insurance policy that specifically covers your trip is advisable. Foreign travelers should check if they are covered by their home insurance companies and see Chapter 3, "For Foreign Visitors," for more information.

You can also protect your travel investment with travel-related insurance to cover you against lost or damaged baggage and trip-cancellation or interruption costs. These coverages are often combined into a single comprehensive plan, sold through travel agents, credit-card companies, and automobile and other clubs.

SAFETY Innocent tourists are rarely the victims of violent crime. In most major cities, crime is usually a domestic affair and is confined to the poorest parts of town. Still, few locals would recommend that you walk alone at night in South Central Los Angeles. There are few tourist attractions in this area; however, it may interest visitors for sociological reasons. Whenever you're traveling in an unfamiliar city or country, stay alert. Be aware of your immediate surroundings. It is best to carry your valuables in a moneybelt. If your camera or purse has a shoulder strap, wear the strap diagonally across your body to minimize the chance that your camera or purse could be snatched away. Every society has its criminals. It's your responsibility to be aware and alert, even in the most heavily touristed areas.

SUNBURN We now know that the sun is healthful only in moderation. Over a long period of time too much exposure to the sun's rays can be detrimental, and even cause cancer. Sunning can be fun, but you should also take it seriously and exercise precautions.

Protect yourself with a high Sun Protection Factor (SPF) lotion or screen and don't expose yourself to too much sun in one day— especially if you've been out of the sun for months. If you burn easily, a product with an SPF of at least 8 is recommended. Also, wear sunglasses—the kind that block out ultraviolet rays—and bring a hat with a wide bill or rim. You may laugh now, but when you're walking on the beach in the middle of the afternoon, or driving west while the sun is setting, you'll want your hat.

EARTHQUAKES There will always be earthquakes in California—most of which you will never notice. However, in the event of an earthquake, there are a few basic precautionary measures to take whether you're inside a high-rise hotel or out driving or walking.

If you are inside a building, do not run out of the building; instead, move away from windows in the direction of what would be the center of the building. Get under a desk or table, or stand against a wall or under a doorway. If you are in bed, get under the bed, or stand in a doorway, or crouch under a sturdy piece of furniture. When exiting the building, use stairwells, NOT elevators.

If you are in your car, pull over to the side of the road and stop, but wait until you are away from bridges or overpasses, and telephone or power poles and lines. Stay in your car.

If you are out walking, stay outside and away from trees or power lines or the sides of buildings. If you are in an area with tall buildings, find a doorway to stand in.

4. WHAT TO PACK

CLOTHING It's unwise to bring more than you can carry. There is no need to overpack and be a slave to your luggage; many smaller hotels do not have porters. Don't worry if you forget something or need an emergency item. Almost anything you could possibly want can be purchased in Los Angeles.

Warm weather translates into informal dress. Few places require jackets and ties; if you're on vacation, you'll rarely feel out of place without them.

From May through October, weather in Los Angeles warrants

lightweight summer clothing, with a sweater or lightweight jacket for the occasional brisk evening or over-cool restaurant. November through April temperatures are milder, and generally require spring-weight clothing and a raincoat. During winter, it's a good idea to plan for cold snaps and cool nights with clothes appropriate to more northerly climes. Of course, you should bring shorts, a bathing suit, and sunglasses. Keep your rain gear at home; there is little chance that you'll need it.

OTHER ITEMS If you are currently taking medication, pack the prescriptions in case your pills are lost. Eyeglass wearers should also carry their prescriptions.

5. TIPS FOR THE DISABLED, SENIORS & FAMILIES

FOR THE DISABLED Most of Los Angeles' major museums and tourist attractions are fitted with wheelchair ramps to accommodate physically challenged visitors. In addition, several hotels offer special accommodations and services for wheelchair-bound and other disabled visitors. These include large bathrooms, ramps, and telecommunication devices for the deaf. The California Travel Industry Association, 2500 Wilshire Blvd., Suite 603, Los Angeles, CA 90057 (tel. 213/384-3178), provides information and referrals to specially equipped sights and hotels around the city and state. California issues special license plates to physically disabled drivers and honors plates issued by other states. Special "handicapped" parking spots are located near the entrances to most buildings.

FOR SENIORS In California, "senior citizen" usually means anyone who is 65 or older. Seniors regularly receive discounts at museums and attractions; when available, they are listed in the following chapters under their appropriate headings. Ask for discounts everywhere—at hotels, movie theaters, museums, restaurants, and attractions. You may be surprised how often you will be offered reduced rates. When making airline reservations, ask about a senior discount, but find out if there is a cheaper promotional fare before committing yourself.

Older travelers are particularly encouraged to purchase travel insurance (see "Insurance" above) and would be well advised to exercise frugality when packing.

In addition to organizing tours, the American Association of Retired Persons (AARP) Travel Service, 100 North Sepulveda Blvd., Suite 1020, El Segundo, CA 90024, provides a list of travel suppliers who offer discounts to members.

FOR FAMILIES Children add joy and a different level of experience to travel. They help you see things in a different way and can sometimes attract reticent local people like a magnet. Taking kids to California obviously means additional, more thorough planning. On airplanes, special-order children's meals as far in advance as possible.

Most airlines don't carry baby food, but they will be glad to heat up any you've brought with you. Pack essential first-aid supplies, such as Band-Aids, a thermometer, children's pain reliever, and cough drops; and always carry with you some snacks, such as raisins, crackers, and fruit, as well as water or juice.

Frommer's Los Angeles with Kids is an excellent, specialized guide to the city for parents with kids in tow. Los Angeles is full of sightseeing opportunities and special activities geared toward children. In this guide, see the "Cool for Kids" listings for restaurant and hotel suggestions.

6. GETTING THERE

Los Angeles is easy to reach, but not all transportation options are created equal. Shopping around will ensure that you get there the right way at the best price.

BY PLANE

Almost every major scheduled airline flies into Los Angeles International Airport (LAX). Many carriers also service the half-dozen smaller gateways located around the city. If you are not planning to visit the city center, it might be wise to avoid it entirely and fly into a smaller regional airport. Airlines often offer special deals that can make it as cheap to fly into Orange County, for instance, as it is to fly into LAX. Explore this possibility before buying your ticket.

THE MAJOR AIRLINES

Some 36 international airlines, and all major American carriers, serve the Los Angeles International Airport (LAX)—one of the busiest airports in the world. Domestic airlines flying in and out of LAX include Alaska Airlines (tel. toll free 800/426-0333), American Airlines (tel. toll free 800/433-7300), Delta Air Lines (tel. toll free 800/221-1212), Northwest Airlines (tel. toll free 800/225-2525), Southwest Airlines (tel. toll free 800/531-5601), Trans World Airlines (tel. toll free 800/221-2000), United Airlines (tel. toll free 800/241-6522), and USAir (tel. toll free 800/428-4322).

Several smaller carriers are known for the excellent and comprehensive service they provide up and down the California coast. America West (tel. toll free 800/247-5692), American Eagle (tel. toll free 800/433-7300), Skywest (tel. toll free 800/453-9417), United Express (tel. toll free 800/241-6522), and USAir (tel. toll free 800/428-4322) are some of the biggest carriers offering regular service between California cities.

REGULAR FARES Depending on your point of origin, travel agents may not feel it is worth their while to help you find a really inexpensive ticket to Los Angeles. To get the lowest price, I usually do the legwork and make the reservation myself, and then visit my travel agent for ticketing. Check the newspapers for advertisements and call a few of the major carriers before committing yourself.

The cheapest standard economy-class fare usually comes with serious restrictions and steep penalties for altering dates and itineraries. When purchasing these tickets, don't use terms like "APEX" and "excursion" or other airline jargon; just ask for the lowest fare. If you are flexible with dates and times, say so. Ask if you can get a cheaper fare by staying an extra day or by flying during the middle of the week; many airlines won't volunteer this kind of information. At the time of this writing, the lowest round-trip fare to Los Angeles from New York was $398 and from Chicago $298; the lowest round-trip fare to Los Angeles from San Francisco was $198. You may find even cheaper fares.

BUSINESS/FIRST CLASS   Business-class seats can easily cost twice the price of coach seats. When buying a full-fare ticket to Los Angeles, expect to pay about $1,600 from New York and about $1,100 from Chicago. Note, however, that competition is stiff for luxury-class passengers, and prices are sometimes more elastic in this category than they are in economy class. Call several airlines and compare prices before committing yourself.

If you fly first class, expect to pay about $2,500 from New York and about $2,000 from Chicago to Los Angeles. Many short hops to L.A. don't have a first-class section, but when they do, they're predictably expensive.

OTHER GOOD-VALUE CHOICES   Alternatives to tickets from a traditional travel agent have their advantages (usually in lower prices) and their drawbacks (usually in lack of freedom). Don't overlook a consolidator, or "bucket shop," when hunting for domestic fares. By negotiating directly with the airlines, the "buckets" can sell tickets at prices below official rates. On the minus side, consolidators usually don't offer advice and don't book hotels or rental cars. Like the most heavily restricted tickets, these often carry heavy penalties for changing or canceling.

The lowest priced bucket shops are usually local operations with low profiles and overheads. Look for their advertisements in the travel or classified section of your local newspaper. Nationally advertised businesses are usually not as competitive as the smaller, boiler-room operations, but they have toll-free telephone numbers and are easily accessible. Two of the best known are Travac, 989 Sixth Ave., New York, NY 10018 (tel. 212/563-3303, or toll free 800/TRAV-800); and Unitravel, 1177 N. Warson Rd. (P.O. Box 12485), St. Louis, MO 63132 (tel. 314/569-0900, or toll free 800/325-2222).

Competition from the bucket shops, not to mention fierce competition among commercial airlines, has pared the number of charters somewhat, but there are still plenty from which to choose. Most charter operators advertise and sell their seats through travel agents, making these local professionals your best source of information for available flights. Before deciding to take a charter flight, check the restrictions on the ticket. You may be asked to purchase a tour package, to pay far in advance of the flight, to be amenable if the day of departure or the destination is changed, to pay a service charge, to fly on an airline with which you are not familiar (usually this is not the case), and to pay harsh penalties if you cancel but to be understanding if the charter does not fill up and is canceled up to 10 days before departure. Summer charters fill up more quickly than others and are almost sure to fly; if you do decide on a charter flight, seriously consider cancellation and baggage insurance (see "Insurance" above).

Since courier flights are primarily for long-distance travel, they are usually not available for short, domestic flights. But if you are crossing the country, or an ocean, becoming a mule might be a good bargain for you. Companies that hire couriers use your luggage allowance for their business baggage; in return, you get a deeply discounted ticket. Flights are often offered at the last minute, and you may have to arrange a pretrip interview to make sure you're right for the job. Now Voyager, Inc. (tel. 212/431-1616 from 11:30am to 6pm), flies from New York and sometimes has flights to Los Angeles for as little as $199 round trip.

BY TRAIN

Traveling by train takes a long time and usually costs as much as, or more than, flying. But if you're afraid of airplanes, or want to take a leisurely ride through America's countryside, rail may be a good option. Amtrak (tel. toll free 800/USA-RAIL), the nation's most complete long-distance passenger railroad network, connects about 500 American cities with points all over California.

Trains bound for Los Angeles leave daily from New York and pass through Chicago and Denver. The journey takes about 3½ days, and seats fill up quickly. As of this writing, the lowest round-trip fare was $339 from New York and $269 from Chicago. These heavily restricted tickets are good for 45 days and allow up to three stops along the way.

Amtrak also runs trains up and down the California coast, connecting Los Angeles with San Francisco and all points in between. A one-way ticket can often be had for as little as $50.

Ask about special family plans, tours, and other money-saving promotions the rail carrier may be offering. Call for an excellent brochure outlining routes and prices for the entire system.

BY BUS

Bus travel should not be overlooked, since it is an inexpensive and often flexible option. Greyhound/Trailways can get you here from anywhere, and offers several money-saving multiday bus passes. Round-trip fares vary, depending on your point of origin, but few, if any, ever exceed $200.

In Los Angeles, the main Greyhound/Trailways terminal is located downtown at 208 East 6th St. The company no longer operates a single nationwide telephone number, so consult your local directory for the office nearest you.

BY CAR

California is well connected to the rest of the United States by several major highways. Among them are Interstate-5, which enters the state

**FROMMER'S SMART TRAVELER:
AIRFARES**

1. Check the fares of all airlines that fly to your destination.
2. Always ask for the lowest fare, not "discount," "APEX," or "excursion."
3. Keep calling the airline—availability of cheap seats changes daily.
4. Seek out budget alternatives. Phone "bucket shops," charter companies, and discount travel agents.
5. Plan to travel midweek, when rates are usually lower.

from the north; Interstate-10, which originates in Jacksonville, Florida, and terminates in Los Angeles; and U.S. 101, which follows the western seaboard from Los Angeles north to the Oregon state line. By car is a great way to go if you want to become acquainted with the countryside; but after figuring in food, lodging, and automobile expenses, it may not be your cheapest option. Still, driving down the California coast is one of the world's ultimate journeys. Always drive within the speed limit, and keep an eye out for "speed traps," where the limit suddenly drops. Buy a good road map of the state before you start your trip and keep it handy in the glove compartment for easy reference. Before setting out for a long drive, call 415/557-3755 for a recorded announcement on California road conditions. See "Getting Around" in Chapter 4 for more information on driving in Los Angeles.

ROAD MAPS California's freeway signs frequently indicate direction by naming a town rather than a point on the compass. If you have never heard of Canoga Park you might be in trouble, unless you have a map. The best state road guide is the comprehensive Thomas Bros. *California Road Atlas*, a 300-plus-page book of maps with schematics of towns and cities statewide. It costs $20 but is a good investment if you plan to do a lot of exploring. Smaller, accordion-style maps are handy for the state as a whole or for individual cities and regions. These foldout maps usually cost $2 to $3 and are available at gas stations, pharmacies, supermarkets, and tourist-oriented shops everywhere.

BREAKDOWNS/ASSISTANCE Before taking a long car trip you should seriously consider joining a major automobile association. Not only do automobile associations offer travel insurance and helpful information, but they can also perform vacation-saving roadside services, including towing. The American Automobile Association (AAA), 8111 Gatehouse Rd., Falls Church, VA 22047 (tel. 703/222-6000), is the nation's largest auto club, with more than 850 offices. Membership fees range from about $20 to $60, depending on where you join.

Other recommendable auto clubs include the Allstate Motor Club, Allstate Place, Northbrook, IL 60062 (tel. 312/402-5461), and the Amoco Motor Club, P.O. Box 9046, Des Moines, IA 50369 (tel. toll free 800/334-3300).

HITCHHIKING   Thumbing a ride is the cheapest and most unpredictable way of traveling. Unfortunately, it can also be dangerous. Small country roads are best, and cities are worst. Use common sense: Sit next to an unlocked door, keep your bags within reach, and refuse a ride if you feel uneasy. The best way to become a rider is to strike up a conversation at a gas station or truck stop. Better still, find a driver through a ride board, located at most colleges, and in some local cafés.

PACKAGE TOURS

Tours and packages, put together by airlines, charter companies, hotels, and tour operators, are sold to travelers either directly or through travel agents. A **tour** usually refers to an escorted group and often includes transportation, sightseeing, meals, and accommodations. The entire group travels together and shares the same pre-planned activities. A **package,** on the other hand, can include any or all of the above components, but travelers are usually unescorted and free to make their own itinerary. Many travelers purchase airfare, hotel, and airport transfers from a travel agent, without even knowing that they are buying a tour operator's package. This is fine since packages can be a good value. Because packagers buy in bulk, they can often sell their services at a discount.

To find out what tours and packages are available to you, check the ads in the travel section of your newspaper or visit your travel agent. Before signing up, however, read the fine print carefully and do some homework:

How reputable is the tour operator?   Ask for references of people who have participated in tours run by the same company. Call travel agents and the local Better Business Bureau, and check with the consumer department of the U.S. Tour Operators Association, 211 E. 51st St., Suite 12B, New York, NY 10022 (tel. 212/944-5727). Be leery of any outfit that doesn't give you details of the itinerary.

What is the size of the tour group?   Decide how you feel about sharing an experience with 40 other people, or if your limit is 20. A smaller group usually means a better-quality tour.

What kinds of hotels have been booked and where are they located?   Get the names of the hotels and then look them up in guidebooks or in your travel agent's hotel guide. If you sense that the hotels provide only minimal essentials, that might be a clue about everything else on the tour. If the hotels are not conveniently located, they will be less expensive; however, if you feel isolated or unsafe, you may have to spend extra money and time getting to and from various attractions and nightspots.

If meals are included, how elaborate are they?   Is breakfast continental, English, or buffet? Is the menu for the group limited to just a few items?

How extensive is the sightseeing?   You may be able to get on and off the bus many times to explore various attractions, or you may be obliged to see them only from the bus window. If you like to explore, pick an attraction you're interested in and ask the operator precisely how much time you can expect to spend there. Find out if all admissions are included in the price of the tour.

Are the optional activities offered at an additional price? This is usually the case, so make sure the activities that particularly interest you are included in the tour price.

What is the refund policy if you decide to cancel? Check this carefully; some tour operators are more lenient than others regarding trip cancellations.

How is the package price paid? If a charter flight is involved, make sure that you can pay into an escrow account (ask for the name of the bank) in order to ensure proper use of the funds or their return in case the operator cancels the trip.

Most of the airlines listed above offer both escorted tours and on-your-own packages. Dozens of other companies also compete for this lucrative business. Discuss your options with a travel agent and compare tour prices with those in this guide.

FOR FOREIGN VISITORS

The pervasiveness of American culture around the world may make you feel that you know the States well. Still, leaving your own country requires an additional degree of planning, as well as some special advance knowledge of what to expect from a major American city. This chapter will help you become fully prepared.

1. PREPARING FOR YOUR TRIP

NECESSARY DOCUMENTS With the exception of Canadian nationals, who need only proof of residence, all foreigners entering the United States must present a valid **passport,** with an expiration date at least six months later than the scheduled end of your visit. Citizens of most countries, including Australia, Ireland, and New Zealand, also need to obtain a **tourist visa.**

To get a tourist or business visa to enter the United States, contact the nearest American embassy or consulate. Present your passport, a passport-size photo of yourself, and a completed visa application. Visa applications are available through the embassy or consulate and are also distributed by many airline offices and travel agents.

You may be asked to provide information about how you plan to finance your trip or show a letter of invitation from a friend with whom you plan to stay. Those applying for a business visa may be asked to show evidence that they will not receive a salary in the United States.

Be sure to check the length of stay on your visa; usually it is six months. If you want to stay longer, you may file for an extension with the Immigration and Naturalization Service once you are in the country. If permission to stay is granted, a new visa is not required unless you leave the United States and want to reenter.

MEDICAL REQUIREMENTS Unless you are arriving from an area known to be in the midst of an epidemic, no inoculations or vaccinations are required to enter the United States. Foreign visitors should be sure to have a doctor's prescription for any controlled substances you are carrying.

INSURANCE Although it is not required of travelers, health insurance is highly recommended. Unlike many European countries, the United States seldom offers free or low-cost medical care to its citizens or visitors. Doctors and hospitals are expensive and usually require advance payment or proof of coverage before they will render any services. Policies can cover everything from the loss or theft of your baggage and trip cancellation to the guarantee of bail in case you are arrested. Good policies will also cover costs of an accident, repatriation, or death. Such packages are sold by automobile clubs as well as by insurance companies and travel agents.

See "Health, Insurance & Other Concerns" in Chapter 2 for more information.

2. GETTING TO & AROUND THE U.S.

In addition to the domestic American airlines listed in Chapter 2, several international carriers also serve Los Angeles International Airport. Among them are Air Canada (tel. toll free 800/776-3000), British Airways (tel. toll free 800/247-9297), Japan Airlines (tel. toll free 800/525-3663), and SAS (tel. toll free 800/221-2350).

Some large airlines, including American Airlines, TWA, Northwest, and Delta, offer travelers on their transatlantic or transpacific flights special discount tickets under the name Visit USA, allowing travel between any U.S. destinations at minimum rates. They are not on sale in the United States and must be purchased abroad in conjunction with your international ticket. See your travel agent or airline ticket office for full details, as well as terms and conditions.

European visitors can also buy a USA Railpass, good for unlimited train travel on Amtrak. The pass is available through some airlines and travel agents, including Thomas Cook in Great Britain and Cuoni on the continent. Various itinerary options are available for $299 and up. Amtrak officials suggest that you make route reservations as soon as possible, since many trains could be sold out.

With a foreign passport and airline ticket, you can also buy the passes at Amtrak offices in Seattle, San Francisco, Los Angeles, Chicago, New York, Boston, Washington, D.C., and Miami. For further information write to Amtrak Distribution Center, P.O. Box 7700, 1549 W. Glen Lake Ave., Itasca, IL 60143, or call within the United States toll free 800/USA-RAIL.

 FOR THE FOREIGN TRAVELER

Accommodations Some of the major hotels listed in this book maintain overseas reservation networks and can be booked either directly or through travel agents. Some hotels are also included in tour operators' package tours. Since tour companies buy rooms in bulk, they can often offer them at a discount. Discuss this option with your travel agent and compare tour prices with those in this guide.

Auto Organizations If you plan on renting a car in the United States, you will probably not need the services of an additional auto organization. If you are planning to buy or borrow a car, automobile association membership is recommended. The American Automobile Association (AAA), 8111 Gatehouse Rd., Falls Church, VA 22047 (tel. 703/222-6000), is the country's largest auto club, supplying members with maps, insurance, and, most important, emergency road service. The cost of joining runs from $20 to $60, but if you are a member of a foreign auto club with reciprocal arrangements, you can enjoy free AAA service in America. See "Getting There" in Chapter 2 for more information.

Business Hours See "Fast Facts: Los Angeles" in Chapter 4.

Climate See "When to Go—Climate" in Chapter 2.

Currency and Exchange The U.S. monetary system has a decimal base: 1 dollar ($1) = 100 cents (100¢). The most common bills (all green) are the $1 (colloquially, a "buck"), $5, $10, and $20 denominations. There are also $2 (seldom encountered), $50, and $100 bills (the last two are not welcome when paying for small purchases).

There are six denominations of coins: 1¢ (1 cent, or a penny); 5¢ (5 cents, or a nickel); 10¢ (10 cents, or a dime); 25¢ (25 cents, or a quarter); 50¢ (50 cents, or a half dollar); and—prized by collectors— the rare $1 piece (both the older, large silver dollar and the newer, small Susan B. Anthony coin).

Foreign-exchange bureaus are rare in the United States, and most banks are not equipped to handle currency exchange. Traveler's checks are widely accepted, however. Make sure that they are denominated in U.S. dollars, since foreign-currency checks are difficult to exchange.

Customs and Immigration Every visitor over 21 years of age may bring in, free of duty, the following: 1 liter of wine or hard liquor; 200 cigarettes, 100 cigars (but not from Cuba), or 3 pounds of smoking tobacco; and $400 worth of gifts. These exemptions are offered to travelers who spend at least 72 hours in the United States and who have not claimed them within the preceding six months. It is altogether forbidden to bring into the country foodstuffs (particularly cheese, fruit, cooked meats, and canned goods) and plants (vegetables, seeds, tropical plants, and the like). Foreign tourists may bring in or take out up to $10,000 in U.S. or foreign currency with no formalities; larger sums must be declared to Customs on entering or leaving.

Drinking Laws The legal age for purchase and consumption of alcoholic beverages is 21; proof of age is required. In California, all types of liquor are sold in supermarkets and grocery stores. When licensed, restaurants are permitted to sell alcohol; however, many eateries are licensed only for beer and wine.

Electricity U.S. wall outlets give power at 110–115 volts, 60 cycles, compared with 220 volts, 50 cycles, in most of Europe. In addition to a 110-volt converter, small foreign appliances, such as hairdryers and shavers, will require a plug adapter with two flat, parallel pins.

Embassies and Consulates All embassies are located in the national capital, Washington, D.C.; some consulates are located in major cities. Most countries maintain a mission to the United Nations in New York City. The embassies and consulates of the major English-speaking countries—Australia, Canada, the Republic of Ireland, New Zealand, and the United Kingdom—are listed below. If you are from another country, you can get the telephone number of your embassy by calling "Information" in Washington, D.C. (tel. 202/555-1212).

Australia: The embassy is located at 1601 Massachusetts Ave. NW, Washington, D.C. 20036 (tel. 202/797-3000). Consulates are maintained at 611 N. Larchmont Blvd., Los Angeles, CA 90004 (tel. 213/469-4300); and 360 Post St., San Francisco, CA 94108 (tel. 415/362-6160).

Canada: The embassy is located at 501 Pennsylvania Ave. NW, Washington, D.C. 20001 (tel. 202/682-1740). Consulates are maintained at 300 S. Grand Ave., 10th Floor, Los Angeles CA 90071 (tel. 213/687-7432); and at One Maritime Plaza, Golden Gateway Center, San Francisco, CA 94111 (tel. 415/981-8541).

Republic of Ireland: The embassy is located at 2234 Massachusetts Ave. NW, Washington, D.C. 20008 (tel. 202/462-3939). A consulate is maintained at 655 Montgomery St., Suite 930, San Francisco, CA 94111 (tel. 415/392-4214).

New Zealand: The embassy is located at 37 Observatory Circle NW, Washington, D.C. 20008 (tel. 202/328-4800). A consulate is maintained in the Tishman Bldg., 10960 Wilshire Blvd., Westwood Suite 1530, Los Angeles, CA 90024 (tel. 213/477-8241).

United Kingdom: The embassy is located at 3100 Massachusetts Ave. NW, Washington, D.C. 20008 (tel. 202/462-1340). A consulate is maintained at 3701 Wilshire Blvd., Suite 312, Los Angeles, CA 90010 (tel. 213/385-7381).

Emergencies In all major cities you can call the police, an ambulance, or the fire department through the single emergency telephone number 911. Another useful way of reporting an emergency is to call the telephone company operator by dialing 0 (zero, not the letter "O"). Outside major cities, call the county sheriff or the fire department directly at the number you will find in the local telephone book.

Gasoline Prices vary, but expect to pay anywhere between $1.10 and $1.45 for one U.S. gallon of "regular" unleaded gasoline (petrol). Higher octane fuels are also available at most gas stations for slightly higher prices. Taxes are already included in the printed price.

Holidays On the following legal national holidays, banks, government offices, post offices, and many stores, restaurants, and museums are closed:

New Year's Day   January 1
Martin Luther King Day   Third Monday in January
Presidents Day   Third Monday in February
Memorial Day   Last Monday in May
Independence Day   July 4

Labor Day   First Monday in September
Columbus Day   Second Monday in October
Veterans (Armistice) Day   November 11
Election Day   The Tuesday following the first Monday in November is a national holiday in presidential-election years
Thanksgiving Day   Last Thursday in November
Christmas Day   December 25

Information   See "Orientation" in Chapter 4.

Legal Aid   Happily, foreign tourists rarely find themselves compelled to come into contact with the American legal system. If you are stopped for a minor driving infraction (speeding, for example), never attempt to pay the fine directly to a police officer; fines should be paid to the clerk of the court, and a receipt should be obtained. If you are accused of a more serious offense, it is wise to say and do nothing before consulting a lawyer. Under U.S. law, an arrested person is allowed one telephone call to a party of his or her choice. You may wish to contact your country's embassy or consulate (see listings above).

Mail   If you want to receive mail but aren't sure exactly where you'll be staying, have it sent to you, in your name, c/o General Delivery (Poste Restante) at the main post office of the city or region you're visiting. The addressee must pick it up in person and produce proof of identity (driver's license, credit card, passport). Most post offices will hold your mail for up to one month.

Generally found at street intersections, mailboxes are blue and carry the inscription U.S. MAIL. If your mail is addressed to a U.S. destination, don't forget to add the five-figure ZIP Code, after the two-letter abbreviation of the state to which the mail is addressed ("CA" for California).

Medical Emergencies   To call an ambulance, dial 911 from any phone. No coins are needed. For a list of hospitals and other emergency information, see "Fast Facts: Los Angeles" in Chapter 4.

Newspapers and Magazines   Most city newsstands offer a small selection of the most popular foreign periodicals and newspapers, such as *The Economist, Le Monde,* and *Der Spiegel.* For information on local publications, see "Fast Facts: Los Angeles" in Chapter 4.

Post   See "Mail" above.

Radio and Television   The audiovisual media play a major role in the cultural life of California, as they do elsewhere in the United States. A variety of radio stations broadcast classical, country, jazz, and pop music, punctuated by regular news reports and advertisements (commercials). Broadcast television offers access to several channels, including those of the three coast-to-coast commercial networks—the American Broadcasting System (ABC), the Columbia Broadcasting System (CBS), and the National Broadcasting Company (NBC)—as well as the noncommercial Public Broadcasting System (PBS) and the emerging commercial Fox network. Also, in most cities local cable franchises offer a number of additional channels delivered by cable to their subscribers, including the Cable News Network (CNN) and Home Box Office (HBO, mostly movies).

Most hotels have TVs in their rooms, and many offer both broadcast and some cable channels (with sports, music, and movies); some may offer special programs or movies on a pay-per-view basis.

Restrooms   See "Toilets" below.

Safety   In general, the United States is a fairly safe place, especially for tourists, who are rarely the victims of crime. However, there are "danger zones" in the big cities that should be approached with extreme caution.

As a general rule, isolated areas, such as parks and parking lots, should be avoided after dark. Elevators and public-transportation systems in off-hours, particularly between 10pm and 6am, are also potential crime scenes. If you're driving through a decaying neighborhood, you should have your car doors locked and the windows closed. Never carry valuables like jewelry or large sums of cash; traveler's checks are much safer.

Taxes   In the United States there is no VAT (Value-Added Tax) or other indirect tax at a national level. Every state, as well as every city, is allowed to levy its own local sales tax on all purchases, including hotel and restaurant checks and airline tickets. Taxes are already included in the price of certain services, such as public transportation, cab fares, telephone calls, and gasoline. The amount of sales tax varies from 4% to 10%, depending on the state and city; so when you're making major purchases, such as photographic equipment, clothing, or high-fidelity components, it can be a significant part of the cost.

Telephone, Telegraph, Telex, and Fax   In cities, pay telephones can be found almost everywhere—at street corners, and in bars, restaurants, and hotels. Outside metropolitan areas, however, public telephones are more difficult to find; stores and gas stations are your best bet. In most parts of California, local calls cost 20¢.

Public pay telephones do not accept pennies, and few will take anything larger than a quarter. Some public telephones, especially those at airports and in large hotels, accept credit cards, among them MasterCard, VISA, and American Express. These are especially handy for international calls; instructions are printed on the telephone itself.

For long-distance or international calls, stock up with a supply of quarters; a recorded voice will instruct you when and in what quantity you should put them into the slot. For direct overseas calls, first dial 011, then dial the country code (Australia, 61; Republic of Ireland, 353; New Zealand, 64; United Kingdom, 44), followed by the city code and the number of the telephone you wish to call. To place a call to Canada or the Caribbean, just dial 1, the area code, and the number you wish to call.

Before calling from a hotel room, always ask the hotel telephone operator whether there are any telephone surcharges. These can sometimes be reduced by calling collect or by using a telephone charge card. Hotel charges, which can be exorbitant, may be avoided altogether by using a public telephone.

For collect (reversed-charge) calls and for person-to-person calls, dial 0 (zero, not the letter "O"), followed by the area code and number you want; an operator will then come on the line, and you should specify that you are calling collect or person-to-person, or both. If your operator-assisted call is international, ask for the overseas operator.

For local "information" (directory inquiries), dial 411; for long-distance information in Canada or the United States, dial 1, then the appropriate area code and 555-1212.

Like the telephone system, telegraph and telex services are provided by private corporations, such as ITT, MCI, and, above all, Western Union. You can take your telegram to a Western Union office or dictate it over the telephone (tel. toll free 800/325-6000). You can also telegraph money, or have it telegraphed to you, very quickly. Look in the telephone book or call Western Union to find out the location of the office nearest you.

Time   The United States is divided into six time zones. From east to west, these are Eastern Standard Time (EST), Central Standard Time (CST), Mountain Standard Time (MST), Pacific Standard Time (PST), Alaska Standard Time (AST), and Hawaii Standard Time (HST). California is on Pacific Standard Time, eight hours behind Greenwich Mean Time. Noon in New York City (EST) is 11am in Chicago (CST), 10am in Denver (MST), 9am in Los Angeles (PST), 8am in Anchorage (AST), and 7am in Honolulu (HST).

Daylight Saving Time is in effect from 1am on the first Sunday in April until 2am on the last Sunday in October, except in Arizona, Hawaii, part of Indiana, and Puerto Rico.

Tipping   Service in America is among the best in the world, and tipping is the reason why. The amount you tip should depend on the service you receive. Good service warrants the following tips: bartenders, 15%; bellhops, $2 to $4; cab drivers, 15%; in cafeterias and fast-food restaurants, no tip; chambermaids, $1 per person per day; at cinemas, no tip; checkroom attendants, 50¢ to $1 (no tip if there's a charge); gas-station attendants, no tip; hairdressers, 15% to 20%; parking valets, $1; redcaps (at airports and in railroad stations), $2 to $4; and in restaurants and nightclubs, 15%.

Toilets   Public toilets can be hard to find. There are none on the streets, and few small stores will allow you access to their facilities. You can almost always find a toilet in restaurants and bars, but if you are not a customer, you should ask permission to use their facilities. Large hotels and fast-food restaurants are probably the best bet for good, clean facilities. Museums, department stores, shopping malls, and, in a pinch, gas stations all have public toilets.

Yellow Pages   The *Yellow Pages* telephone directory lists all local services, businesses, and industries by category; it also has an index for quick reference. Categories range from automobile repairs (listed by make of car) and drugstores, or pharmacies, to places of worship and restaurants (listed according to cuisine and geographical location). The *Yellow Pages* directory is also a good source for information of particular interest to the traveler; among other things, it has maps of the city, showing sights and transportation routes, "hotline" telephone numbers, and interesting facts about local attractions.

THE AMERICAN SYSTEM OF MEASUREMENTS

LENGTH

1 inch (in.)	=	2.54cm			
1 foot (ft.)	=	12 in.	=	30.48cm	= .305m
1 yard	=	3 ft.	=	.915m	
1 mile (mi.)	=	5,280 ft.	=	1.609km	

To convert miles to kilometers, multiply the number of miles by 1.61 (for example, 50 mi. × 1.61 = 80.5km). Note that this conversion can be used to convert speeds from miles per hour (m.p.h.) to kilometers per hour (km/h).

To convert kilometers to miles, multiply the number of kilometers by .62 (for example, 25km × .62 = 15.5 mi.). Note that this same conversion can be used to convert speeds from kilometers per hour to miles per hour.

CAPACITY

1 fluid ounce (fl. oz.)	=	.03 liter		
1 pint	=	16 fl. oz.	=	.47 liter
1 quart	=	2 pints	=	.94 liter
1 gallon (gal.)	=	4 quarts	=	3.79 liter
	=	.83 Imperial gal.		

To convert U.S. gallons to liters, multiply the number of gallons by 3.79 (example, 12 gal. × 3.79 = 45.58 liters.)

To convert U.S. gallons to Imperial gallons, multiply the number of U.S. gallons by .83 (example, 12 U.S. gal. × .83 = 9.95 Imperial gal.).

To convert liters to U.S. gallons, multiply the number of liters by .26 (example, 50 liters × .26 = 13 U.S. gal.).

To convert Imperial gallons to U.S. gallons, multiply the number of Imperial gallons by 1.2 (example, 8 Imperial gal. × 1.2 = 9.6 U.S. gal.).

WEIGHT

1 ounce (oz.)		= 28.35 grams	
1 pound (lb.) = 16 oz.		= 453.6 grams	= .45 kilograms
1 ton		= 2,000 lb. = 907 kilograms	= .91 metric ton

To convert pounds to kilograms, multiply the number of pounds by .45 (example, 90 lb. × .45 = 40.5kg).

To convert kilograms to pounds, multiply the number of kilos by 2.2 (example, 75kg × 2.2 = 165 lb.).

AREA

1 acre	= .41 hectare (ha)	
1 square mile (sq. mi.) = 640 acres	= 2.59 hectares = 2.6km	

To convert acres to hectares, multiply the number of acres by .41 (example, 40 acres × .41 = 16.4ha).

To convert square miles to square kilometers, multiply the number of square miles by 2.6 (example, 80 sq. mi. × 2.6 = 208km).

To convert hectares to acres, multiply the number of hectares by 2.47 (example, 20ha × 2.47 = 49.4 acres).

To convert square kilometers to square miles, multiply the number of square kilometers by .39 (example, 150km × .39 = 58.5 sq. mi.).

TEMPERATURE

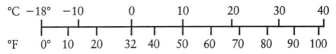

To convert degrees Fahrenheit to degrees Celsius, subtract 32 from °F, multiply by 5, then divide by 9 (example, 85°F − 32 × 5/9 = 29.4°C).

To convert degrees Celsius to degrees Fahrenheit, multiply °C by 9, divide by 5, and add 32 (example, 20°C × 9/5 + 32 = 68°F).

CLOTHING SIZE CONVERSION

The following charts should help foreign visitors choose the correct clothing sizes in the U.S. However, sizes can vary, so the best guide is to simply try things on.

WOMEN'S DRESSES, COATS, AND SKIRTS

American	6	8	10	11	12	13	14	15	16	18
Continental	36	38	40	40	42	42	44	44	46	48
British	8	10	12	13	14	15	16	17	18	20

WOMEN'S BLOUSES AND SWEATERS

American	10	12	14	16	18	20
Continental	38	40	42	44	46	48
British	32	34	36	38	40	42

WOMEN'S SHOES

American	5	6	7	8	9	10
Continental	36	37	38	39	40	41
British	3½	4½	5½	6½	7½	8½

MEN'S SUITS

American	34	36	38	40	42	44	46	48
Continental	44	46	48	50	52	54	56	58
British	34	36	38	40	42	44	46	48

MEN'S SHIRTS

American	14½	15	15½	16	16½	17	17½	18
Continental	37	38	39	41	42	43	44	45
British	14½	15	15½	16	16½	17	17½	18

MEN'S SHOES

American	7	8	9	10	11	12	13
Continental	39½	41	42	43	44½	46	47
British	6	7	8	9	10	11	12

CHILDREN'S CLOTHING

American	3	4	5	6	6X
Continental	98	104	110	116	122
British	18	20	22	24	26

CHILDREN'S SHOES

American	8	9	10	11	12	13	1	2	3
Continental	24	25	27	28	29	30	32	33	34
British	7	8	9	10	11	12	13	1	2

GETTING TO KNOW LOS ANGELES

Even natives have trouble negotiating their way around this sprawling city. The freeways, which cross and connect L.A.'s disparate regions are your lifeline to the sights; they will take a little time to master. This chapter will help familiarize you with the city and its various parts.

1. ORIENTATION

ARRIVING

BY PLANE   Los Angeles International Airport (LAX) is situated on the water, at the southwestern corner of the city. Two main roads connect LAX with the rest of the city: Century Boulevard, which runs east-west; and Sepulveda Boulevard, which runs north-south. Going north on Sepulveda Boulevard will take you directly to the airport; going south, you should turn right on 96th Street to get to the airport entrance.

The San Diego Freeway (I-405)—it's called that even in Los Angeles—has an exit to West Century Boulevard, which leads to the airport. There are directional signs on all airport area roads.

Many city hotels provide free shuttles for their guests; ask about transportation when you make reservations. Super Shuttle (tel. 310/338-1111), a private ride-sharing service, offers regularly scheduled minivans from LAX to any location in the city. The set fare can range from about $10 to $20, depending on your destination. When traveling to the airport, reserve your shuttle at least one day in advance.

Unless you're staying at one of the nearby airport hotels, taxis are not recommended; the cost of a taxi often seems more like a down payment on one.

The city's RTD buses also go between LAX and many parts of the city. Phone RTD Airport Information (tel. 800/252-7433) for the schedules and fares. Free Blue, Green, and White Airline Connections shuttle buses (tel. 213/646-8021) connect the terminals at LAX and stop in front of each ticket building. Special handicapped-accessible minibuses are also available.

Other Airports   LAX is the city's largest airport, but Los

Angeles is full of smaller regional airports that are usually easier to reach and may be closer to your destination. To the north is the Burbank-Glendale-Pasadena Airport, 2627 N. Hollywood Way, Burbank (tel. 818/840-8840); to the south are the Long Beach Municipal Airport, 4100 Donald Douglas Dr., Long Beach (tel. 310/421-8293), and the John Wayne Airport, 19051 Airport Way North, Anaheim (tel. 714/755-6510); and to the east is the Ontario International Airport, Terminal Way, Ontario (tel. 714/988-2700).

BY TRAIN   Amtrak service to and from San Diego to the south and Oakland and Seattle to the north, as well as to and from points in between, operates out of Union Station at 800 N. Alameda (tel. 213/624-0171), on the north side of downtown L.A.

BY BUS   The Greyhound/Trailways bus system serves most cities in California. In Los Angeles, the main terminal is downtown at 208 E. 6th St., at Los Angeles St. (tel. 213/620-1200), a rather seedy part of the city. Although there are other Greyhound stations around L.A., not all of them are serviced by interstate buses. If you are planning to arrive by bus, tell the operator where you want to go, and see if there's a stop closer to your destination.

BY CAR   All of the interstate highways that crisscross L.A. run right through the downtown area. From the east, you'll arrive on I-10, the San Bernardino Freeway. From the north or south, the most direct route is via I-5. You may wish to avoid the clogged downtown area entirely, in which case you should turn off I-5 onto I-405, which runs by LAX. Noninterstate entries include U.S. 101, which comes into the downtown area from Santa Barbara and the north; and Calif. 1, which follows the coast through Santa Monica.

TOURIST INFORMATION

The Los Angeles Convention and Visitors Bureau, 515 S. Figueroa St., 11th Floor, Los Angeles, CA 90071 (tel. 213/689-8822) is the city's main source for information. Write for a free visitor's kit. The bureau staffs a Visitors Information Center at 695 S. Figueroa St., between Wilshire Boulevard and 7th Street, which is open Monday through Saturday from 8am to 5pm.

Many Los Angeles–area communities also have their own tourist offices, including:

The Visitor Information Center Hollywood, The Janes House, 6541 Hollywood Blvd., Hollywood, CA 90028 (tel. 213/461-4213), open Monday through Saturday from 9am to 5pm.

Beverly Hills Chamber of Commerce and Visitors Bureau, 239 S. Beverly Dr., Beverly Hills, CA 90212 (tel. 213/271-8174, or toll free 800/345-2210).

The Hollywood Arts Council, P.O. Box 931056, Dept. 1991, Hollywood, CA 90093 (tel. 213/462-2355), distributes the free magazine *Discover Hollywood*. It contains good listings of the area's many theaters, galleries, music venues, and comedy clubs.

Long Beach Convention and Visitors Council, 1 World

Trade Center, Suite 300, Long Beach, CA 90831 (tel. 213/436-3645, or toll free 800/234-3645).

Marina del Rey Chamber of Commerce, 4629-A Admiralty Way, Marina del Rey, CA 90292 (tel. 213/821-0555).

Pasadena Convention and Visitors Bureau, 171 S. Los Robles Ave., Pasadena, CA 91101 (tel. 818/795-9311).

Santa Monica Convention and Visitors Bureau, 2219 Main St., Santa Monica, CA 90405 (tel. 310/393-7593). The Santa Monica Visitors Center is located near the Santa Monica Pier, at 400 Ocean Avenue.

CITY LAYOUT

Los Angeles is an incongruous patchwork of communities sewn into an ever expanding quilt. Sprawled between sea and mountains, the city encompasses both seaside resorts and treeless desert foothills. With notable exceptions, the better homes are in the hills—built on shelves of granite in shrub-covered mountains.

"Sky-high" Mulholland Drive rolls along the crest of the Santa Monica mountain chain through part of Beverly Hills and Holly-wood. Popular with sightseeing tourists and teenage locals, the drive offers excellent views of the city to the west, and the San Fernando Valley to the north. The valley, located between the Hollywood Hills and the Mojave Desert mountains, was once covered with orange groves, but is now both residential and commercial.

Downtown Los Angeles lies about 12 miles east of the Pacific Ocean on a direct line with the coastal town of Santa Monica. This is the city's primary business district, but by no means the only one.

Most of the commercial areas of Los Angeles have remained in the flatlands, including Wilshire Boulevard ("Miracle Mile"), which runs from the downtown area to the sea. The highest point in the city is Mount Hollywood. Sunset and Hollywood boulevards—the main thoroughfares—run along the foot of the mountains.

Because of earthquake concerns, skyscrapers weren't permitted in the city of Los Angeles until recent times—which partially explains why the city is so spread out, encompassing more than 450 square miles.

MAIN ARTERIES & STREETS The city's main arteries are freeways that crisscross L.A. in a complicated maze. U.S. 101 runs across L.A. from the San Fernando Valley to the center of downtown. I-5 bisects the city on its way from San Francisco to San Diego. I-10 connects the downtown area with Santa Monica and nearby beach areas. And I-405 skirts the downtown area completely, connecting the San Fernando Valley with LAX and the city's southern beach areas.

Hollywood, located northwest of downtown, is best reached by the Hollywood Freeway (U.S. 101). Beverly Hills, which adjoins Hollywood on the southwest, is most accessible by taking the Hollywood Freeway from the Civic Center to Santa Monica Boule-vard.

Wilshire Boulevard, L.A.'s main drag, connects the downtown

area with Beverly Hills, then continues on through Westwood en route to Santa Monica. As Wilshire Boulevard enters Beverly Hills, it intersects La Cienega Boulevard. The portion of La Cienega that stretches north from Wilshire Boulevard to Santa Monica Boulevard is known as Restaurant Row.

Hollywood's Sunset Boulevard, between Laurel Canyon Boulevard and La Brea Avenue, is the famed Sunset Strip. Just north of the strip lies the equally famous Hollywood Boulevard.

Farther north still, via the Hollywood Freeway, is the San Fernando Valley; here you'll find Universal City. A right turn on the Ventura Freeway takes you to downtown Burbank.

Venice, the yacht-filled harbors of Marina del Rey, and the Los Angeles International Airport (LAX) are located on Calif. 1, south along the shore from Santa Monica.

FINDING AN ADDRESS   Use a map—there's no other way. It's important to know in what area of the city the address you're looking for is located. When you know, for instance, that the hotel is in Santa Monica, finding it is much easier. For that reason, all Los Angeles addresses in this guide either include the city area or are listed under a helpful heading.

NEIGHBORHOODS IN BRIEF

Hollywood   The legendary city where actresses once posed with leashed leopards is certainly on everyone's must-see list. Unfortunately, the glamour—what's left of it—is badly tarnished, and Hollywood Boulevard has been accurately labeled "the Times Square of the West." But Hollywood seems unaware of its own decline. For one thing, the HOLLYWOOD sign is still on the hill, and the prices keep going up.

The legend of Hollywood as the movie capital of the world still persists, though many of its former studios have moved to less-expensive and more spacious venues. The corner of Hollywood and Vine is legendary—its fame larger than it deserves. Architecturally dull, it was known for the stars who crossed the intersection—all the big names in Hollywood.

Beverly Hills   The aura of Beverly Hills is unique. Beneath its veneer of wealth, it's a curious blend of small-town neighborliness and cosmopolitan worldliness. Many of southern California's most prestigious hotels, restaurants, high-fashion boutiques, and department stores are located here. Don't miss that remarkable group of European-based super-upscale stores along Rodeo Drive. A shopping guide is available from the Beverly Hills Chamber of Commerce and Visitors Bureau (see "Tourist Information," above).

Downtown Los Angeles   This ever expanding sprawl of a city did have a point of origin: in and around the Old Plaza and Olvera Street. The first buildings included some (now demolished) elegant residences and the (still standing) deluxe-class Biltmore Hotel. Due to concern about earthquakes, city-planning authorities originally prohibited the construction of buildings over 150 feet in

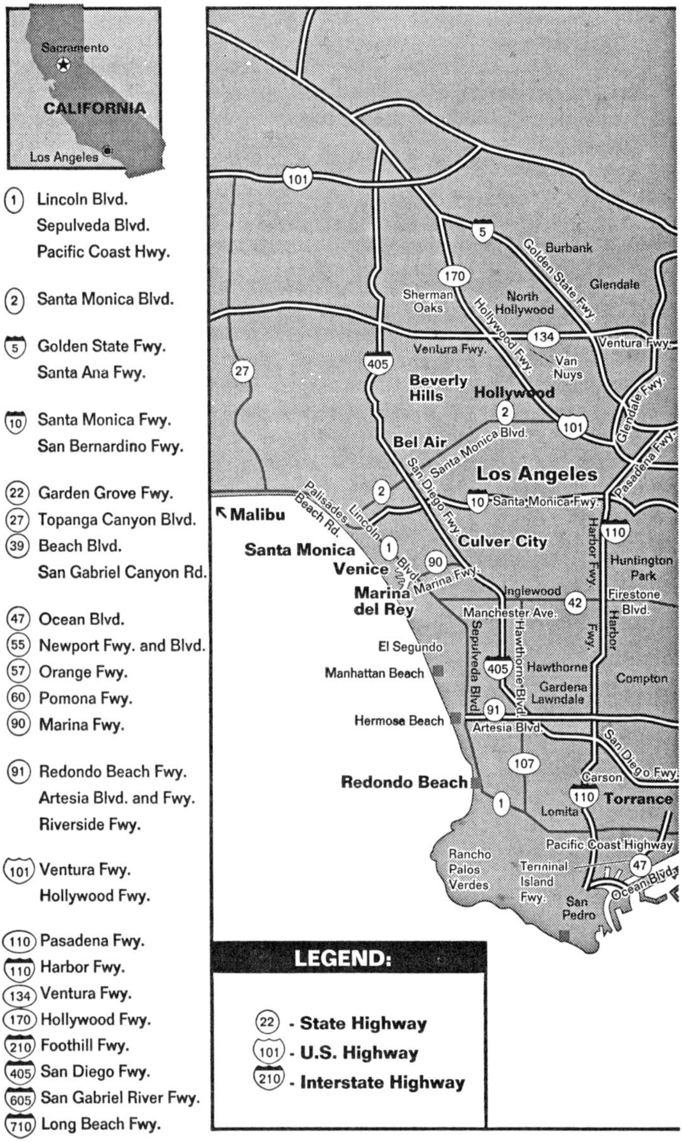
Sacramento
CALIFORNIA
Los Angeles
1 Lincoln Blvd.
Sepulveda Blvd.
Pacific Coast Hwy.
2 Santa Monica Blvd.
5 Golden State Fwy.
Santa Ana Fwy.
10 Santa Monica Fwy.
San Bernardino Fwy.
22 Garden Grove Fwy.
27 Topanga Canyon Blvd.
39 Beach Blvd.
San Gabriel Canyon Rd.
47 Ocean Blvd.
55 Newport Fwy. and Blvd.
57 Orange Fwy.
60 Pomona Fwy.
90 Marina Fwy.
91 Redondo Beach Fwy.
Artesia Blvd. and Fwy.
Riverside Fwy.
101 Ventura Fwy.
Hollywood Fwy.
110 Pasadena Fwy.
110 Harbor Fwy.
134 Ventura Fwy.
170 Hollywood Fwy.
210 Foothill Fwy.
405 San Diego Fwy.
605 San Gabriel River Fwy.
710 Long Beach Fwy.
Burbank
Golden State Fwy.
Glendale
Sherman Oaks
North Hollywood
Hollywood Fwy.
Ventura Fwy.
Van Nuys
Beverly Hills
Hollywood
Santa Monica Blvd.
Bel Air
Glendale Fwy.
Pasadena Fwy.
Los Angeles
Santa Monica Fwy.
Malibu
Palisades Beach Rd.
Lincoln Blvd.
San Diego Fwy.
Santa Monica
Culver City
Venice
Marina Fwy.
Marina del Rey
Harbor Fwy.
Huntington Park
Inglewood
Firestone Blvd.
Manchester Ave.
El Segundo
Sepulveda Blvd.
Hawthorne Blvd.
Manhattan Beach
Hawthorne
Compton
Gardena
Lawndale
Hermosa Beach
Artesia Blvd.
San Diego Fwy.
Redondo Beach
Carson
Torrance
Lomita
Pacific Coast Highway
Rancho Palos Verdes
Terminal Island Fwy.
San Pedro
Ocean Blvd.
LEGEND:
22 - State Highway
101 - U.S. Highway
210 - Interstate Highway

height. This limitation led many companies to move to Wilshire Boulevard and outlying areas, leaving the original downtown to fall into relative disrepair. In 1957 new construction technology permitted tall buildings to be constructed safely. Construction of the shimmering $35-million Music Center in the '60s marked the beginning of a long-overdue renaissance for downtown Los Angeles, which later included new office buildings and several major new hotels. One of the most magnificent new buildings in the downtown area is the Museum of Contemporary Art (MOCA), designed by the Japanese architect Arata Isozaki. MOCA is the only Los Angeles institution that is devoted exclusively to art from 1940 to the present.

Chinatown and Little Tokyo   Neither is on the scale of its San Francisco equivalent, and neither is worth going out of your way to see. Still, both offer a group of ethnic shops and restaurants that you might enjoy exploring. Chinatown, bounded by North Broadway, North Hill Street, Bernard Street, and Sunset Boulevard, centers on a Chinese mall called Mandarin Plaza at 970 N. Broadway.

Little Tokyo is located close to City Hall, bordered by Alameda and Los Angeles Streets and 1st and 3rd Streets. It is the site of the luxury class Japanese hotel, the New Otani, as well as many Japanese shops and restaurants.

Century City Nestled between Beverly Hills and Westwood, this compact and busy area bustles with businesses, shops, cinemas, and theaters. It's a good, central place to locate.

Malibu Located 25 miles from downtown Los Angeles, Malibu occupies a long stretch of northern L.A. shoreline from Topanga Canyon to the Ventura County line. Once a privately owned ranch—purchased in 1857 for 10¢ an acre—Malibu is now a popular seaside resort, and substantially more expensive. During the 1920s the emerging movie colony flocked here, and Malibu became famous for wild parties and extravagant lifestyles. Although many famous people still live here, they tend to keep a low profile.

At its widest point, the Malibu strip is only 3 miles across; at its narrowest, just 1 mile. Malibu's wide, sandy beaches are among the best in the county for bathing, surfing, and sunning.

Wilshire Boulevard In many ways, Wilshire Boulevard is Los Angeles' primary thoroughfare; the city's "Fifth Avenue" or "Champs Elysées." Commencing in downtown Los Angeles, near Grand Street, Wilshire runs all the way to the beach in Santa Monica. Along the way it's the address for an impressive string of hotels, contemporary apartment houses, department stores, office buildings, and plush restaurants. In the 1930s, some optimistic developers dubbed one stretch of Wilshire—between Highland and Fairfax—"Miracle Mile." Only recently, however, is their ambitious label becoming a reality as new stores and glass-and-steel office buildings locate here.

Wilshire Boulevard passes by MacArthur and Lafayette parks, as well as the Los Angeles County Museum and La Brea Tar Pits in Hancock Park. The boulevard also runs through a portion of the Beverly Hills shopping section.

Marina del Rey Located oceanside, just south of Venice, Marina del Rey is best known for its small-craft harbor, which may be the largest of its kind in the world. You can watch the boats negotiate their way through a maze of piers, while strolling along an excellent Restaurant Row, packed with eateries for all palates and pocketbooks.

Santa Monica Los Angeles' premier beach community is one of the most dynamic, fun, and pretty places in the entire city. Filled with art deco buildings and fronting a sizable swath of beach, the town is known for its long ocean pier and cutting-edge, artistic lifestyle. The new Third Street Promenade, lined with great shops and restaurants, is one of the most successful revitalization projects in the United States. Main Street, which runs south to Venice Beach, is also crammed with creative shops and eateries.

Redondo Beach and San Pedro Established in the 1880s by railway tycoon Henry E. Huntington, Redondo Beach experienced a great land boom as it became the largest shipping port between San Diego and San Francisco. Located south of Marina del Rey and the Los Angeles International Airport, the area has since settled into a modest oceanside resort. Still largely commercial, Redondo fronts King Harbor, which now anchors a small fishing fleet, and about 2,000 pleasure craft.

Now L.A.'s busiest commercial port, San Pedro handles an

estimated 2 million tons of cargo annually. There's not much for tourists here, but it's worth going out of your way to drive along the San Pedro coast, past seemingly never ending, huge container ships and docks.

Long Beach   L.A.'s biggest beach town is actually the sixth-largest city in California. True to its name, it does, in fact, have a very long beach—5½ miles of sand. It's also well equipped with tennis, golf, sailing, fishing, and boating facilities.

Pasadena   The grande dame of the Greater Los Angeles area, Pasadena is a residential city 11 miles northwest of the downtown district, hugging the foothills of the Sierra Madre mountain range in the San Gabriel Valley. It features street after street of large estates, surrounded by semitropical gardens—a haven for "old money."
    The city is known chiefly for its Rose Bowl and its annual Tournament of Roses Parade. Since its beginnings in 1890—with "flower-bedecked buggies and surreys"—the parade has included such "grand marshals" as Bob Hope and Mary Pickford, even Richard Nixon and Shirley Temple. Downtown Pasadena has recently seen a tremendous renaissance, attracting young, upscale professionals, top restaurants, and terrific nightlife.

San Fernando Valley   The media popularized The Valley by focusing on the "Valley Girl" stereotype—a Galleria (mall) hopping teen whose favorite word is "ohmygod." The Valley snuggles between the Santa Monica and the San Gabriel mountain ranges, just west of Hollywood. It is mostly residential and commercial, and off the beaten tourist track. Cities in The Valley include Studio City, Sherman Oaks, Van Nuys, Tarzana, Reseda, and Encino.

STREET MAPS   Because Los Angeles is so spread out, a good map is essential. Good, foldout accordion-style maps are available at gas stations, hotels, bookshops, and tourist-oriented shops all around the city.

2. GETTING AROUND

BY PUBLIC TRANSPORTATION

With the exception of a single commuter rail line that operates from downtown Los Angeles to Long Beach, the city's extensive public transportation system relies primarily on a complex network of local and express buses. Public transportation is operated by Southern California Rapid Transit District (RTD), 425 S. Main St., Los Angeles, CA 90013 (tel. 213/626-4455). The regular fare for both buses and commuter rail is $1.10 for adults and 55¢ for seniors and the physically disabled; children under 5 ride free.
    Stop in, write, or call RTD for maps, schedules, and detailed trip

information. The office publishes a handy pamphlet outlining about two dozen self-guided RTD tours, including visits to Universal Studios, Beverly Hills, and Disneyland. A second, more convenient RTD office is located in ARCO Towers, 515 S. Flower St., adjacent to the Visitors and Convention Bureau.

BY BUS   Quite frankly, I have never heard of a tourist who traveled throughout Los Angeles completely by city bus. Spread-out sights, sluggish service, and frequent transfers make this kind of touring impractical. If you are not planning to move around too much, however, buses could prove to be economical. Be sure to take a good book along to while away ride time (*War and Peace*, perhaps?).

The basic bus fare is $1.10 for all local lines. Express buses, which travel along the freeways, and buses on intercounty routes charge higher fares. Exact fare is required, since drivers carry no change.

BY RAIL   In June 1990, the first line of a planned network of commuter rail lines opened. The new Blue Line service connects downtown's 7th Street and Flower Street stations with the 1st Street station in Long Beach. The nonstop trip takes 55 minutes and operates daily every 10 to 20 minutes from 5:30am to about 7pm.

BY TAXI

Distances are long in L.A., and cab fares are high. Even the shortest trip will cost $10 or more. Taxis charge $2 for the first $\frac{2}{10}$ mile, and $1.50 for each additional mile after that. You can sometimes hail a cab in the street, especially in the downtown area. To assure a ride, however, order one in advance from Independent Cab Co. (tel. 213/653-5050), Checker Cab Co. (tel. 213/654-8400), or Yellow Cab Co. (tel. 213/221-2331).

BY CAR

Need I tell you that Los Angeles is a car city? The elaborate network of freeways that connects this incredible urban sprawl is often jammed, especially during rush hours, when parking lots of traffic can seemingly slog along for hours. The golden rule of Los Angeles is always to allow more time to get to your destination than you reasonably think it will take.

RENTALS   Los Angeles is one of the cheapest places in America in which to rent a car. Major national car-rental companies usually offer their cheapest economy vehicles for about $30 per day and $100 per week with unlimited mileage. The best-known firms, with locations throughout the city, include: Alamo (tel. 800/327-9633), Avis (tel. 800/331-1212), Budget (tel. 800/527-0700), Dollar (tel. 800/421-6868), General (tel. 800/327-7607), Hertz (tel. 800/654-3131), National (tel. 800/328-4567), and Thrifty (tel. 800/367-2277).

Most rental firms pad their profits by selling Loss/Damage Waiver (LDW), which usually costs an extra $9 per day. Before agreeing to this, however, check with your insurance carrier and credit-card companies. Many people don't realize that they are already covered by either one or both. If you're not already protected, the LDW is a wise investment.

For renters, the minimum age is usually 19 to 25. Some agencies have also set maximum ages. If you are concerned that these limits may affect you, ask about rental requirements at the time of booking to avoid problems later.

Finally, think about splurging on a convertible. Few things in life can match the feeling of flying along warm California freeways with the sun smiling on your shoulders and the wind whipping through your hair.

PARKING Since practically everyone drives, parking throughout the city is ample. In most places you will be able to find metered street parking (carry plenty of quarters). Space gets scarce downtown, however, where you'll probably have to pay in excess of $10 for a spot in an indoor garage. Most of the hotels listed in this book offer off-street parking, usually for an additional charge. This can get pricey—up to $20 per day. Check the listings and ask at the hotel before committing yourself.

DRIVING RULES You may turn right at a red light (unless otherwise indicated), after yielding to traffic and pedestrians, and making a complete stop. Pedestrians have the right-of-way at intersections and crosswalks. Pay attention to signs and arrows on the streets and roadways or you may find that you're in a lane that requires exiting or turning when you wanted to go straight. What's more, the city's profusion of one-way streets can create a few small difficulties; most road maps of the city, however, indicate which way traffic flows.

BY BICYCLE

If you care about your life, you won't try to bicycle in the city as a means of getting around. Traffic is heavy, and often you just can't get there from here with a bike. Cycles are terrific for recreation, however, especially along the car-free beach bike path in Venice and Santa Monica. See "Sports & Recreation," in Chapter 7, for complete information.

 ***FAST* LOS ANGELES**

American Express There are several American Express Travel Service offices including 327 N. Beverly Dr. in Beverly Hills, and 901 W. 7th St. in downtown Los Angeles. To report lost or stolen cards, call toll free 800/528-4800. To report lost or stolen traveler's checks, call toll free 800/221-7282.

Area Code All phone numbers in this guide are prefaced with area codes. You'll need to use them when calling from one calling area to another.

There are three area codes in Los Angeles. Most numbers,

including Hollywood and downtown L.A. are within the 213 code. Phone numbers in the city's beach communities, including the Los Angeles International Airport (LAX), Malibu, and Santa Monica, begin with a 310 prefix. Many inland suburbs, including Pasadena and towns of the San Fernando Valley, are within the 818 calling area.

Babysitters If you're staying at one of the larger hotels, the concierge can usually recommend a reliable babysitter. If they can't, contact Baby Sitters Guild, P.O. Box 3418, South Pasadena, CA 91031 (tel. 818/441-4293). This company, in business since 1948, provides mature, bonded sitters, on call 24 hours.

Business Hours Stores are usually open Monday through Saturday from 10am to 6pm; closed on Sunday.

Car Rentals See "Getting Around" in this chapter.

Climate See "When to Go—Climate" in Chapter 2.

Currency Exchange Foreign-currency exchange services are provided by the Bank of America at 555 S. Flower St., 3rd floor, (tel. 213/228-4567). Thomas Cook International, at 677 S. Figueroa, and Hilton Hotel Center, 900 Wilshire Blvd. (tel. 213/624-4221), also offer foreign-currency exchange services.

Dentists Hotels usually have a list of dentists in case you need one. For other referrals, you can call the Los Angeles Dental Society (tel. 800/422-8338).

Doctors Here again, hotels usually have a list of doctors on call. For referrals, you can contact the Los Angeles Medical Association (tel. 213/483-6122).

Drugstores Walgreens Pharmacies are all over town. Ask at your hotel, or check the local phone directory for a location near you.

Embassies and Consulates See Chapter 3, "For Foreign Visitors."

Emergencies For police, fire, highway patrol, or in case of life-threatening medical emergencies, dial 911.

Eyeglasses Lenscrafters makes glasses in about an hour. Offices include 301 Wilshire Blvd. in Santa Monica (tel. 213/394-6692); and 4520 Van Nuys Blvd., Sherman Oaks (tel. 818/501-6474).

Hairdressers/Barbers If your hotel does not have a hair salon on the premises, they can usually make a recommendation. Beverly Hills Hair Design, 9171 Wilshire Blvd., Beverly Hills (tel. 213/274-8197) is well known for its stylish cuts.

Holidays See "Fast Facts: For the Foreign Traveler," in Chapter 3.

Hospitals In an emergency, dial 911 from any phone. Santa Monica Hospital Medical Center, 1250 16th St., Santa Monica (tel. 213/319-4000), is just one of many hospitals in the city. Ask at your hotel or check the front pages of a telephone directory for the hospital closest to you.

Information See "Tourist Information" in this chapter.

Laundry/Dry Cleaning Any major hotel can take care of these services for you, but allow two days for the job.

Liquor Laws Liquor and grocery stores can sell packaged alcoholic beverages between 6am and 2am. Most restaurants, nightclubs, and bars are licensed to serve alcoholic beverages during the same hours. The legal age for purchase and consumption is 21, and proof of age is required. In California you can purchase packaged liquor with your credit card; however, most stores usually have a minimum dollar amount for charging.

Newspapers and Magazines *The Los Angeles Times* is distributed throughout the county. Its Sunday "Calendar" section is an excellent and interesting guide to the world of entertainment in and around L.A., and includes listings of what's doing and where to do it. The free weekly events magazine *L.A. Weekly* is packed with news of events and a calendar of happenings around town. It's available from sidewalk newsracks and in many stores and restaurants around the city.

Photographic Needs Photofinishing labs can be found in almost every shopping mall and on major streets around the city. Fromex, 406 Broadway, Santa Monica (tel. 213/395-5177), is one of southern California's largest developers.

Police See "Emergencies" above.

Post Office Post offices are located all over the city. Call 213/586-1467 to find the one closest to you.

Radio Stations There are literally dozens of radio stations in L.A. FM classical music stations include KCSN (88.5), KCPB (91.1), KUSC (91.5), and KKGO (105.1). Country music stations include KFOX (93.5), KIKF (94.3), and KFRG (95.1). Rock music stations include KUCI (88.9), KLOS (95.5), KLSX (97.1), and KROQ (106.7). The top AM news and information station is KNX (1070).

Religious Services Los Angeles has hundreds of churches and synagogues, and at least 100 denominations, formal and informal. Should you be seeking a house of worship, your hotel desk person or bell captain can usually direct you to the nearest church of most any denomination.

Restrooms Stores rarely let customers use the restrooms, and many restaurants offer their facilities to customers only. But most malls have bathrooms, as do the ubiquitous fast-food restaurants. Many public beaches and large parks provide toilets, though in some places you have to pay, or tip an attendant. If you have the time to find one, go into a large hotel. Most have well-stocked, clean restrooms in their lobbies.

Safety Innocent tourists rarely become victims of violent crime. Still, few locals would recommend walking alone late at night. South Central L.A., an inland area where tourists rarely venture, is the city's most infamous area. See Chapter 2 for additional safety tips.

Taxes California state sales tax is 7¾%; hotel taxes range from 11% to 13%.

Taxis See "Getting Around" in this chapter.

Television Stations All the major networks and several independent stations are represented. They are KCBS, Channel 2; KNBC, Channel 4; KTLA, Channel 5; KABC, Channel 7; KCAL, Channel 9; KTTV (Fox), Channel 11; and KCOP, Channel 13.

Transit Information See "Getting Around" in this chapter.

Useful Telephone Numbers Call for the correct time at 213/853-1212; information on local highway conditions can be obtained at 213/620-3270. For nonemergency police matters, phone 213/485-2121 or, in Beverly Hills, 213/550-4951.

Weather   Call Los Angeles Weather Information (tel. 213/554-1212) to find out that it will once again be 74° F. and sunny tomorrow.

3. NETWORKS & RESOURCES

FOR STUDENTS   Students will find that their valid high school or college I.D. often entitles them to discounts at museums and other attractions, as well as at many bars during "college nights." When student prices are available, I have noted them in this book under the appropriate listing.

FOR GAY MEN & LESBIANS   Like everything else in Los Angeles, the gay and lesbian community is spread throughout the city; you'll have to drive to get to bars, businesses, and other congregating places. The city's many gay-oriented publications are the best places to find out what's happening when you're there. Popular titles, available at most good newsstands, include *The Advocate,* a biweekly national magazine; *Frontiers Magazine,* a southern California–based biweekly serving the local community; and *Nightlife,* which offers good listings of entertainment places complete with maps.

A Different Light, 8853 Santa Monica Blvd., West Hollywood (tel. 310/854-6601), is Los Angeles' best gay bookshop; in fact, it's one of the largest of its kind on the West Coast. A second shop is located at 4014 Santa Monica Blvd. (tel. 213/668-0629).

See Chapter 10 "Evening Entertainment" for listings of clubs and bars that cater primarily to gays and lesbians.

FOR WOMEN   Several Los Angeles women's bookstores are the best places in the city to get up-to-date information on feminist issues and happenings. Page One Bookstore, 966 N. Lake Ave., Pasadena (tel. 818/798-8694), is one of the best, selling feminist music, books by and for women, and tickets to women's events. Sisterhood Bookshop, 1351 Westwood Blvd. (tel. 310/477-7300), provides similar services in Westwood.

FOR SENIORS   Seniors aged 62 and older often receive discounts at attractions, museums, movies, and some restaurants. It can't hurt to ask if there is a senior price. You'd be surprised how often your proof of age will save you money during your travels in L.A.

CHAPTER 5

LOS ANGELES ACCOMMODATIONS

In Los Angeles, location is everything. When searching for a hotel here, think about the areas where you plan to spend most of your time, and locate nearby. In sprawling Los Angeles no place is convenient to everything; wherever you stay, count on doing a lot of driving to somewhere else.

Generally, the most elegant accommodations are in Beverly Hills and Bel Air. For hard-core tourists, Hollywood is probably the most central place to stay. Businesspeople are more likely to prefer a downtown location. Santa Monica and Marina del Rey are great areas right on the beach; they are coolest in summer and trendiest year round. Finally, families with kids might want to head straight to Anaheim or Buena Park in order to be close to the theme parks.

You'll notice that there are a disproportionate number of deluxe hostelries listed here—there are simply more of them in star-studded L.A. than in other cities. Budget inns in the city are few and far between. Nevertheless, they do exist, and I've described them below. Nearly all of my selections quote daily rates, though the budget-conscious will find weekly prices lower at some hotels.

The prices listed below do not include state and city taxes which run from a whopping 11% to 13%. Be aware that most hotels make additional charges for parking (with in-and-out privileges, except where noted), and levy heavy surcharges for telephone use. Many have their own on-site health facilities. When they don't, they often have an arrangement with a nearby club, allowing you to use their facilities on a per-day basis. Charges are usually from $8 to $15. Inquire about these extras before committing yourself.

Finally, even in the budget categories, all of the following listings meet my pretty exacting standards of comfort and cleanliness.

There are so many hotels in Los Angeles—in every price range—that few regularly fill to capacity. Even during the height of the tourist season, you can usually drive right into the city and find decent accommodations fairly quickly. But be careful. If you really want a specific hotel, must have an ocean view, or want to be in an

FROMMER'S SMART TRAVELER: HOTELS

1. A hotel room is a perishable commodity; if it's not rented, there is no revenue. Always ask if a hotel has a lower rate, and make it clear that you're shopping around.
2. For the best rates, seek out business-oriented hotels on weekends and in the summer; and tourist-oriented bed-and-breakfasts during the off-season.
3. Ask about summer discounts, corporate rates, and special packages. Most hotel reservations offices won't tell you about promotional rates unless you ask.
4. Always inquire about parking and telephone charges. In Los Angeles, it could add $20 per night for your car and $1 per local call.

area where accommodations are somewhat scarce, you should book your room in advance.

Hotel-operated toll-free telephone numbers can also help you with your search. These "800" numbers will save you time and money when inquiring about rates and availability. Toll-free numbers (if offered) are listed below for each hotel. Some of the larger hotel chains with properties in the Los Angeles area include: Best Western (tel. 800/528-1234), Days Inn (tel. 800/325-2525), Holiday Inn (tel. 800/465-4329), Quality Inn (tel. 800/228-5151), Ramada Inn (tel. 800/272-6232), and TraveLodge (tel. 800/255-3050).

To help you decide what accommodations are best for you, the hotels listed below are categorized first by area, then by price, according to the following guide: Very Expensive—over $160, Expensive—$120–$159, Moderate—$80–$119, Inexpensive—below $80. These categories reflect the price of an average double room during the high season. Read it carefully. Many hotels also offer rooms at rates above and below the assigned price range.

The city's tourist season is loosely defined; it runs from about April through September. In general, hotel rates are rather inelastic; they don't vary much throughout the year. However, the recent economic sluggishness has led to small rate reductions throughout the city, and bargains and special packages are available. Ask about weekend discounts, corporate rates, and family plans.

1. DOWNTOWN LOS ANGELES

VERY EXPENSIVE

BILTMORE, 506 S. Grand Ave., Los Angeles, CA 90071. Tel. 213/624-1011, or toll free 800/245-8673. Fax 213/612-1545. 700 rms, 40 suites. A/C MINIBAR TV TEL **Directions:**

Beverly Crest Hotel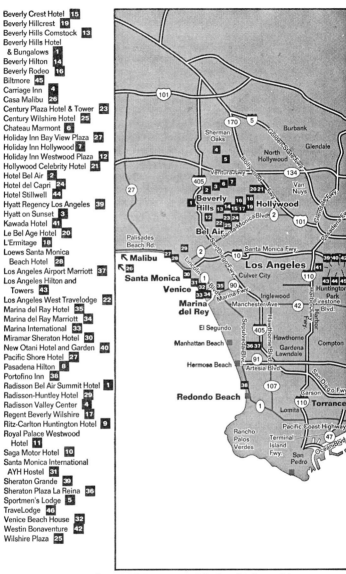
Beverly Hillcrest **19**
Beverly Hills Comstock **13**
Beverly Hills Hotel
& Bungalows **1**
Beverly Hilton **14**
Beverly Rodeo **16**
Biltmore **45**
Carriage Inn **4**
Casa Malibu **26**
Century Plaza Hotel & Tower **23**
Century Wilshire Hotel **25**
Chateau Marmont **6**
Holiday Inn Bay View Plaza **27**
Holiday Inn Hollywood **7**
Holiday Inn Westwood Plaza **12**
Hollywood Celebrity Hotel **21**
Hotel Bel Air **2**
Hotel del Capri **24**
Hotel Stillwell **44**
Hyatt Regency Los Angeles **39**
Hyatt on Sunset **3**
Kawada Hotel **41**
Le Bel Age Hotel **20**
L'Ermitage **18**
Loews Santa Monica
Beach Hotel **28**
Los Angeles Airport Marriott **37**
Los Angeles Hilton and
Towers **43**
Los Angeles West Travelodge **22**
Marina del Ray Hotel **35**
Marina del Ray Marriott **34**
Marina International **33**
Miramar Sheraton Hotel **30**
New Otani Hotel and Garden **40**
Pacific Shore Hotel **27**
Pasadena Hilton **8**
Portofino Inn **38**
Radisson Bel Air Summit Hotel **1**
Radisson-Huntley Hotel **29**
Radisson Valley Center **4**
Regent Beverly Wilshire **17**
Ritz-Carlton Huntington Hotel **9**
Royal Palace Westwood
Hotel **11**
Saga Motor Hotel **10**
Santa Monica International
AYH Hostel **31**
Sheraton Grande **39**
Sheraton Plaza La Reina **36**
Sportmen's Lodge **5**
TraveLodge **46**
Venice Beach House **32**
Westin Bonaventure **42**
Wilshire Plaza **25**

From U.S. 101, take Grand Avenue exit. The hotel is located between 5th and 6th Streets.

$ Rates: $175–$245 single; $205–$275 double; from $400, suite. AE, CB, DC, MC, V. **Parking:** $18.

Built in 1923, this gracious and elegant hotel was the site of the Academy Awards ceremonies during the 1930s and 1940s, including the year *Gone with the Wind* swept them all. The always beautiful Biltmore now looks better than ever following a $40-million facelift completed in 1987. Contemporary additions now complement traditional styles, including Jim Dine prints in the guest rooms and state-of-the-art door locks and other mechanical systems.

Lavishly appointed rooms are spacious and attractively decorated in pastel tones. Modern marble bathrooms, color TVs, and in-room minibars are offset by traditional French furniture.

Dining/Entertainment: The grand Rendezvous Court serves afternoon tea and evening cocktails. Its ornate cathedral-like vaulted ceiling was hand-painted by Italian artist Giovanni Smeraldi.

Bernard's, the hotel's top dining room, features fluted columns and hand-painted beamed ceilings. The cuisine combines classical French and regional American dishes. Smeraldi's Ristorante is open daily for breakfast, lunch, and dinner. The full-service dining room features homemade pastas and California cuisine with an Italian flair. The Grand Avenue Bar offers a cold lunch buffet, and showcases top-name jazz entertainment in the evening.

Services: 24-hour room service, concierge, evening turndown, overnight shoeshine.

Facilities: Health club, including Roman spa pool, steam room, sauna, Jacuzzi, Nautilus equipment, and free weights; business center.

HYATT REGENCY LOS ANGELES, 711 S. Hope St., Los Angeles, CA 90017. Tel. 213/683-1234, or toll free 800/233-1234. Fax 213/612-3179. 484 rms, 40 suites. A/C TV TEL **Directions:** From U.S. 101, exit at Grand Avenue and turn left at 7th Street. The hotel is on the corner of 7th and Hope Streets.

$ Rates: $129–$209 single; $174–$234 double; from $225, suite. AE, CB, DC, DISC, MC, V. **Parking:** $13.50.

The 24-story Hyatt Regency is a dazzlingly ultramodern fixture in Broadway Plaza, a 21st-century-style complex of shops, restaurants, offices, and galleries in the middle of downtown L.A. Topped by bright skylights, the two-story ground-floor lobby entrance has a garden plaza, lounges, a sidewalk café, and several boutiques. Wide escalators glide down to the lobby/reception area and lower gardens. Giant wall graphics and exposed brick surround potted plants, trees, old-fashioned gaslight streetlamps, and overstuffed furniture.

The hotel's guest rooms are of the same high comfort and unquestionable taste. Both innovative and attractive, the accommodations boast enormous windows that provide surprisingly nice views for a downtown hotel. Deep pile carpeting, oversize beds, and small sofas are all futuristic in design and utilize the same bold textures and russet-gold color scheme that's prevalent throughout the hotel.

Dining/Entertainment: Both the informal, lobby-level Brasserie and the more opulent Pavan restaurant are open for lunch and dinner Monday through Saturday. There is also the Lobby Bar.

Services: Room service, concierge, evening turndown.

Facilities: Fitness center, business center.

LOS ANGELES HILTON AND TOWERS, 930 Wilshire Blvd., Los Angeles, CA 90017. Tel. 213/629-4321, or toll free 800/445-8667. Fax 213/488-9869. 900 rms, 32 suites. A/C MINIBAR TV TEL **Directions:** From Calif. 110 north, exit onto Wilshire Boulevard; the hotel is located at the corner of Figueroa Street.

$ Rates: $160–$201 single; $180–$221 double; from $375, suite. AE, CB, DC, MC, V. **Parking:** $16.50.

This hotel is centrally located, near many downtown attractions, and it offers easy access to major freeway entrances. The hotel's modern exterior is matched by equally modern rooms outfitted with comfortable furnishings colored in soft shades. Like other Hiltons, this is a business-oriented hotel, offering a good, if unremarkable, standard of service. Furnishings are contemporary and clean; such amenities as in-house movies, a writing desk, and double-panel glass windows to minimize outside noise are also included. No-smoking rooms are available, as are those specially equipped for handicapped guests. The best rooms overlook the oval swimming pool, where there are poolside tables for drinking and dining.

The premium Towers rooms—on the 15th and 16th floors—have separate check-in facilities and a dedicated staff. Premium rates include a two-line telephone, morning newspaper delivery, continental breakfast, and a daily cocktail hour with complimentary hors d'oeuvres.

Dining/Entertainment: There are four hotel restaurants. The Gazebo Coffee Shop serves breakfast and burgers 24 hours a day; the City Grill, open for lunch only, specializes in California cuisine; and Minami of Tokyo serves Japanese breakfasts, lunches, and dinners. Cardini, a northern Italian restaurant, is the hotel's top eatery and offers good pastas, as well as a good selection of fish and veal dishes.

Services: 24-hour room service, concierge, evening turndown.

Facilities: Fitness center, swimming pool, business center, car rental, tour desk, beauty salon.

NEW OTANI HOTEL AND GARDEN, 120 S. Los Angeles St., Los Angeles, CA 90012. Tel. 213/629-1200, or toll free 800/421-8795 (800/273-2294 in California). Fax 213/622-0980. 440 rms, 15 suites. A/C MINIBAR TV TEL **Directions:** From U.S. 101, take the Los Angeles Street exit south to the corner of 1st Street.

$ Rates: $135–$170 single; $160–$195 double; from $340, Japanese-style suite. AE, CB, DC, MC, V. **Parking:** $9.

This 21-story triangular tower is the city's only Japanese-style hotel; its classical 16,000-square-foot tea garden is for the exclusive use of guests. Most of the luxurious rooms are Western in style and are furnished with refrigerators, oversize beds, bathroom telephones and radios, and individual doorbells. For a special treat, choose a Japanese-style suite, with tatami-mat bedrooms, deep whirlpool baths, and balconies overlooking the hotel garden.

Dining/Entertainment: The Canary Garden is an informal coffee shop serving breakfast, lunch, and dinner (fresh-baked breads and pastries are a specialty). Commodore Perry's, named for the infamous naval officer who forced Japan to open trade with the West, features American and continental specialties in an intimate setting. A Thousand Cranes is the evocative name of the Otani's Japanese restaurant, which serves traditional breakfasts, lunches, and dinners, including sushi.

Services: 24-hour room service, concierge, evening turndown, same-day valet cleaning.

Facilities: Japanese-style health club with saunas, baths, and shiatsu massages; shopping arcade with more than 30 shops, car-rental desk, airport limousine service. Golf and tennis are available in conjunction with a nearby country club.

SHERATON GRANDE, 333 S. Figueroa St., Los Angeles, CA 90012. Tel. 213/617-1133, or toll free 800/325-3535.

Fax 213/613-0291. 469 rms, 69 suites. A/C MINIBAR TV TEL
Directions: From Calif. 110 (Pasadena Freeway), exit onto
Wilshire Boulevard and turn left onto Figueroa Street. The hotel is
located between 3rd and 4th Streets.

$ Rates: $165–$210 single; $200–$235 double; from $250, suite.
AE, CB, DC, DISC, MC, V. **Parking:** $17.

One of downtown's newest hotels, the Sheraton Grande is a splendid
smoky-mirrored-glass structure located right in the heart of the
hustle. The large open lobby and lounge are decorated with skylights
and plants. A pianist entertains in the lounge daily from noon to
10:30pm.

Pastel-colored guest rooms are well lit and outfitted with the usual
furnishings, including a writing desk, minibar, color TV, and firm
mattresses. Bathrooms are equally functional, featuring good-quality
fittings and hotel-quality Italian marble.

Dining/Entertainment: The Back Porch, an informal dining
room overlooking the pool, serves three meals a day. The gourmet
room, Ravel, features California cuisine nightly.

Services: 24-hour room service, concierge, evening turndown,
overnight shoeshine.

Facilities: Four movie theaters, heated outdoor swimming pool
and sun deck, access to an off-premises health club.

**WESTIN BONAVENTURE, 404 S. Figueroa St., Los Ange-
les, CA 90071. Tel. 213/624-1000,** or toll free 800/228-
3000. Fax 213/612-4800. 1,500 rms, 94 suites. A/C MINIBAR TV
TEL **Directions:** From Calif. 110 (Pasadena Freeway), exit onto
Wilshire Boulevard, and turn left onto Figueroa Street. The hotel is
located between 4th and 5th Streets.

$ Rates: $150–$195 single; $175–$215 double; from $335, suite.
AE, DC, CB, MC, V. **Parking:** $22.

One of California's most innovative hotels, the space-age Westin
Bonaventure is known for its five gleaming cylindrical towers which
constitute one of downtown's most distinctive landmarks. Designed
by architect John Portman (who also designed San Francisco's Hyatt
Regency), the Westin features a beautiful six-story skylight lobby that
houses a large lake, trees, splashing fountains, and gardens. Twelve
glass-enclosed elevators appear to rise from the reflecting pools.

The best city views are available from the highest guest rooms in
this 35-story hotel. Like the lobby, accommodations are elegantly
modernistic, complete with floor-to-ceiling windows and every
amenity you'd expect at a top big-city hotel. It's even nice to know
that despite the hotel's large size, no bedroom is more than six doors
from an elevator.

Dining/Entertainment: The Sidewalk Cafe, a California bistro, and the adjacent Lobby Court, with tables under large fringed
umbrellas, are the focus of the hotel's nightly entertainment, which
varies from jazz combos to cocktail-hour music, and dancing. The
Flower Street Bar, a mixture of marble, brass, and mahogany, is a
popular spot for cocktails.

The Top of Five rooftop restaurant features panoramic views
and gourmet continental cuisine. A revolving cocktail lounge, the

Bona Vista, is located just below, on the 34th floor. Beaudry's, on the lobby level, features haute cuisine in a stunning contemporary setting.

Services: 24-hour room service, concierge, evening turndown, overnight shoeshine, car-rental desk.

Facilities: Outdoor swimming pool and sun deck, tennis courts, health club, five levels of shops and boutiques (which comprise the Shopping Gallery above the lobby).

INEXPENSIVE

THE KAWADA HOTEL, 200 S. Hill St., Los Angeles, CA 90012. Tel. 213/621-4455, or toll free 800/752-9232. Fax 213/687-4455. 116 rms, 1 suite. No-smoking rooms available. A/C TV TEL **Directions:** From Calif. 110, exit at 4th Street. Turn left on Broadway, left on 2nd Street, and left again on Hill Street. The hotel is on the corner of Hill and 2nd Streets.

$ Rates: $58–$75 single; $62–$80 double; $135 suite. AE, DISC, MC, V. **Parking:** $6.50.

This pretty, well-kept, and tightly managed hotel is a pleasant oasis in the otherwise gritty heart of downtown L.A. Behind the three-story, clean red-brick exterior can be found almost 10 dozen pristine rooms, all with handy kitchenettes and simple rose-color furnishings. Although the rooms are not large, they are extremely functional, providing both VCRs with complimentary movie rentals and two phones.

The hotel's popular lobby-level Epicentre restaurant features an eclectic international menu, and is open for breakfast, lunch, and dinner.

HOTEL STILLWELL, 838 S. Grand Ave., Los Angeles, CA 90017. Tel. 213/627-1151, or toll free 800/553-4774. Fax 213/622-8940. 250 rms, 4 suites. A/C TV TEL **Directions:** From U.S. 101, exit at Grand Avenue. The hotel is located between 8th and 9th Streets.

$ Rates: $30–$40 single; $40–$55 double; from $69, suite. AE, DC, MC, V. **Parking:** $5.

Conveniently situated in the downtown area, the hotel is close to the Civic Center's Ahmanson Theater and Dorothy Chandler Pavilion. It's also close to the Museum of Contemporary Art, Little Tokyo, Olvera Street, Union Station, and a variety of exceptional restaurants.

Decently decorated rooms include no-smoking accommodations, and larger rooms for guests traveling with children. The simple, yet comfortable, facilities are decorated in soft blue and gray tones. It's not a fancy place, but the Stillwell is relatively clean and a good choice for modestly priced accommodations in an otherwise expensive neighborhood.

There are two restaurants on the premises: Gills Cuisine of India, serving competent North Indian dishes; and Lily's, offering simple American meals. There's also a business center and tour desk.

2. HOLLYWOOD

VERY EXPENSIVE

LE BEL AGE HOTEL DE GRANDE CLASSE, 1020 N. San Vicente Blvd., West Hollywood, CA 90069. Tel. 310/ 854-1111, or toll free 800/434-4443. Fax 310/854-0926. 189 suites. No-smoking rooms available. A/C TV TEL MINIBAR **Directions:** From I-405, exit onto Santa Monica Boulevard and continue east about 4½ miles. Turn left onto San Vicente Boulevard; the hotel will be on your right.

$ Rates: $245–$330 single/double; $500 suite. AE, CB, DC, MC, V. **Parking:** $14.

One of the darlings of the hip record and film industry crowd, this luxurious, all-suite hotel is as opulent as it is pretentious. The hotel's most notable attribute is its vast collection of quality contemporary oil paintings and collages which are liberally spread throughout the lobby, hallways, and guest rooms.

Dark wood, large retro sofas and chairs, and modern smoked-glass cocktail bars complete the art-filled suites. Extras in every suite include VCRs with complimentary movie rentals; hairdryers; terry-cloth robes; multiline telephones; and milled soaps, lotions, and shampoos. Guests are welcomed with mineral water and a fruit basket upon arrival. Rooms facing the neighboring Hollywood foothills are nice, but accommodations on the other side have an even better view of the city and the valley.

Dining/Entertainment: The Bel Age Restaurant serves continental dinners Tuesday through Saturday, as well as a good Sunday brunch from 11am to 3pm. The Brasserie, which is less formal, serves California cuisine in dining rooms with great views of the city. The Brasserie bar regularly features top-notch jazz performers, and is one of the prettiest drinking rooms in the neighborhood.

Services: 24-hour room service, concierge, overnight laundry, complimentary shoeshine, business services.

Facilities: Rooftop swimming pool and Jacuzzi, hair salon, gift shop, art gallery, florist.

EXPENSIVE

CHATEAU MARMONT, 8221 Sunset Blvd., West Holly-wood, CA 90046. Tel. 213/656-1010, or toll free 800/242-8328. Fax 213/655-5311. 63 rms, 53 suites. A/C TV TEL **Directions:** From U.S. 101, exit onto Highland Avenue and turn right onto Sunset Boulevard. The hotel is located between La Cienega and Crescent Heights Boulevards, at Marmont Lane.

$ Rates: $140 single or double; from $190, suite; from $395, bungalow. AE, CB, DC, MC, V.

There isn't enough space here to list all the famous people who have stayed at this chateau-style apartment hotel situated on a cliff just above Sunset Strip. Humphrey Bogart, Jeanne Moreau, Boris Karloff, Al Pacino, James Taylor, Richard Gere, Bianca Jagger, John and Yoko, Sophia Loren, Sidney Poitier, and Whoopi

Goldberg are just a few famous former guests. Carol Channing met her husband here; Greta Garbo used to check in under the name Harriet Brown; and even Howard Hughes once maintained a suite here.

Now a historical monument, the hotel was built in 1927. It mimics the architectural style of the French Normandy region and is surrounded by private gardens with views of the city and the Hollywood hills. Chateau Marmont is famous for its privacy and personal attention; not to mention its magnificently stocked wine cellar.

Guests often gather in the great baronial living room that is furnished with local antiques. On warm days, you might lounge around the oval swimming pool amid semitropical trees and shrubbery. Guest rooms are beautifully furnished in a tasteful English style. Suites have fully equipped kitchens, and most pets are welcome.

Services: Room service, concierge.

Facilities: Swimming pool, car-rental desk.

HYATT ON SUNSET, 8401 Sunset Blvd., West Hollywood, CA 90069. Tel. 213/656-1234, or toll free 800/233-1234. Fax 213/650-7024. 262 rms. A/C TV TEL **Directions:** From U.S. 101, exit onto Highland Avenue and turn right onto Sunset Boulevard. The hotel is located 2 blocks east of La Cienega Boulevard.

$ Rates: $99–$155 single; $145–$175 double; $350–$550 suite. Special weekend rates are available. AE, CB, DC, DISC, MC, V. **Parking:** $8.

This lively place is well located: close to Restaurant Row on La Cienega Boulevard and to Sunset Strip nightlife. Spacious bedrooms on 13 floors have views of the Los Angeles skyline and the Hollywood hills; most have private balconies. Rooms have modern furnishings and dressing areas, plus all the conveniences you'd expect from a Hyatt, including in-room movies on color TVs and large, modern bathrooms.

Dining/Entertainment: The Silver Screen Restaurant pays homage to the old days of Hollywood. Giant stills from old movies surround ancient movie cameras and lights. Meals are served daily from 7am to midnight. The Sunset Lounge is a good place for a drink, and live jazz is featured several nights a week.

Services: Room service, concierge, evening turndown, car rental, tour desk.

Facilities: Rooftop swimming pool/sun deck, business center, gift shop.

MODERATE

HOLIDAY INN, 1755 N. Highland Ave., Hollywood, CA 90028. Tel. 213/462-7181, or toll free 800/465-4329. Fax 213/466-9072. 470 rms, 22 suites. A/C TV TEL **Directions:** From U.S. 101, take the Franklin Avenue exit and head west. At Highland Avenue, turn left; the hotel is located between Franklin and Hollywood Boulevards.

$ Rates: $100–$120 single or double; from $125, suite. Extra person $12. Children 18 and under stay free in parents' room. AE, DC, DISC, MC, V. **Parking:** Free.

This 22-story hostelry in the heart of Old Hollywood offers perfectly acceptable rooms that are both pleasant and comfortable. Each room is equipped with a clock radio and a digital safe. There are three laundry rooms and on every floor ice and soda machines. Suites here are a particularly good buy, since they include a small kitchenette which can help you save on restaurant meals. There's a swimming pool and sun deck on the hotel's second floor.

A revolving circular rooftop restaurant, called Windows on Hollywood, features great Hollywood views while dancing and dining. The Show Biz Café, an unusually plush coffee shop, serves breakfast, lunch, and dinner. The Front Row Lounge, an intimate cocktail lounge, is open daily until 2am.

INEXPENSIVE

HOLLYWOOD CELEBRITY HOTEL, 1775 Orchid Ave., Hollywood, CA 90028. Tel. 213/850-6464, or toll free 800/222-7017 (800/222-7090 in California). Fax 213/850-6464. 39 rms. A/C TV TEL **Directions:** From U.S. 101, take the Highland Avenue exit and turn right onto Hollywood Boulevard. Take the first right onto Orchid Avenue.

$ Rates (including continental breakfast): $68 single, $78 double, $85 twin. Extra person $8. AE, CB, DC, DISC, MC, V. **Parking:** Free.

One of the best budget buys in Hollywood is this small but centrally located hotel, just half a block behind Mann's Chinese Theatre. Spacious and comfortable units are decorated in an original art deco style. Breakfast is brought to your room along with the morning newspaper. Each room has cable TV and a radio. Small pets are allowed, but require a $50 deposit.

3. BEVERLY HILLS & CENTURY CITY

VERY EXPENSIVE

BEVERLY HILLS HOTEL & BUNGALOWS, 9641 Sunset Blvd., Beverly Hills, CA 90210. Tel. 213/276-2251, or toll free 800/283-8885. Fax 310/271-0319. 268 rms, 21 bungalows and garden suites. A/C TV TEL **Directions:** From I-405, exit at Sunset Boulevard and drive east. The hotel is located on the corner of Sunset Boulevard and Rodeo Drive.

$ Rates: $185–$295 single; $230–$320 double; from $395, suite; from $545, bungalow. AE, DC, MC, V. **Parking:** $15.

This is the real stomping ground of millionaires and maharajahs, jet-setters and movie stars. There are hundreds of anecdotes about this famous hotel, most of which took place in the hotel's Polo Lounge, one of the world's most glamorous bars. For years Howard Hughes maintained a complex of bungalows, suites, and rooms here, using some of the facilities for an elaborate electronic-communications security system, and a separate room to house his personal food-taster. Years ago Katharine Hepburn did a flawless dive into the pool—fully clad in her tennis outfit, shoes and all. Dean Martin and Frank Sinatra once got into a big fistfight with other Polo Lounge habitués. And in 1969 John Lennon and Yoko Ono checked into the most secluded bungalow under assumed names, then stationed so many armed guards around their little hideaway that discovery was inevitable. So it goes. The stories are endless and relate to everyone from Charlie Chaplin to Madame Chiang Kai-shek.

What attracts them all? For one thing, each other. And, of course, you can't beat the service—not just the catering to such eccentricities as a preference for bear steak, but little things like being greeted by your name every time you pick up the phone. It doesn't hurt that the Beverly Hills Hotel is a beauty; its green and pink stucco buildings are set on 12 carefully landscaped and lushly planted acres. There are winding paths lined with giant palm trees throughout, and the privacy of each veranda is protected by flowering and leafy foliage.

Each gorgeous accommodation is custom-designed with tropical overtones and equipped with every amenity from hairdryers to in-room VCRs.

Dining/Entertainment: The world-famous Polo Lounge has been the rendezvous headquarters of international society for more than 40 years. The Loggia and Patio (which adjoin the Polo Lounge) serve breakfast and lunch in a delightful garden setting.

Services: 24-hour room service, concierge, evening turndown, overnight laundry, shoeshine.

Facilities: Olympic-size swimming pool, cabanas, two tennis courts, fitness room, Cinema Room for private screenings.

BEVERLY HILTON, 9876 Wilshire Blvd., Beverly Hills, CA 90210. Tel. 310/274-7777, or toll free 800/445-8667. Fax 310/285-1313. 581 rms, 90 suites. A/C MINIBAR TV TEL **Directions:** From I-405 north, exit onto Santa Monica Boulevard and go east 3 miles to the hotel at Wilshire Boulevard.

$ Rates: $200–$240 single; $225–$265 double. Children and teens stay free in parents' room. Extra adult $25. AE, CB, DC, DISC, MC, V. **Parking:** $14.

Easily one of the poshest in the Hilton chain, this luxuriously decorated hotel is like a mini-city, complete with a small shopping mall and several restaurants, making it unnecessary to leave the premises.

Individually decorated rooms are full of amenities, including refrigerators and in-room, first-run movies. Most rooms have balconies that overlook an Olympic-size pool and the surrounding hillsides. The more expensive rooms are on higher floors.

Dining/Entertainment: L'Escoffier, the rooftop restaurant, combines gourmet French cuisine with a panoramic view of the city. It's open for dinner Tuesday to Saturday. The award-winning Trader Vic's sports a nautical theme, and serves South Seas and continental dishes along with exotic drinks.

Mr. H, another elegant continental-style eatery is known for its

Sunday champagne brunch and daily lunch and dinner buffets. Cafe Beverly and the lively Lobby Bar round out the offerings.

Services: 24-hour room service, concierge, evening turndown, overnight shoeshine.

Facilities: Two heated swimming pools, health club, business center; shops include Princess Ermine Jewels, Cecily L. boutique, a gift and sundry shop.

CENTURY PLAZA HOTEL AND TOWER, Avenue of the Stars, Century City, CA 90067. Tel. 310/277-2000, or toll free 800/228-3000. Fax 310/551-3355. 1,072 rms and suites. A/C TV TEL **Directions:** From Santa Monica Boulevard, exit south onto the Avenue of the Stars. The hotel is 2 blocks ahead on your left.

$ Rates: Hotel $190–$215 single; $220–$245 double; from $300, suite. Tower $225–$275 single; $285–$305 double; from $1,100, suite. AE, CB, DC, MC, V. **Parking:** $9 self, $15 valet.

The imposing Century Plaza Hotel and Tower complex is comprised of two separate and distinctive properties on 10 tropical plant-covered acres. Occupying a commanding position near Beverly Hills and right across the street from the ABC Entertainment Center and the 1,850-seat Shubert Theater, the Westin-owned hotel was built on what was once a Twentieth-Century-Fox back lot.

The 20-story, 750-room hotel is enormous—it appears to be roughly the size of New York's Grand Central Terminal—complete with vaulted cathedral ceilings, two-story windows, and sunken lounge areas. It has the feel of a bustling city of tomorrow. Rooms follow a garden motif with marble-topped oak furnishings and beautiful teal-blue or forest-green carpeting. Each has a balcony and is equipped with every amenity, including a color TV discreetly hidden in an oak armoire; three phones (bedside, tableside, and bath); refrigerator; AM/FM radio; clock; big closet; and tub/shower bath with marble sink, hairdryers, oversize towels, and scales. Special hotel extras range from a dedicated kitchen elevator in which food is kept warm on its way to your room, to the homey practice of leaving a mint and a good-night note from the management on each guest's pillow when the beds are turned down for the night.

The 30-story, $85-million Tower at Century Plaza (where former President Reagan once stayed) has 322 exceptionally spacious rooms—that's only 14 rooms per floor. All have private balconies, a wet bar and refrigerator, three conveniently located phones, an all-marble bathroom with separate soak tub and shower, double vanity and washbasins, and a heat lamp. Writing desks have travertine marble tops, and there's a live tree or green plant in each room. All Tower guests receive a complimentary newspaper each morning, as well as such deluxe bath amenities as robes, slippers, and oversize bath towels. Tower suites are all fitted with marble Jacuzzis.

The Tower and Hotel are linked by a marble corridor hung with more than $4 million worth of art. The property underwent a $16.5-million renovation in 1990.

Dining/Entertainment: The Lobby Court cocktail lounge features nightly entertainment and is surrounded by two-story windows that overlook the hotel's pools and garden. The Water's

Edge Seafood Bar & Grill also has floor-to-ceiling windows looking out onto lush tropical gardens, reflecting pools, and fountains. Fresh seafood and pasta dishes are highlighted at both lunch and dinner. La Chaumiere restaurant blends contemporary California ingredients and classic French techniques to produce an innovative cuisine in a setting reminiscent of a fine European club. Bill Marx, son of Harpo, plays piano every Tuesday to Saturday night in the adjacent bar. The Terrace is an excellent choice for classic California dining. Filled with greenery and located on the lobby level, it serves breakfast, lunch, and dinner daily, as well as a champagne brunch on Sunday. The Cafe Plaza, a provincial-style coffee shop with a simple bakery, deli, and charcuterie, is decorated with French travel posters. It's open from 6am to 1am.

Services: 24-hour room service, concierge, evening turndown, business center, multilingual staff, same-day laundry, complimentary car service to and from Beverly Hills.

Facilities: Two large outdoor heated swimming pools, three Jacuzzis, a children's pool, 10 shops, airline desk, car-rental office, ticket agency, tour desk, free access to an off-premises health club.

L'ERMITAGE, 9291 Burton Way, Beverly Hills, CA 90210. Tel. 213/278-3344, or toll free 800/424-4443. Fax 213/278-8247. 112 suites. A/C MINIBAR TV TEL **Directions:** From Santa Monica Boulevard, exit onto Burton Way. The hotel is located 10 blocks ahead, at the corner of Maple Drive.

$ Rates: $285–$325 one-bedroom executive suite; $385–$475 one-bedroom town-house suite; $455–$625 two-bedroom town-house suite; $1,000 three-bedroom town-house suite. AE, CB, DC, MC, V. **Parking:** $12.

Ⓕ FROMMER'S COOL FOR KIDS: HOTELS

Century Plaza Hotel and Tower (see p. 64) Although it is not inexpensive, older children will love exploring this labyrinthine hotel, which features two large outdoor heated swimming pools, three Jacuzzis, and a children's pool. Kids are given free amenity packs filled with games, crayons, coloring books, and an inflatable beach ball.

Loews Santa Monica Beach Hotel (see p. 77) One of the few beachfront hotels in Los Angeles, it offers a complete children's program during summer. For $25 per day, kids are treated to tours, classes, and activities monitored by a trained staff.

Hotel Stillwell (see p. 59) Ask for one of their larger guest rooms, and the kids will have plenty of room for romping. It's an inexpensive hotel in an otherwise pricey neighborhood.

L'Ermitage is one of the finest hotels in the world. In addition to a kitchenette, each of the small suites includes a sunken living room, wet bar, dressing area, and powder room. Town-house suites are slightly larger and have fully equipped kitchens. Accommodations here are furnished residentially, like rooms in a fine home. The rooms and hallways are hung with oil paintings, and every unit has a fireplace.

Strawberries and brown sugar are delivered to each suite at 4pm, and complimentary caviar is served each afternoon in the elegant bar on the top floor.

Dining/Entertainment: The Club restaurant, which is hung with original paintings by Renoir, Braque, and de la Pena, caters exclusively to hotel guests.

Services: 24-hour room service, concierge, overnight shoeshine, limousine service, morning newspaper.

Facilities: Rooftop garden, mineral spa, heated swimming pool, private solarium.

REGENT BEVERLY WILSHIRE, 9500 Wilshire Blvd., Beverly Hills, CA 90210. Tel. 310/275-5200, or toll free 800/421-4354. Fax 310/274-2851. 300 rms, 144 suites. A/C TV TEL **Directions:** From Santa Monica Boulevard, exit onto Wilshire Boulevard and continue east 8 blocks to the hotel.

$ Rates: $255 single or double; $325 deluxe single or double; from $425, suite. Additional person $30. Children under 15 stay free in parents' room. AE, DC, DISC, MC, V. **Parking:** $15.

This grand Beverly Hills hotel has long attracted international royalty, media celebrities, stage personalities, presidents, and the usual smattering of rich and famous. Parts of *Pretty Woman,* with Richard Gere and Julia Roberts, were filmed here. The spacious lobby contains French Empire (Directoire) furnishings, French and Italian marble flooring, restored bronze and crystal chandeliers, hand-wrought sconces, and two paintings by Verhoven.

Upon arrival, visitors are greeted by a guest-relations officer who personally escorts you to your room; luggage is recorded by computer and arrives by a separate elevator. There is steward service on every floor (a concept that began with the Regent's Hong Kong property), as well as 24-hour concierge service.

El Camino Real, a private cobblestone and gas lamp street separates the Beverly and Wilshire wings of the hotel. On average, guest rooms here are larger than those in comparable hotels. Wilshire Wing rooms are largest, but many on the Beverly side are prettier, with balconies overlooking the pool area. Every room is beautifully appointed with a mix of period furniture, three telephones, three color cable TVs, and special double-glazed windows that ensure absolute quiet.

The bathrooms, which are lined with marble, feature a large vanity, excellent lighting, deep soaking tubs, and a separate glass-enclosed shower that's large enough for three or more. Amenities include fresh flowers in each room, plush deep-pile white bathrobes, scales, hairdryers, and specially packaged toiletries.

Dining/Entertainment: The Cafe, an elegant, updated version of the old-fashioned soda fountain, serves lox and eggs, cheese blintzes, sandwiches, salads, and changing daily main courses. It's open from 6am to midnight. The Lobby Lounge is an elegant European-style salon for tea (served from 3 to 5pm), light menus, late-night dinner fare, and cocktails—a place "to be seen." There's live entertainment in the evening. The Dining Room, outfitted in lush woods and soft fabrics, offers a lengthy list of elegant American lunch and dinner fare. Reservations are recommended.

Services: 24-hour room service, concierge, evening turndown, overnight shoeshine.

Facilities: Health club, swimming pool, hot tubs, massage, business center, shops (including Tiffany and Buccellati).

EXPENSIVE

BEVERLY HILLCREST, 1224 S. Beverwil Dr., Beverly Hills, CA 90212. Tel. 213/277-2800, or toll free 800/421-3212 (800/252-0174 in California). Fax 213/203-9537. 150 rms, 4 suites. A/C TV TEL **Directions:** From Santa Monica Boulevard, exit south onto the Avenue of the Stars and turn left onto Pico Boulevard. The hotel is about 10 blocks ahead, at Beverwil Drive.

$ Rates: $85–$100 single; $100–$140 double; $215–$345 suite. Weekend rates available. AE, DC, MC, V. **Parking:** $6.

A multimillion-dollar luxury hostelry at the southern edge of Beverly Hills, the Hillcrest offers particularly spacious and elegant accommodations on 12 floors. Rooms are appointed in a restrained French provincial decor, many with half-canopied beds. Each has a refrigerator, marble bathroom with an extra phone, and a balcony.

Dining/Entertainment: A steel-and-glass exterior elevator whisks guests to the Top of the Hillcrest, a rooftop restaurant offering views of Beverly Hills, Hollywood, and the Pacific Ocean. Its lavish interior, complete with gold-leather upholstered chairs and glittering crystal chandeliers, is a good setting for choice continental meals that include coq au vin, steak, and lobster. Breakfast, lunch, and dinner are served daily at Portofino, a candlelit Old World Italian eatery with tufted red-leather booths and exposed brick and wood-paneled walls.

Services: Room service, concierge, evening turndown, business center, tour desk, car-rental.

Facilities: Swimming pool.

BEVERLY RODEO, 360 N. Rodeo Dr., Beverly Hills, CA 90210. Tel. 310/273-0300, or toll free 800/356-7575. Fax 310/859-8730. 88 rms, 4 suites. A/C TV TEL MINIBAR **Directions:** From Santa Monica Boulevard, turn south onto Rodeo Drive. The hotel is located 1 block north of Wilshire Boulevard.

$ Rates: $140–$160 standard single or double; $150–$170 deluxe single or double; $160–$180 executive single or double; from $250, suite. AE, DC, MC, V. **Parking:** $9.

Owner Max Baril has seen to it that his intimate, European-style hotel feels luxurious. Once you get past the courteous doorman, you enter a recently redecorated French provincial–style world with opulent wall hangings and plush carpets.

Accommodations don't disappoint either—they're outfitted with matching floral-print spreads and draperies, and marble baths with extra phones. Many rooms enjoy balconies and refrigerators.

Dining/Entertainment: Cafe Rodeo, with its large windows facing the street, is great for Rodeo Drive people-watching. The dining room is furnished with contemporary natural wood and rattan furniture. Breakfast, lunch, dinner, and Sunday brunch are also served in the adjoining, charming outdoor courtyard. A pianist performs each evening.

Services: Room service, concierge, evening turndown, overnight shoeshine, same-day laundry, morning newspaper.

MODERATE

BEVERLY CREST HOTEL, 125 S. Spalding Dr., Beverly Hills, CA 90212. Tel. 213/274-6801, or toll free 800/247-6432. Fax 213/273-6614. 53 rms. A/C TV TEL **Directions:** From I-405 north, exit onto Santa Monica Boulevard. Continue east for 3 miles, turn east onto Wilshire Boulevard and after 1 block turn right onto Spalding Drive to the hotel.

$ Rates: $95–$100 single; $100–$110 double. Special senior rates available. AE, MC, V. **Parking:** Free.

Although somewhat small, the rooms here are pleasantly decorated in cool shades of blue, peach, or orange. White- or black-lacquer furnishings are contemporary in style, and complement good closet space, full-length mirrors, and individual air conditioning and heating controls. The most desirable rooms overlook the swimming pool courtyard, which is surrounded by palm trees.

The hotel's Venetian Grill serves competent continental-style breakfasts, lunches, and dinners. Guests have access to an off-premises health club; and they may also use the services of a tour desk with car-rental facilities.

HOTEL DEL CAPRI, 10587 Wilshire Blvd., Los Angeles, CA 90024. Tel. 310/474-3511, or toll free 800/444-6835. Fax 310/470-9999. 81 rms, 48 suites. No-smoking rooms available. A/C TV TEL **Directions:** From I-405 north, exit onto Wilshire Boulevard and turn right. Continue down Wilshire Boulevard about 1¼ miles; the hotel is on the left at the corner of Westholme Avenue and Wilshire Boulevard.

$ Rates (including continental breakfast): $85–$105 single or double; from $110, suite. Additional person $10. AE, CB, DC, MC, V. **Parking:** Free.

Although it sits squarely in the middle of L.A., the hotel's muted aqua and pink exterior seems to come right from "Miami Vice." The Del Capri is actually two buildings, one a two-story motel surrounding a kidney-shaped swimming pool, the other a four-story hotel overlooking the courtyard and the boulevard.

Although each room is a little different, most are outfitted with pretty pastels and contemporary black accents. Many look out onto the courtyard through lace curtains that cover floor to ceiling windows. All the beds here are electrically adjustable—a nice, if unconventional, touch. The more expensive rooms are slightly larger, and have whirlpool baths and an extra phone in the bathroom.

In addition to continental breakfast, the hotel provides free shuttle service to nearby shopping and sights in Westwood, Beverly Hills, and Century City.

4. BEL AIR

VERY EXPENSIVE

HOTEL BEL AIR, 701 Stone Canyon Rd., Bel Air, CA 90077. Tel. 310/472-1211, or toll free 800/648-4097. Fax 310/476-5890. 92 rms, 33 suites. A/C MINIBAR TV TEL **Directions:** From I-405, exit onto Sunset Boulevard east. After 2 miles, turn left onto Stone Canyon Road.

$ Rates: $225–$395 single; $245–$435 double; from $480, suite. AE, CB, DC, MC, V. **Parking:** $11.

Yet another top hotel in one of the world's fanciest neighborhoods, the Spanish-style Hotel Bel Air regularly wins praise from guests for its attentive service and ultra-deluxe guest rooms. Set on exquisite tropical grounds and surrounded by the Santa Monica hills, the Bel-Air is entered via a long awning-covered pathway, actually an arched stone bridge over a swan- and duck-filled pond. A large oval swimming pool is set amid the lush gardens and surrounded by a flagstone terrace. Inside, you'll find richly traditional public rooms furnished with fine antiques, and a fire that is kept burning in the entrance lounge.

The individually decorated rooms and garden suites, all of which have large picture windows, are equally stunning; many have patios or terraces, and some have wood-burning fireplaces. Each room has two telephones, and VCRs are delivered to your room on request.

Dining/Entertainment: Even if you're not staying here, it's worth showing up for a drink at the Bougainvillea Court or dinner in The Restaurant. Main courses include Muscovy duck with tangerine sauce and loin of lamb Wellington baked in phyllo dough. Terrace seating overlooks a small lake. The Bar, a cozy drinkery adjacent to The Restaurant, has a wood-burning fireplace and nightly entertainment.

Services: 24-hour room service, concierge, evening turndown.

Facilities: Swimming pool, tennis courts, access to off-premises health club.

EXPENSIVE

RADISSON BEL AIR SUMMIT HOTEL, 11461 Sunset Blvd., Los Angeles, CA 90049. Tel. 310/476-6571, or toll free 800/333-3333. Fax 310/471-6310. 161 rms, 6 suites. A/C MINIBAR TV TEL **Directions:** From I-405, exit onto Sunset Boulevard west. The hotel is immediately ahead on your right.

$ Rates: $109–$139 single; $119–$149 double; from $179, suite. Additional person $15. AE, CB, DC, DISC, MC, V. **Parking:** $3.50.

Set in an 8-acre garden estate, The Bel Air Summit is just minutes away from Beverly Hills, Westwood Village and UCLA, and Century City; and 8 miles north of LAX.

Spacious rooms and suites all feature large balconies and have subtle color schemes and understated decor. All rooms have VCRs, hairdryers, refrigerators, coffee-makers, electronic security keys, radios, and two telephones. There is a heated swimming pool and a single unlit tennis court on the premises.

Dining/Entertainment: Echo, the hotel dining room, serves breakfast, lunch, dinner, and a fabulous Sunday brunch. The Oasis bar serves cocktails nightly, and complimentary hors d'oeuvres Monday through Saturday from 5 to 7pm.

Services: Room service, concierge, evening turndown, car-rental, tour desk.

Facilities: Swimming pool, tennis court, gift shop, beauty salon with spa treatments.

5. WILSHIRE

Wilshire is a very long street that connects Beverly Hills with downtown L.A. The two listings below are on opposite ends of the street.

EXPENSIVE

WILSHIRE PLAZA, 3515 Wilshire Blvd., Los Angeles, CA 90010. Tel. 213/381-7411, or toll free 800/382-7411. Fax 213/386-7379. 400 rms, 5 suites. A/C TV TEL **Directions:** From U.S. 101, take the Melrose/Normandie exit and turn south onto Normandie Avenue. The hotel is located about 2 miles ahead, at the corner of Wilshire Boulevard.

$ Rates: $110–$140 single; $120–$160 double; from $250, suite. AE, DC, DISC, MC, V. **Parking:** $8 self, $10 valet.

Located close to downtown, this 12-story luxury hotel is popular with businesspeople for its push-button comfort and convenient location. Rooms are attractively furnished in a modern style; each has a glass-brick wall and functional furniture. One- and two-bedroom suites have two bathrooms and an additional living room.

Dining/Entertainment: Hugo's is open for breakfast, lunch, and dinner, serving basic American fare such as prime rib and grilled swordfish.

Services: Room service, concierge, car rental, tour desk, business center.

Facilities: Heated outdoor swimming pool, barbershop.

MODERATE

BEVERLY HILLS COMSTOCK, 10300 Wilshire Blvd., Los Angeles, CA 90024. Tel. 310/275-5575, or toll free 800/800-1234. Fax 310/278-3325. 116 suites. A/C MINIBAR TV TEL **Directions:** From I-405 south, exit onto Wilshire Boulevard

WESTWOOD & WEST LOS ANGELES • **71**

east. The hotel is located just before Beverly Hills, at Comstock Street.

$ Rates: $95–$130 standard suite; $150–$195 one-bedroom kitchen suite; $210–$295 two-bedroom kitchen suite. Monthly rates available. AE, CB, DC, DISC, MC, V. **Parking:** $5.

Dedicated to the comfortable, homelike suite business, this quiet, peaceful hotel offers a standard of intimacy and privacy not usually available at larger hotels. Understandably, the Comstock, located just outside Beverly Hills, attracts many celebrity guests.

The large rooms are decorated in either a traditional hotel style or a colorful California modern flair. The units, which surround a central courtyard pool and garden area, have private balconies or patios. There are telephones and TVs in both bedrooms and bathrooms. The kitchen suites are particularly large, ranging from 1,000–2,000 square feet. These well-equipped accommodations have a living room, a dining area, and completely equipped kitchens with china service.

Dining/Entertainment: Le Petit Cafe, a continental restaurant, serves breakfast, lunch, and dinner, and has a full-service bar.

Services: Room service, concierge, overnight laundry.

Facilities: Swimming pool, Jacuzzi, access to an off-premises health club.

6. WESTWOOD & WEST LOS ANGELES

Wedged between Santa Monica and glamorous Beverly Hills, the UCLA-student-dominated community of Westwood has more than 400 shops, about 100 restaurants, and 15 first-run movie theaters. West Los Angeles, as a glance at your L.A. map will show you, is just slightly south of Westwood, and within easy reach of Beverly Hills, Century City, and Santa Monica.

EXPENSIVE

HOLIDAY INN WESTWOOD PLAZA, 10740 Wilshire Blvd., Los Angeles, CA 90024. Tel. 310/475-8711, or toll free 800/472-8556 (800/235-7973 in California). Fax 310/475-5220. 295 rms, 8 suites. A/C MINIBAR TV TEL **Directions:** From I-405, take the Westwood exit and follow Wilshire Boulevard east 1 mile to the hotel, at the corner of Selby Avenue.

$ Rates: $120–$130 single; $130–$140 double; from $225, suite. Children 18 or under stay free in parents' room. AE, CB, DC, DISC, MC, V. **Parking:** Free.

Attractively furnished twin-bedded rooms are decorated according to an English Tudor theme, which includes hunting prints on most walls. Special touches include marble sinks in the bathrooms, and complimentary morning newspapers delivered to your door. Services include a tour desk, car rental, laundry, concierge, gift shop, and an exercise room. The hotel also provides complimentary shuttle service to anyplace within a 2½-mile radius.

Dining/Entertainment: The hotel restaurant, Cafe Le Dome, is best known for its cocktail lounge, which is popular with basketball and football players, many of whom stay at the hotel.

Facilities: Swimming pool, sun deck, sauna, Jacuzzi.

INEXPENSIVE

CENTURY WILSHIRE HOTEL, 10776 Wilshire Blvd., Los Angeles, CA 90024. Tel. 310/474-4506, or toll free 800/421-7223. Fax 310/474-2535. 100 rms, 58 suites. No-smoking rooms available. TV TEL **Directions:** From I-405 north, exit onto Wilshire Boulevard and turn right. Continue down Wilshire Boulevard about 1 mile; the hotel is on the right between Malcolm and Selby Avenues.

$ Rates (including continental breakfast): $65–$75 single; $65–$85 double; $80–$95 junior suite; $125–$150 one-bedroom suite. AE, CB, DC, MC, V. **Parking:** Free.

This large white hotel in downtown Westwood is conveniently located near UCLA and Beverly Hills. The otherwise sparsely decorated rooms are enlivened with floral wallpaper and certain special touches. Some rooms feature French doors which open onto balconies, and many other rooms come complete with kitchenettes. The hotel surrounds a quiet courtyard, and has an Olympic-size swimming pool out back. Breakfast is served each morning in the small lobby.

LOS ANGELES WEST TRAVELODGE, 10740 Santa Monica Blvd., Los Angeles, CA 90025. Tel. 213/474-4576, or toll free 800/631-0100. Fax 213/470-3117. 36 rms. A/C TV TEL **Directions:** From I-405, exit onto Santa Monica Boulevard. The hotel is 2 miles ahead, at Overland Avenue.

$ Rates: $60–$90 single; $66–$96 double. Extra person $6. AE, CB, DC, MC, V. **Parking:** Free.

This clean and friendly establishment offers good value for the area. The pleasant, modern rooms are equipped with clocks, in-room coffee-makers, and refrigerators. There is no restaurant or health facilities in the hotel, but there is an enclosed private heated swimming pool with a sun deck, plus plenty of parking.

ROYAL PALACE WESTWOOD HOTEL, 1052 Tiverton Ave., Los Angeles, CA 90024. Tel. 310/208-6677, or toll free 800/631-0100. Fax 310/824-3732. 36 rms, 6 suites. A/C TV TEL **Directions:** From I-405, take the Westwood exit and follow Wilshire Boulevard east ½ mile. Turn left onto Glendon Avenue and bear right onto Tiverton Avenue to the hotel.

$ Rates: $60 single; $66–$76 double; from $90, suite. Extra person $8. AE, CB, DC, DISC, MC, V. **Parking:** Free.

Located between Beverly Hills, Century City, Santa Monica, West Los Angeles, and Bel Air, the Royal Palace is convenient to Hollywood, the beach, the airport, and most importantly, the San Diego Freeway. There are dozens of shops and restaurants within easy walking distance of the hotel.

This is not a fancy place by any stretch of the imagination, but each comfortable, redecorated room has a bed, desk, dresser, and color TV. Some accommodations have stoves, refrigerators, and stainless steel countertops, while others have microwave ovens. There are marble vanities in the bathrooms. Facilities include a free exercise room, lounge, and a tour desk for area activity information and reservations.

7. SAN FERNANDO VALLEY

MODERATE

CARRIAGE INN, 5525 Sepulveda Blvd., Sherman Oaks, CA 91411. Tel. 818/787-2300, or toll free 800/854-2608. Fax 818/782-9373. 183 rms, 2 suites. A/C TV TEL **Directions:** From I-405 north, take the Burbank Boulevard exit and turn right onto Sepulveda Boulevard. The hotel will be straight ahead on your right.

$ Rates: $80 single or double; from $150, suite. **Parking:** Free.

The Carriage Inn is on "motel row," near the San Diego Freeway (I-405) at Burbank Boulevard. It's a super structure, with a seemingly endless maze of accommodations. In the middle is a small swimming pool, a Jacuzzi, a coffee shop and dining room, and a cocktail bar, which features nightly entertainment. The rooms are not new, but large, each with a small sitting area.

RADISSON VALLEY CENTER, 15433 Ventura Blvd., Sherman Oaks, CA 91403. Tel. 818/981-5400, or toll free 800/248-0446. Fax 818/981-3175. 215 rms, 7 suites. A/C TV TEL **Directions:** From either U.S. 101 or I-405 north, exit at Sherman Oaks and continue on Ventura Boulevard to the hotel.

$ Rates: $70 single or double during the week; $80 single or double on the weekend; from $225, suite. Special discount packages available. AE, CB, DC, MC, V. **Parking:** $5.

Well located, in the heart of the valley, the Radisson Valley Center sits at the crossroads of two major freeways—San Diego (I-405) and Ventura (U.S. 101). Universal Studios, NBC, Magic Mountain, Griffith Park, Hollywood, and Beverly Hills are all nearby. The spacious rooms are attractively decorated with only slightly out-of-date baths and furnishings, and each has a private balcony.

Hotel facilities include a heated rooftop swimming pool, Jacuzzi, and sun deck. The ground floor Orion Cafe and Lounge serves breakfast, lunch, and dinner, and is open late for cocktails.

SPORTSMEN'S LODGE, 12825 Ventura Blvd., Los Angeles, CA 91604. Tel. 818/769-4700, or toll free 800/821-8511 (800/821-1625 in California). Fax 213/877-3898. 193 rms, 13 suites. A/C TV TEL **Directions:** From U.S. 101 north, take the Coldwater Canyon exit and turn left. After 1 mile, turn left onto Ventura Boulevard. The hotel will be about ¼ mile ahead on your left.

$ Rates: $94–$104 single, $104–$140 double; poolside executive studio $154 single, $159 double. Extra person $10. AE, CB, DC, DISC, MC, V. **Parking:** Free.

Movie, TV, and recording industry people all know about the Sportsmen's Lodge. Out in the valley, it is so near many of the studios that actors sometimes stay here during a stretch of shooting.

While here, you'd hardly know you're in the middle of a big city. Located just west of Universal City, the Sportsmen's Lodge is surrounded by redwood trees, waterfalls, rock gardens, lush tropical greenery, and rustic wooden footbridges that cross freshwater ponds. In fact, the hotel's name derives from the fact that guests used to fish for trout right on the premises.

Rooms are large and comfortable, but not luxurious in any way. They have AM/FM radios, many have balconies, and refrigerators are available. The poolside executive studios are the most appealing accommodations.

The hotel's attractive restaurant features a glass-enclosed dining room overlooking a tropical lagoon-style pond and small waterfall. You might begin a meal here with an order of baked clams topped with bacon bits and pimento, then order a main dish of veal piccata or duckling à l'orange with wild rice, priced from $15 to $28. Cakes and rolls are baked fresh daily. An adjacent coffee shop serves simpler breakfasts, lunches, and dinners.

Facilities include an Olympic-size, heated swimming pool with a Jacuzzi and large sun deck. A well-equipped exercise room has life cycles, rowing machines, and weights. There are also a variety of shops and service desks in the hotel, and both bowling and golf are available nearby. Complimentary afternoon tea is served in the lobby at 4pm.

8. PASADENA

EXPENSIVE

THE PASADENA HILTON, 150 S. Los Robles Ave., Pasadena, CA 91101. Tel. 818/577-1000, or toll free 800/445-8667. Fax 818/584-3148. 291 rms, 15 suites. A/C MINIBAR TV TEL **Directions:** From I-210, take the Lake Avenue South exit and turn right on Cordova Street. The hotel is straight ahead, on the corner of Cordova Street and Los Robles Avenue.

$ Rates: $120–$150 single; $135–$165 double; from $250, suite. AE, CB, DC, MC, V. **Parking:** $8.

This 13-story hostelry is 15 minutes from downtown Los Angeles, and only 1½ blocks south of Colorado Boulevard, which is famous for the annual route of the Rose Parade. The rooms have been redecorated in soft earth tones. Some have beds with elaborate high headboards, and all have refrigerators and in-room movies. The higher rates command accommodations with king-size beds and balconies.

The hotel does a lot of convention business. It is also affiliated with the nearby, exclusive L.A. Canada/Flintridge Country Club, which allows hotel guests to use its facilities.

Dining/Entertainment: The Trevos restaurant, serving a California cuisine, offers breakfast, lunch, and dinner. There is an all-you-can-eat, fresh buffet daily. The Lobby Bar is a favorite rendezvous during happy hour.

Facilities: Outdoor swimming pool; exercise room with Universal equipment, StairMasters, life cycles, and free weights; business center.

Services: Room service, concierge, evening turndown, overnight laundry.

THE RITZ-CARLTON HUNTINGTON HOTEL, 1401 S. Oak Knoll Ave., Pasadena, CA 91109. Tel. 818/568-3900, or toll free 800/241-3333. Fax 818/568-3700. 383 rms, 21 suites. A/C MINIBAR TV TEL **Directions:** From LAX, take Century Boulevard to I-405 north. Exit onto I-10 east (Santa Monica Freeway) and continue to Calif. 110 north (Pasadena Freeway). At the first traffic signal, turn right onto Glenarm Avenue. Turn right again onto El Molino, then left onto Elliot, and left again onto Oak Knoll Avenue. The hotel is on the corner of Wentworth Avenue.

$ Rates: $145–$240 single or double; from $350, suite. AE, DC, MC, V. **Parking:** $10.

Originally built in 1906, the landmark Huntington Hotel quickly became the place to be seen, as celebrated writers, entertainers, political leaders, royalty, and business leaders discovered the elegance of this special place. The hotel managed to survive the 1929 stock market crash, the Great Depression, and World War II, but it could not survive the major earthquake that struck in 1985. After a painstaking 2½-year restoration, the Huntington reopened in 1991 under the Ritz-Carlton banner. The fantastically beautiful hotel is set on 23 meticulously landscaped acres nestled in the shadows of the San Gabriel Mountains and overlooking the San Gabriel Valley.

Throughout the hotel, careful attention has been given to re-create the genteel, timeless ambience of the original resort. Overstuffed sofas and club chairs upholstered in natural fabrics sit on oriental carpets and are surrounded by fine 18th- and 19th-century oil paintings.

The hotel consists of a main building and six suite-filled cottages. Each room is oversized and elegantly appointed with marble bathrooms, sitting areas, desks, large closets, and two telephones. There are remote-controlled color TVs, thick terry bathrobes, and in-room minibars.

Dining/Entertainment: The Grill offers a comfortable clublike setting for grilled meats, chops, and fresh fish. The 100-seat Georgian Room is the hotel's premiere restaurant, serving continental cuisine prepared by renowned French chef Bernard Bordaris. The Cafe serves breakfast, lunch, and dinner, either inside or outdoors. The menu offers American standards, as well as light spa cuisine. A fixed-price, four-course dinner is offered on Friday and Saturday nights, and champagne brunch is served on Sundays. The Bar serves lunch and cocktails into the night. The Lobby Lounge offers continental breakfast, cocktails, and traditional afternoon tea with—a pleasant touch—classical music accompaniment.

Facilities: Olympic-size swimming pool, outdoor whirlpool, fitness center, three tennis courts, pro shop, business center, gift shop, Japanese gardens.

Services: 24-hour room service, concierge, evening turndown, complimentary airport transportation, babysitting, car rental, mountain bike rental.

INEXPENSIVE

SAGA MOTOR HOTEL, 1633 E. Colorado Blvd., Pasadena, CA 91106. Tel. 818/795-0431. 69 rms. A/C TV TEL **Directions:** From I-210, exit Fair Oaks Avenue south, and turn left on Colorado Boulevard, the second major street. The hotel is about 1 mile ahead, between Allan Avenue and Sierra Bonita.

$ Rates (including continental breakfast): $55 single; $57 double; $59 single or double with king-size bed and refrigerator; $75 suite. AE, CB, DC, MC, V. **Parking:** Free.

The Saga Motor Hotel is about 1 mile from the Huntington Library, and reasonably close to Pasadena City College, Cal Tech, and the Jet Propulsion Lab. It's also within easy distance of the Rose Bowl. But the bottom line is that the Saga has, by far, some of the most attractive rooms in its price range, as well as an inviting, sunlit, and spotlessly clean reception area.

Comfortable accommodations, which include cable TVs, are nicely decorated with brass beds, blue-and-white-checked spreads, and blue-and-white tile baths with both showers and tubs. Guest rooms are split between two buildings: the first is a single-story structure wrapped around a swimming pool; the other is a small three-story building between the pool and a quiet street at the rear of the building.

9. MALIBU

MODERATE

CASA MALIBU, 22752 Pacific Coast Hwy., Malibu, CA 90265. Tel. 310/456-2219, or toll free 800/831-0858. Fax 310/456-5418. 21 rms. TV TEL **Directions:** From Santa Monica, take Calif. 1 north to Malibu. The hotel is located directly on Calif. 1 about ¼ mile before the Malibu Pier.

$ Rates: $85 single or double with garden view; $105 single or double with ocean view; $115 oceanfront single or double. $10 additional for rooms with kitchens. Extra person $10. MC, V. **Parking:** Free.

Inexpensive accommodations in Malibu are hard to obtain. Your best bet is the Casa Malibu, a ranch-style motel built around a palm-studded inner courtyard with well-tended flowerbeds and cuppa d'oro vines growing up the balcony. The squat hostelry sits directly on the ocean, in front of a large swath of private, sandy beach. The rooms are cheerful and attractively furnished—some with private balconies. Each is equipped with oversize beds, a coffee-maker, and refrigerator. Oceanfront rooms are particularly lovely, since they have private decks hanging over the sandy beach.

10. SANTA MONICA & VENICE

Not only does choosing Santa Monica or adjacent Venice mean being near the beach, it means getting away from the smog and staying in one of the most attractive, dynamic neighborhoods in L.A.

VERY EXPENSIVE

LOEWS SANTA MONICA BEACH HOTEL, 1700 Ocean Ave., Santa Monica, CA 90401. Tel. 310/458-6700, or toll free 800/223-0888. Fax 310/458-6761. 349 rms, 22 suites. A/C MINIBAR TV TEL **Directions:** From the Santa Monica Freeway (I-10), exit west onto 4th Street and turn left toward the ocean. Turn right onto Ocean Drive, then left to the hotel.

$ Rates: $155–$285 single; $175–$305 double; from $300, suite. Children under 18 stay free in parents' room. Additional person $20. AE, CB, DC, MC, V. **Parking:** $10.

Loews is one of the few beachfront hotels in all of Los Angeles. Located just two blocks from Santa Monica Pier, this relatively new lavish hotel is easily the best in the area.

In addition to all the amenities you'd expect from a top hotel, each room is equipped with three TVs, three telephones (with two phone lines), plush terry bathrobes, hairdryers, and VCRs on request.

Dining/Entertainment: There are two restaurants and poolside snack service. A pianist entertains in the lounge most afternoons, and during the evening, when the bar gets busy.

Services: 24-hour room service, concierge, twice-daily maid service, overnight shoeshine, bike and roller-skate rental, babysitting, summer children's program.

Facilities: Swimming pool, Jacuzzi, fitness center, business center.

MIRAMAR SHERATON HOTEL, 101 Wilshire Blvd., Santa Monica, CA 90401. Tel. 310/394-3731, or toll free 800/325-3535. Fax 310/458-7912. 303 rms, 62 suites. A/C MINIBAR TV TEL **Directions:** From the Santa Monica Freeway (I-10), exit west onto 4th Street. After 5 blocks, turn left onto Wilshire Boulevard. The hotel is 4 blocks ahead on your left, between Ocean Avenue and 2nd Street.

$ Rates: Winter: $150–$175 single; $170–$195 double. Summer: $160–$185 single; $180–$205 double; year round from $245, suite. Extra person $20. AE, CB, DC, MC, V. **Parking:** $5.

Miramar means "ocean view" and that's just what this hotel offers from its cliff-top perch overlooking Santa Monica Beach. The hotel was originally built in the 1920s, and that era's elegance is clearly in evidence throughout the public areas. In the courtyard is a century-old fig tree that casts its shadow over the garden and adjacent swimming pool.

Guest rooms are split between older low buildings and the newer tower. Each is comfortable and luxurious for a beach hotel. Amenities include a king-size bed or two double beds, in-room safe, and digital clock radio. Bathrooms are plush, outfitted with extra phones, honor bars, special soaps and shampoos, and oversize towels.

Dining/Entertainment: The International Room, serving continental and American cuisine, is open for dinner; the Garden Room, overlooking the pool and garden, serves breakfast and lunch; and The Cafe serves continuously from breakfast to dinner. The Stateroom Lounge offers live entertainment, cocktails, and dancing several nights a week.

Services: 24-hour room service, concierge, evening turndown, same-day laundry and valet service, complimentary newspaper, bike rental.

Facilities: Heated swimming pool, access to an off-premises health club, gift shop, beauty salon, women's boutique.

EXPENSIVE

PACIFIC SHORE HOTEL, 1819 Ocean Ave. (at Pico Boulevard), Santa Monica, CA 90401. Tel. 310/451-8711, or toll free 800/622-8711. Fax 310/394-6657. 168 rms. A/C TV TEL **Directions:** From the Santa Monica Freeway (I-10) south, exit at 4th Street and turn right. After 2 blocks, turn right onto Pico Boulevard. The hotel is straight ahead, at the corner of Ocean Avenue.

$ Rates: $125–$135 single or double. AE, MC, V. **Parking:** Free.

An eight-story hotel, just a half block from the beach, Pacific Shore lives up to its name, offering excellent views from the higher priced rooms. Every guest room looks out onto the ocean or pool through an entire wall of tinted glass; you can see out but nobody can see in. Accommodations are attractively decorated in cheerful colors. Each has a small dressing area, rattan and walnut furnishings, and an AM/FM radio. There are ice and soft-drink machines on every floor. A cocktail lounge offers nightly entertainment.

Facilities: Shops, car-rental, tour desk, guest laundry, outdoor heated swimming pool, whirlpool, Jacuzzi, saunas for men and women.

RADISSON-HUNTLEY HOTEL, 1111 2nd St., Santa Monica, CA 90403. Tel. 310/394-5454, or toll free 800/333-3333. Fax 310/458-9776. 213 rms, 6 suites. A/C TV TEL **Directions:** From the Santa Monica Freeway (I-10), exit west onto 4th Street. After 5 blocks, turn left onto Wilshire Boulevard, then right onto 2nd Street to the hotel.

$ Rates: $120–$145 single; $135–$160 double; from $150, suite. Ask about the "Supersaver Rates" promotion. AE, CB, DC, DISC, MC, V. **Parking:** $5.

One of the tallest buildings in the neighborhood, the Radisson-Huntley offers nondescript rooms just two blocks from the beach. Accommodations are basic yet comfortable; attractive, with ocean or mountain views; and equipped with AM/FM radios, color TVs, and other modern amenities. Toppers, the rooftop Mexican restaurant, has a great view, serves good margaritas, and offers free live entertainment nightly. The lobby-level Garden Cafe is a classy coffee shop serving American standards.

MODERATE

HOLIDAY INN BAY VIEW PLAZA, 530 Pico Blvd. (at 6th Street, west of Lincoln), Santa Monica, CA 90405. Tel. 310/399-9344, or toll free 800/465-4329. Fax 310/399-2504. 309 rms, 9 suites. A/C MINIBAR TV TEL **Directions:** From the Santa Monica Freeway (I-10), exit onto 4th Street and turn left onto Lincoln Boulevard south. After 6 blocks, turn right onto Pico Boulevard to the hotel.

$ Rates: $95–$115 single or double; from $225, suite. AE, CB, DC, MC, V. **Parking:** Free.

Although not particularly cheap, this Holiday Inn represents some of the best value on the beach, with good-sized, well-outfitted rooms. Accommodations on the highest floors of this 10-story hotel offer nice views of either the ocean or the city. There is a heated, outdoor swimming pool and adjacent spa pool, as well as a small exercise room for guests' use. The hotel's Bay View Café is open daily for breakfast, lunch, and dinner. Guests are provided with free shuttle service to and from Los Angeles International Airport.

VENICE BEACH HOUSE, 15 30th Ave., Venice, CA 90291. Tel. 310/823-1966. Fax 310/823-1842. 7 rms, 2 suites. TV TEL **Directions:** From Calif. 1, turn west onto Washington Boulevard, then right onto Pacific Avenue. Thirtieth Avenue is a small walkway on the left. There's a parking lot behind the house.

$ Rates (including continental breakfast): Mon–Thurs: $80–$130 single or double without bath; $110 single or double with bath. Fri–Sun: $90–$150 single or double without bath; $120 single or double with bath; from $110, suite. Additional person $10. No smoking allowed. AE, DC, MC, V. **Parking:** Free.

Built in 1911 by Warren Wilson, this former family home is now one of the area's finest bed-and-breakfasts. While admiring the Victorian building's hardwood floors, bay windows, lattice porch, and large oriental rugs, it's easy to forget the hustle and bustle of the beach that's just steps away.

Each of the inn's seven rooms is different, outfitted with white rattan dressers and nightstands, or antique wood furnishings. Some are punctuated with country prints, or shelves packed with worn hardcover books. Every room has an alarm clock and access to a fan, and one particularly romantic room has a fireplace. The inn provides bicycles for guests and can make picnic baskets for day excursions.

Continental breakfasts that include cereal, breads, juice, and coffee are served each morning in the comfortable downstairs sitting room. Afternoon tea or cool lemonade is also served every day.

Be aware that the Venice Beach House can get noisy, and despite this simple B&B's relative homeyness, it is not for everyone.

INEXPENSIVE

SANTA MONICA INTERNATIONAL AYH HOSTEL, 1436 2nd St., P.O. Box 575, Santa Monica, CA 90406. Tel. 310/393-9913. Fax 310/393-1769. 38 rms. **Directions:** From the Santa Monica Freeway (I-10), exit on 4th Street and make a right turn. Turn left on Colorado and then right on 2nd Street.

$ Rates: $14 per person with an IYHF card; $17 per person without; $3 surcharge for twin rooms. MC, V. **Parking:** 50¢ per hour.

Opened in April 1990, the Santa Monica hostel is just two blocks from the beach and Santa Monica Pier, and about 1 mile from Venice Beach. It's within walking distance of shops and restaurants and about two blocks from regional bus lines, including a direct bus to Los Angeles International Airport (about 7 miles).

This is one of the largest specifically built hostels in this country and can accommodate up to 200 guests, including groups and families on a space-available basis. Accommodations are dormitory style, with shared bedrooms and bathrooms. The hostel has guest kitchen facilities, a travel library, and a travel center. It's pretty nice too, designed in muted earth tones and centered around an open courtyard. Six twin rooms are reserved for couples, and four family rooms cater to families.

There is a TV lounge, laundry room, game room, information desk, vending machines, a dining room, library, and secure lockers. You must provide sheets; you are asked to be quiet after 11pm; and you are not permitted to smoke or drink alcohol.

Reservations are highly recommended, especially from May to October. Write them at least two weeks in advance and include your dates of stay; number of males and females in your party; your name, address, and telephone number; and the first night's deposit. To reserve by phone, call between 1pm and 5pm Monday through Saturday.

IYHF membership is required during peak times. Individual membership in the American Youth Hostel organization costs $25 per year and entitles you to discounted rates in any AYH-affiliated hostel. You can buy a membership at the hostel. Guests are limited to three-night stays; however, this can be extended to five nights with the approval of the manager.

11. MARINA DEL REY

Sandwiched between Santa Monica and the Los Angeles International Airport, Marina del Rey is a popular waterfront resort, just two minutes from major freeways that connect with most L.A. attractions. More than 6,000 pleasure boats dock here, making its marina the world's largest small-craft harbor.

EXPENSIVE

MARINA DEL REY HOTEL, 13534 Bali Way, Marina del Rey, CA 90292. Tel. 310/301-1000, or toll free 800/882-4000 (800/862-7462 in California). Fax 310/301-8167. 156 rms, 6 suites. A/C TV TEL **Directions:** From I-405, exit onto Calif. 90, which ends at Lincoln Boulevard. Turn left onto Lincoln Boulevard, then right onto Bali Way to the hotel.

$ Rates: $120–$185 single; $140–$205 double; from $350, suite. AE, CB, DC, MC, V. **Parking:** Free.

Located at the tip of a pier jutting into the harbor, this hotel specializes in rooms that look out over one of the world's largest yacht-filled harbors. The only hotel located on a harbor pier, the Marina del Rey is almost completely surrounded by water. First-class guest rooms are decorated in a soothing blue-and-tan color scheme and are fitted with all the expected amenities. Most rooms have balconies or patios. If yours doesn't, go down to the heated waterside swimming pool where great views can be enjoyed from the beautifully landscaped sun deck area.

Dining/Entertainment: The Dockside Cafe, a coffee shop, is open daily for breakfast and lunch. The Crystal Seahorse serves continental dinners from 6 to 11pm daily. The restaurant overlooks the marina, and its mirrored tables, walls, and ceilings reflect the view.

Services: Room service, concierge, evening turndown, complimentary airport limousine, car-rental desk.

Facilities: Heated swimming pool; putting green; nearby tennis, golf, and beach.

MARINA DEL REY MARRIOTT, 13480 Maxella Ave., Marina del Rey, CA 90292. Tel. 310/822-8555, or toll free 800/228-9290. Fax 310/823-2996. 283 rms, 3 suites. A/C MINIBAR TV TEL **Directions:** From I-405, exit onto Calif. 90, which ends at Lincoln Boulevard. Turn right onto Lincoln Boulevard, and right again onto Maxella Avenue.

$ Rates: $90–$135 single; $130–$160 twin or double; from $275, suite. AE, CB, DC, DISC, MC, V. **Parking:** Free.

This delightful, resort-like hotel offers excellently appointed rooms with AM/FM clock radios, first-run movies, and bright tropical-style rooms accented with splashy floral-design spreads and drapes. Tile bathrooms, in-room minibars, pretty furnishings, and good service make this an excellent place to stay. Many rooms have patios or balconies.

The hotel is conveniently located next to the Villa Marina Center, a small mall with about 30 shops.

Dining/Entertainment: Maxfield's Restaurant and Lounge serves American-continental dishes in cheery surroundings. The outdoor pool bar is in a landscaped courtyard complete with a rock waterfall, pond, and bridge over a stream.

Services: Room service, concierge, evening turndown, complimentary airport transportation.

Facilities: Swimming pool, whirlpool, car and bicycle rental.

MARINA INTERNATIONAL, 4200 Admiralty Way, Marina del Rey, CA 90292. Tel. 310/301-2000, or toll free 800/882-4000 (800/862-7462 in California). Fax 310/301-6687. 135 rms, 24 suites, 25 bungalows. A/C TV TEL **Directions:** From I-405, exit onto Calif. 90, which ends at Lincoln Boulevard. Turn left onto Lincoln Boulevard, right onto Bali Way, and then right onto Admiralty Way to the hotel.

$ Rates: $110–$150 single; $125–$298 double; from $130, suite; from $150, bungalow. AE, CB, DC, MC, V. **Parking:** Free.

Located at the top end of the harbor, the Marina International's lovely rooms are both bright and contemporary; many offer unobstructed water views. Suites have an additional sitting room and an extra phone in the bathroom. The hotel's bungalows are located off a private courtyard. An especially good value, the spacious bungalows offer truly private accommodations. They're fitted with luxuriously appointed sitting areas, bedrooms, and bathrooms. Larger than suites, some bungalows have raised ceilings, while others are split-level duplexes. Most rooms are decorated in a warm, casual, contemporary California style, with soft pastel colors and comfortable textured fabrics.

Dining/Entertainment: The Crystal Fountain features continental cooking served indoors or out. It's open daily for breakfast and lunch.

Services: Room service, concierge, complimentary airport shuttle.

Facilities: Heated swimming pool, whirlpool, tour desk, business center, nearby golf and tennis.

12. AIRPORT

EXPENSIVE

LOS ANGELES AIRPORT MARRIOTT, Century Blvd. and Airport Blvd., Los Angeles, CA 90045. Tel. 310/641-5700, or toll free 800/228-9290. Fax 310/337-5358. 1,020 rms, 19 suites. A/C TV TEL **Directions:** From I-405, take Century Boulevard west toward the airport. The hotel is on your right, at Airport Boulevard.

$ Rates: $89 single; $154 double; from $375, suite. AE, CB, DC, DISC, MC, V. **Parking:** $8.

Built in 1973 and last renovated in 1987, this business hotel is not on the cutting edge, but it is a good choice near the airport. There are cheerfully decorated bedrooms with AM/FM-stereo radios and alarm clocks. The hotel is designed for travelers on the fly; you can use ironing boards, irons, and hairdryers if needed. There's also a guest laundry room on the premises.

Dining/Entertainment: The Lobby Bistro serves buffet breakfasts, lunches, and dinners. The Capriccio Room offers continental specialties in a Mediterranean ambience. The Fairfield Inn coffee shop serves American food and is open all day. Cocktails and entertainment are offered in Champions lounge.

Services: Room service, concierge, car rental, tour desk, complimentary airport limousine service.

Facilities: Giant swimming pool, swim-up bar, garden sun deck, whirlpool, business center.

SHERATON PLAZA LA REINA, 6101 W. Century Blvd., Los Angeles, CA 90045. Tel. 310/642-1111, or toll free 800/325-3535. Fax 310/410-1267. 807 rms, 91 suites. A/C MINIBAR TV TEL **Directions:** From I-405, take Century Boulevard west toward the airport. The hotel is on your right, near Sepulveda Boulevard.

$ Rates: $115–$155 single; $135–$175 double; from $300, suite. AE, CB, DC, DISC, MC, V. **Parking:** $8.

The airport area has been developing in the last few years, and this Sheraton is one of the newer additions. Rooms have a quintessential California look, with rattan chairs and live plants; color-coordinated drapes and bedspreads are dark green and burgundy. All rooms are equipped with digital alarm clocks; TVs with free sports, news, and movie channels; and AM/FM radios. Bathrooms are carpeted and are fitted with shower heads over bathtubs.

Dining/Entertainment: The Plaza Brasserie, an airy, contemporary café, is open from 6am to 11pm. At Landry's, which is open for lunch and dinner, the focus is on steak, chops, and seafood, including a sushi bar. The Plaza Lounge serves cocktails nightly.

Services: 24-hour room service, concierge, evening turndown, car-rental desk, tour desk, business center, same-day laundry, complimentary airport shuttle, complimentary morning newspaper.

Facilities: Heated outdoor swimming pool, spa, shops, boutiques, unisex hair salon, exercise room with Universal equipment.

13. REDONDO BEACH & LONG BEACH

EXPENSIVE

PORTOFINO INN, 260 Portofino Way, Redondo Beach, CA 90277-2092. Tel. 213/379-8481, or toll free 800/468-4292. Fax 213/372-7329. 170 rms, 3 suites. No-smoking rooms available. A/C TV TEL MINIBAR **Directions:** From Calif. 1 south, turn west onto Beryl Street. Continue straight on Beryl Street as it turns into Portofino Way; follow signs to the hotel.

$ Rates: $140–$150 single or double with marina view; $160–$170 king room with marina view; $170–$180 single or double with ocean view; $190–$200 king room with ocean view; $245 double with ocean view and private Jacuzzi; $275 one-bedroom suite. Children under 12 stay free in parents' room. Weekend and other packages available. AE, CB, DC, MC, V. **Parking:** Free.

Resting on its own little peninsula between the Pacific Ocean and the Redondo Beach Marina, this large, salmon-colored inn offers dated, yet elegant seclusion in this busy seaside community.

An imposing fireplace and spectacular two-story oceanfront windows make the hotel's large lobby a natural gathering place.

While the standard single or double rooms are a little small, the slightly more expensive king rooms are well worth the extra money. No matter which you choose, all have lattice balconies, a refrigerator, and a view of either the ocean or the marina. The large bathrooms come with complimentary robes, plush towels, and the usual package of shampoos and soaps.

Dining/Entertainment: The Marina Cafe, which serves breakfast and lunch, has outdoor seating. The Marina Grill is open for dinner only, and serves fresh seafood and steaks, as well as salads and sandwiches. The Bayside 240 bar and grill enjoys excellent water views and is open for dinner and Sunday brunch.

Services: Room service, complimentary coffee and tea service, afternoon and evening snacks served in the lobby, complimentary airport shuttle, bicycle rental.

Facilities: Exercise room, pool, spa.

INEXPENSIVE

TRAVELODGE, 80 Atlantic Ave., Long Beach, CA 90802. Tel. 310/435-2471. Fax 310/437-1995. 63 rooms. A/C TV TEL **Directions:** From the Long Beach Freeway (I-710) south, exit at 6th Street and turn right onto Atlantic Avenue. The hotel is on your left, on the corner of 1st Street and Atlantic Avenue.

$ Rates: $49 single; $54 double; $59 twin. AE, DC, DISC, MC, V. **Parking:** Free.

Literally surrounded by budget hotels, this chain motel is consistently one of the cleanest and cheapest; it represents one of the best values in the area. Nothing fancy here, but the location is good, right in downtown Long Beach, adjacent to an all-night coffee shop.

CHAPTER 6

LOS ANGELES DINING

As recently as 10 years ago, it was hard to get a great meal in Los Angeles. Today, however, the city boasts some of the most interesting and inventive eateries in the world, and consistently rates among the top culinary venues anywhere. Supported by a diverse range of ethnic choices, year-round outdoor seating, and California-inspired imaginative interiors, the many eateries in the city are also blessed with creative and skilled chefs.

In the past decade or so Angelenos have become more knowledgeable about their food. They eat well and love to discuss restaurants and their respective chefs. Dining out is an important part of the entertainment industry; it's where you see and are seen, meet important contacts, and, ultimately, make significant deals.

New restaurants and chefs are regular topics of conversation in Los Angeles. Deciding where to eat can spark a lengthy debate about the positive and negative aspects of various restaurants. In general, Angelenos are well versed about their city's restaurants and the city's continually changing chefs.

Like so many other aspects of externally oriented L.A., dining places are a major part of the local status scene—to the see-and-be-seen crowd, it matters not only which restaurant you patronize, but the table where you are seated. Although it hardly matters to the average tourist, almost every "important" restaurant has its "A" tables and its socially less-important sections. Some film industry watchers even infer who's "in" and who's "out" according to where they are seated in some of the more famous restaurants.

There are lots of places to eat for less than $5. The problem is that you can "starve" in the time it takes to get from one place to another. On the other hand, you can also spend as much as $75 for a meal, per person, without wine or even valet parking. Los Angeles has restaurants for everyone—from American to Lithuanian to Vietnamese.

To help you choose where to eat, the restaurants listed below are categorized first by area, then by price, according to the following guide: Expensive (over $35 per person); Moderate ($20–$35 per person); and Inexpensive (under $20 per person). These categories reflect the price of most dinner menu items, including appetizer, main course, coffee, dessert, tax, and tip. Keep in mind that many of the restaurants listed as "expensive" are moderately priced at lunch. Also, many of the hotel restaurants listed should be considered. Reservations are usually advised at most Los Angeles–area restaurants.

1. DOWNTOWN LOS ANGELES

EXPENSIVE

HORIKAWA, 111 S. San Pedro St. Tel. 213/680-9355.
Cuisine: JAPANESE. **Reservations:** Recommended at dinner.
Directions: From U.S. 101, exit onto Alameda Street south. After 2 blocks, turn right on 1st Street, then left on San Pedro Street.
$ Prices: Appetizers $5–$9; lunch $10–$15; main courses $18–$30; complete dinner $35–$75; Ryotei dinner $110. AE, CB, DC, MC, V.
Open: Lunch, Mon–Fri 11:30am–2pm; dinner, Mon–Thurs 5–10pm, Fri 6–10:30pm, Sat 5:30–11pm, Sun 5–9:30pm.

This tranquil restaurant is an excellent choice for good Japanese cooking. At the entrance there's a small fountain similar to those found in traditional Japanese gardens. Reproductions of works by the Japanese artist Shiko Munakata hang in the separate Teppan Grill Room. It's worth coming here just to see them.

You can begin your dinner at Horikawa with a sushi sampler or seafood teriyaki. A complete dinner might include shrimp tempura, sashimi appetizer, dobin-mushi (a seafood and vegetable soup served in a minipot), kani (crab) salad, filet mignon tobanyaki (served on a sizzling minicooker), rice, tea, and ice cream or sherbet. You can also order à la carte. In the Teppan Grill Room you might opt for filet mignon and lobster tail served with fresh vegetables.

PACIFIC DINING CAR, 1310 W. 6th St. Tel. 310/483-6000.
Cuisine: AMERICAN. **Reservations:** Recommended. **Directions:** From U.S. 101, exit onto Alvarado Street south, and take the third left onto 6th Street. The restaurant is 1 block ahead on your right.
$ Prices: Appetizers $5–$10; main courses $20–$35; lunch $10–$29; breakfast $9–$19. AE, MC, V.
Open: Daily 24 hours; breakfast, 11pm–11am; lunch, 11am–4pm; dinner anytime.

Located just a few short blocks from the center of downtown Los Angeles, this restaurant has been authentically decorated to evoke the golden age of rail travel. Walls are paneled in warm mahogany with brass luggage racks (complete with luggage) overhead. Old menus and prints from early railroading days line the walls, and brass wall lamps with parchment shades light some tables.

Steaks are prime, aged on the premises, and cooked over a mesquite-charcoal fire. At dinner, top sirloin, a New York steak, fresh

FROMMER'S SMART TRAVELER: RESTAURANTS

1. Go ethnic. The city has some great, inexpensive ethnic dining establishments.
2. Eat your main meal at lunch when prices are lower; you can sample gourmet hot spots for a fraction of the price charged at dinner.
3. Watch the liquor; it can add greatly to the cost of any meal.
4. Look for fixed-price menus, two-for-one specials, and coupons in local newspapers and magazines.

seafood, veal, and lamb are all available. For starters, try the excellent calamari; weight watchers, however, might prefer the beefsteak tomato and onion salad. Menu items are basically the same at lunch. On a recent visit I enjoyed a perfectly charbroiled boneless breast of chicken, with choice of potato or tomato. There's an outstanding wine list too. Desserts are simple fare, such as apple pie. There's also a breakfast menu featuring egg dishes, salads, and steaks.

A second restaurant is located in Santa Monica, at 2700 Wilshire Blvd., 1 block east of 26th Street (tel. 310/453-4000).

MODERATE

GRAND STAR, 943 Sun Mun Way. Tel. 213/626-2285.
   Cuisine: CHINESE. **Reservations:** Recommended. **Directions:** From U.S. 101, exit to North Broadway and continue north about 7 blocks to Sun Mun Way, between College and Bernard Streets.
$ Prices: Appetizers $3–$7; main courses $8–$16. Fixed-price meals from $20. AE, CB, DC, MC, V.
   Open: Lunch, Mon–Fri 11:30am–3pm, Sat–Sun noon–3pm; dinner, Mon–Thurs and Sun 3–10pm, Fri–Sat 3pm–midnight.

Owned and operated by the Quon family since 1967, Grand Star offers an unusual selection of top-notch Chinese dishes. There are four complete meals, including a gourmet selection of spicy shrimp in a lettuce shell, wonton soup, spicy chicken wings, Mongolian beef with mushrooms, lobster Cantonese, barbecued pork with snow peas, fried rice, tea, and dessert. If there are four or five people in your party, Mama Quon's chicken salad is added, along with larger portions of everything else. A la carte items are also available, ranging from rum-flamed dumplings to lobster sautéed in ginger and green onion. Steamed fish, priced according to size, is a house specialty, as are the cashew chicken, Mongolian beef, and Chinese string beans.

The building began life as a penny arcade. On the street level the Grand Star looks more Italian than Chinese; it's dimly lit, with black-leather booths and big bunches of dried flowers here and

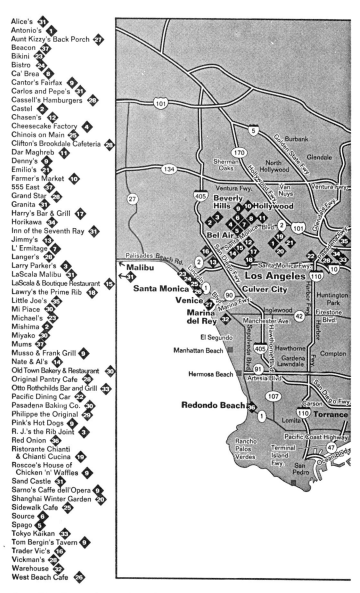

there. I prefer to sit upstairs, where tables are covered with red cloths and the family's fine collection of Chinese embroideries adorns the walls. Entertainment—usually a female vocalist with piano accompaniment—is featured at cocktail time and most evenings.

LITTLE JOE'S, 900 N. Broadway. Tel. 213/489-4900.
Cuisine: ITALIAN. **Reservations:** Recommended. **Directions:** From U.S. 101, exit to North Broadway and continue north

about 5 blocks to the restaurant, at the corner of College Street.

$ Prices: Appetizers $5–$8; main courses $10–$18; 6-course dinner $15–$22; lunch $6–$13. AE, CB, DC, DISC, MC, V.

Open: Mon–Sat 11am–9pm.

Little Joe's, a vestige of this once-Italian neighborhood, now finds itself in touristy New Chinatown. Opened as a grocery in 1927, Joe's has grown steadily over the years; it now encompasses several bars and six dining rooms. It's a wonderfully cozy restaurant with sawdust on the floors, hand-painted oil murals of Rome and Venice, soft lighting, and seating in roomy leather booths.

A meal here ought to begin with a plate of the special hot hors d'oeuvres—fried cheese, zucchini, and homemade ravioli. A complete six-course meal will consist of soup, antipasto, salad, pasta, vegetable or potato, bread and butter, and dessert; main dishes include veal scaloppine, scallops, or halibut steak. You can also get a full pasta dinner, or order à la carte. Less expensive lunches include dishes like eggplant parmigiana, sausage and peppers, and rigatoni. Without doubt, Little Joe's is the best occidental restaurant in Chinatown.

OTTO ROTHSCHILDS BAR AND GRILL, ground floor of the Dorothy Chandler Pavilion, 135 N. Grand Ave. Tel. 213/972-7322.

Cuisine: CONTINENTAL. **Reservations:** Required. **Directions:** From U.S. 101, exit onto Grand Street and go 1 block to the Music Center.

$ Prices: Appetizers $6–$9; main courses $14–$25; after-theater dinner $12–$19; lunch $8–$13; breakfast $6–$10. AE, CB, DC, MC, V.

Open: Mon 7:30am–6pm, Tue–Fri 7:30am–midnight, Sat–Sun 11:30am–midnight.

This restaurant celebrates the unparalleled visual history of the motion picture industry and its stars. Photographs of stage and screen celebrities taken by Otto Rothschild over a period of 40 years adorn the walls of this handsome eatery. At breakfast, traditional egg dishes are offered, as well as some exceptional omelets (including one with crab, avocado, and mushrooms); you might also consider the carameled apple pancake filled with sliced apples and dusted with a hint of cinnamon.

There's nothing commonplace about lunch, either. I tend to focus on the appetizers and light dishes such as the Szechuan grilled chicken tenderloins with two dipping sauces, or the prime rib chili served with corn chips. Heavier dishes like garden fettuccine with wild mushrooms, asparagus, sun-dried tomatoes, broccoli, and zucchini; and pan-seared chicken breast served over wild mushrooms appear regularly.

The list of dinner main courses includes excellent choices of prime meats, seafood, and pastas. Herb-roasted prime rib is served with whipped horseradish sauce; the rack of lamb comes crusted with Dijon herb crumbs; and if you take your seafood spicy, try the Cajun broiled colossal shrimp. An after-theater menu, served from 9pm to midnight, ranges from light main dishes (smoked ham and Cheddar omelet, Rothschild burger, salad) to the more substantive (pasta, fresh fish, even the herb-roasted prime rib of beef).

TOKYO KAIKAN, 225 S. San Pedro St. Tel. 213/489-1333.

Cuisine: JAPANESE. **Reservations:** Recommended. **Directions:** From U.S. 101, exit onto Alameda Street south. After 2 blocks, turn right on 1st Street, then left onto San Pedro Street. The restaurant is located between 2nd and 3rd Streets.

$ Prices: Appetizers $4–$8; main courses $10–$17; complete dinner $16–$22; complete lunch $8–$15. AE, DISC, MC, V.
Open: Lunch, Mon–Fri 11:30am–2pm; dinner, Mon–Sat 5–10pm.

Tokyo Kaikan is among the most popular Japanese restaurants in Los Angeles. It's designed to look like a traditional Japanese country inn, with colored globe lights overhead, barnwood, and bamboo-and-rattan-covered walls adorned with straw baskets and other provincial artifacts.

A la carte dinner main dishes, served with soup and rice, include beef sukiyaki, shrimp and vegetable tempura, and chicken and beef teriyaki. Several combination plates let you try a number of native dishes without ordering everything on the menu. Green tea, sake, and beer are served at both lunch and dinner, as is ginger ice cream.

INEXPENSIVE

CASSELL'S HAMBURGERS, 3266 W. 6th St., in New Chinatown. Tel. 480-8668.

Cuisine: AMERICAN. **Reservations:** Not accepted. **Directions:** From the Pasadena Freeway (Calif. 110), exit at 6th Street and head west. The restaurant is just ahead on your right.
$ Prices: $4–$7. No credit cards.
Open: Lunch, Mon–Sat 10:30am–4pm.

Yellow Formica tables with bridge chairs and linoleum floors prove that the owner prefers to put profits into the hamburger, not the "ambience." And it's agreed, Cassell's flips one of the best burgers in town. For more than 30 years this dive has been importing its own steer beef, almost daily, from Colorado. You can order your burger medium, rare, well done, or "blue" (simply whisked over the fire). Help yourself to fixings which include lettuce, homemade mayonnaise, Roquefort dressing, freshly sliced tomatoes, onions, and pickles. You can also have all the peaches, pineapple slices, cottage cheese, and delicious homemade potato salad you want.

CLIFTON'S BROOKDALE CAFETERIA, 648 S. Broadway. Tel. 213/627-1673.

Cuisine: AMERICAN. **Reservations:** Not accepted. **Directions:** From the Pasadena Freeway (Calif. 110), exit at 6th Street and head east. Turn right onto Spring Street, another right onto 7th Street, and then right again onto Broadway.
$ Prices: Appetizers $1–$3; main courses $3–$7. No credit cards.
Open: Daily 7am–7pm.

This is one of a chain of economy cafeterias that has kept the less prosperous of Los Angeles nourished for more than five decades. Clifford Clinton—not Clifton—founded the business on what, today, would seem to be a unique principle: "We pray our humble service be measured not by gold, but by the Golden Rule." During the Depression he kept thousands from starving by honoring an extraordinary policy: "No guest need go hungry. Pay what you wish, dine free unless delighted."

Those shopping or sightseeing downtown can enjoy a huge,

economical meal that might consist of split-pea soup, hand-carved roast turkey with dressing, baked squash with brown sugar, and Bavarian cream pie—an excellent meal for under $10. There are more than 100 à la carte items at modest prices. However, since there is a charge for everything, including bread and butter, you must limit your choices to keep your meal inexpensive. It's all fresh, delicious, and homemade too; even the baking is done on the premises. Fresh bakery items are sold at the front counter.

A second Clifton's is located nearby, at 515 W. 7th St. at Olive Street (tel. 213/485-1726). It's open Monday through Saturday from 7am to 3:30pm.

VICKMAN'S, in the produce market, 1228 E. 8th St. Tel. 213/622-3852.

Cuisine: AMERICAN. **Reservations:** Recommended. **Directions:** From U.S. 101, exit at Alameda Street and turn right onto 8th Street. The produce market is located at Central Avenue.

$ Prices: Breakfast $6–$9; main courses $4–$7. No credit cards.
Open: Mon–Sat 3am–3pm.

Established in 1930, this is one of the oldest restaurants in downtown Los Angeles. During Depression days Vickman's sold a beef-tip sandwich for 10¢, less than today's tax on the same item. Still, prices are low by current standards. Practically unchanged, however, are the unusual hours and the decor (or lack thereof)—creamy walls, linoleum floors, fluorescent lighting, big Formica tables, and wooden booths. Vickman's managers are always on the scene making sure the service and food are up to snuff. It is, and their clientele is so loyal it almost amounts to a cult.

Patrons come for hearty breakfasts, perhaps a Spanish omelet, fresh-baked Danish pastries, or the market omelet with fresh mushrooms and shallots. Fresh-squeezed orange juice is also available. At lunch there are blackboard specials like cold poached salmon with caper sauce, stuffed pork chops, and boiled chicken. On the other hand, you could order a bagel with cream cheese and lox, a chopped-liver sandwich, or a bowl of chili and beans. Leave room for a big hunk of home-baked fresh-fruit (possibly strawberry or peach) pie with gobs of real whipped cream. It's all cafeteria style; there is no table service. Dinner is not available.

LANGER'S, 704 S. Alvarado St. Tel. 213/483-8050.

Cuisine: JEWISH. **Reservations:** Not accepted. **Directions:** From the Pasadena Freeway (Calif. 110), exit west onto Olympic Boulevard. After 10 blocks turn right (north) on Alvarado Street. The restaurant is 3 blocks ahead, on the corner of 7th Street.

$ Prices: Appetizers $4–$10; main courses $6–$14. MC, V.
Open: Daily 6:30am–9pm.

Dating from 1947, Langer's is a big, roomy place with counter seating and brown tufted-leather booths. The walls are lined with portraits of the Langer family and grandchildren, and the corner location (two windowed walls) is light and airy.

The food is kosher style rather than kosher, which means that you can mix milk and meat and order the likes of pastrami and Swiss cheese on rye. The main dishes include: stuffed kishka with soup or salad, vegetable, and potatoes; meat blintzes with gravy; and an interesting sandwich combination of cream cheese and cashews.

THE ORIGINAL PANTRY CAFE, 877 S. Figueroa St. Tel. 213/972-9279.

Cuisine: AMERICAN. **Reservations:** Not accepted. **Directions:** From Calif. 110 (Pasadena Freeway), exit onto Wilshire Boulevard and turn left onto Figueroa Street. The restaurant is located at 9th Street.

$ Prices: Appetizers $2–$4; main courses $6–$10. No credit cards.

Open: Daily 24 hours.

This place has been open 24 hours a day for more than 60 years; they don't even have a key to the front door. Its well-worn decor consists of shiny cream-colored walls with old patined oil paintings and hanging globe lamps overhead; big stainless-steel water pitchers and bowls of celery, carrots, and radishes are placed on every Formica table. Besides the bowl of raw veggies, you also get a whopping big portion of homemade creamy coleslaw and all the homemade sourdough bread and butter you want—a meal in itself—before you've even ordered.

When you do order, you'll be amazed at the bountiful portions. A Pantry breakfast might consist of a huge stack of hotcakes, big slabs of sweet cured ham, home fries, and cup after cup of freshly made coffee. A huge T-bone steak, home-fried pork chops, baked chicken, and macaroni and cheese are served later in the day. The Pantry is an original—don't miss it.

PHILIPPE THE ORIGINAL, 1001 N. Alameda St. Tel. 213/628-3781.

Cuisine: AMERICAN. **Reservations:** Not accepted. **Directions:** From U.S. 101, exit onto North Broadway and turn right on Ord Street. The restaurant is located 4 blocks ahead at the intersection of North Main, Alameda, and Ord Streets.

$ Prices: Appetizers $1–$3; main courses $3–$7. No credit cards.

Open: Breakfast, daily 6–10:30am; lunch and dinner, daily 10:30am–10pm.

Good old-fashioned value and quality is what this establishment is all about—people come here for the good beef, pork, ham, turkey, or lamb French-dip sandwiches served on the lightest, crunchiest French rolls. Philippe's has been around since 1908, and there's nothing stylish about the place. Stand in line while your French-dip sandwich is being assembled, then carry it to one of several long wooden tables. Other menu items include homemade beef stew, chili, two different soups daily, and pickled pigs' feet. A variety of desserts include New York–style cheesecake, cream and fruit pies, puddings, and custards.

A hearty breakfast is served until 10:30am daily, including Philippe's special cinnamon-dipped French toast. All the egg dishes can be topped with their zesty homemade salsa. Beer and wine are available, and there's free parking in the rear and in a lot across the street.

2. HOLLYWOOD

EXPENSIVE

DAR MAGHREB, 7651 Sunset Blvd. Tel. 213/876-7651.
Cuisine: MOROCCAN. **Reservations:** Recommended. **Directions:** From U.S. 101, exit onto Highland Avenue, and turn right onto Sunset Boulevard. The restaurant is straight ahead, between Fairfax and La Brea Avenues, at the corner of Stanley Avenue.
$ Prices: Set dinners $18-$29. DC, MC, V.
Open: Dinner, daily 6-11pm.

When you pass through these immense carved brass doors, you enter an exotic Arab world. Step into a Koranic patio, at the center of which is an exquisite fountain under an open skylight. The floor is marble, and the carved wood-and-plaster walls are decorated with handmade tiles in geometric designs. A kaftaned hostess greets you and leads you to either the Rabat Room or the Berber Room. The former features rich Rabat carpets, marquetry tables, and silk cushions with spun-gold-thread designs. The Berber Room is more rustic, with warm earth tones, mountain rugs, and brass furniture from Marrakech. In both rooms diners sit on low sofas against the wall and on goatskin poufs (cushions). Berber and Andalusian music are played in the background, and there is belly dancing nightly.

The set meal is a multicourse feast, including a choice of chicken, lamb, rabbit, squab, quail, or shrimp, eaten with your hands and hunks of bread, and shared, from the same dish, with other members of your party. There are eight possible dinners, most of which come with Moroccan salads of cold raw and cooked vegetables; and b'stilla, an appetizer of shredded chicken, eggs, almonds, and spices wrapped in a flaky pastry shell and topped with powdered sugar and cinnamon. Other dishes include a tajine of chicken cooked with pickled lemons, onions, and fresh coriander; and couscous, with lamb and vegetables—squash, carrots, tomatoes, garbanzo beans, turnips, onions, eggplant, and raisins. In addition, all of the feasts include another main dish of either lamb and honey, or a mixed grill of lamb, rabbit, quail, shrimp, or turkey.

MODERATE

CA' BREA, 346 S. La Brea Ave. Tel. 213/938-2863.
Cuisine: ITALIAN. **Reservations:** Recommended. **Directions:** From U.S. 101 south, take the Normandie Avenue exit and turn right (south). Turn right again, onto Beverly Boulevard, and then left onto La Brea Avenue. The restaurant will be 2 blocks ahead on your left, between 3rd and 4th Streets. From the Santa Monica Freeway, take the La Brea Avenue exit and head north. The restaurant is located about 2½ miles ahead on your right.
$ Prices: Appetizers $5-$8; main courses $8-$15; lunch $5-$15. AE, CB, DC, MC, V.

Open: Lunch, Mon–Sat 11:30am–2:30pm; dinner, Mon–Thurs 5:30–11pm, Fri–Sat 5:30–11:30pm. **Closed:** Sun.

★ Even with reservations you can expect a wait here, since Ca' Brea is one of the most celebrated new restaurants in Los Angeles.

The restaurant's refreshingly bright dining room is hung with oversized, contemporary oil paintings, and backed by an open prep-kitchen where you can watch your sautéed seafood cakes being made. The booths are the most coveted seats, but with only 20 tables, surrounded by colorfully upholstered, heavy wooden chairs, be thankful you are sitting anywhere.

Chef Antonio Tommasi watches over a gifted kitchen that turns out consistently excellent dishes that are as pretty as they are tasty. New Italian dishes like roasted pork sausage with braised Napa cabbage, homemade ravioli stuffed with butter squash, and duck served with a light honey-balsamic vinegar sauce are typical of the restaurant's offerings. The menu is the same for both lunch and dinner.

EMILIO'S, 6602 Melrose Ave. Tel. 213/935-4922.

Cuisine: ITALIAN. **Reservations:** Recommended. **Directions:** From U.S. 101, exit onto Highland Avenue and continue straight to the corner of Melrose Avenue, where you will find the restaurant.

$ Prices: Appetizers $5–$10; main courses $10–$24. Sunday buffet $22. AE, CB, DC, MC, V.

Open: Lunch, Thurs–Fri 11:30am–2:30pm; dinner, daily 5pm–midnight; Sun buffet, 5–9pm.

This award-winning restaurant attracts a celebrity clientele with its authentic Italian cooking. The downstairs dining room surrounds a colorfully lit "Fountain de Trevi." The decor is ornate Italian, with marble columns from floor to lofty ceiling, brick archways, stained-glass windows, gilt-framed oil paintings, and fresh flowers on every table.

Order lavishly and savor every bite. You might begin with the antipasti of mussels with spicy tomato sauce and garlic, or the scallops with oil and garlic. For your second course, the brodetto adriadico (it's like cioppino) is heartily recommended, as are any of the several veal main dishes. Homemade pastas are also excellent, including linguine with shrimp and lobster, and rondelli stuffed with ricotta, mortadella, and spinach. Homemade noodles with sun-dried tomatoes, baby corn, carrots, and peas are less caloric, but good. Depending on the day, you may also find roast suckling pig or osso buco on the menu.

MUSSO & FRANK GRILL, 6667 Hollywood Blvd. Tel. 213/467-7788.

Cuisine: AMERICAN. **Reservations:** Recommended. **Directions:** From U.S. 101, exit onto Cahuenga Boulevard and continue to the restaurant at the corner of Hollywood Boulevard.

$ Prices: Appetizers $5–$9; main courses $10–$32. AE, CB, DC, MC, V.

Open: Mon–Sat 11am–11pm.

By the restaurant's own estimation, this is Hollywood's oldest extant eatery, established in 1919. People have kept coming back for the comfortable ambience, superb service, and consistently excellent food for more than half a century; it's also where Faulkner and Hemingway hung out during their screenwriting days. Musso & Frank Grill is a favorite of Jonathan Winters, Merv Griffin, Raymond Burr, and Sean Penn—to name just a few.

The setting is richly traditional—oak beamed ceilings, red-leather booths and banquettes, mahogany room dividers (complete with coathooks)—enhanced by soft lighting from wall sconces and chandeliers with tiny shades.

The menu is extensive; everything from soups to salads to seafood is served à la carte. Try the delicious seafood salads such as the chiffonade or shrimp Louie, perhaps with some Camembert that comes with crusty bread and butter. Diners desiring heartier fare might consider the veal scaloppine marsala, roast spring lamb with mint jelly, or broiled lobster. Sandwiches and omelets are also available. The back of the menu lists an equally extensive liquor and wine selection.

RISTORANTE CHIANTI & CHIANTI CUCINA, 7383 Melrose Ave. Tel. 213/653-8333.

Cuisine: ITALIAN. **Reservations:** Recommended. **Directions:** From U.S. 101, exit onto Highland Avenue. Turn right onto Melrose Avenue and continue straight for about 10 blocks to the restaurant, at the corner of Martel Avenue, between Fairfax and La Brea Avenues.

$ Prices: Appetizers $6–$8; main courses $13–$19. AE, CB, DC, MC, V.

Open: Ristorante Chianti, daily 5:30–11:30pm; Chianti Cucina Mon–Sat noon–11:30pm, Sun 5pm–midnight.

Begun in 1938 by the famous New York restaurateur Romeo Salta, this charming northern Italian restaurant has a long history in Hollywood: The cast party for *Gone with the Wind* was held here. The restaurant has won several prestigious awards, including accolades for its excellent wine list. Although it operates as a single entity, Ristorante Chianti & Chianti Cucina offers two completely different dining experiences and menus.

Ristorante Chianti is traditional Italian in looks—quiet, intimate, complete with red-velvet seating and sepia-tone murals. Hot and cold appetizers range from fresh handmade mozzarella and prosciutto to lamb carpaccio with asparagus and marinated grilled eggplant filled with goat cheese, arugula, and sun-dried tomatoes. As for main dishes, the homemade pasta is both exceptional and deliciously untraditional. Try black tortellini filled with fresh salmon, or giant ravioli filled with spinach, ricotta, and quail eggs topped with shaved black truffle. Other dishes include fresh fish and prawns, poultry, and a fine selection of meat dishes.

Chianti Cucina is bright, bustling, attractive, and loud; it makes you feel as if you are dining right in the kitchen. Although the menu changes frequently, it typically features exceptional antipasti, pastas, and a pleasing main dish selection that is somewhat more limited than

Ristorante Chianti's. Good first-course selections include smoked duck with pearls of mozzarella and steamed spinach, and carpaccio with alfalfa sprouts and Parmesan cheese. Of the pasta dishes, you might try the lobster-and-shrimp-filled tortellini, or the simpler pasta dumplings with roasted pepper sauce, basil, and Parmesan.

SARNO'S CAFFÈ DELL'OPERA, 1714 N. Vermont. Tel. 213/662-3403.

Cuisine: ITALIAN. **Reservations:** Accepted, necessary on weekends. **Directions:** From U.S. 101, exit east onto Sunset Boulevard. Drive straight for about 15 blocks and turn left onto Vermont to the restaurant at the corner of Hollywood Boulevard.

$ Prices: Appetizers $4–$9; main courses $10–$12; pasta dishes $8–$10; complete dinner $13–$17; pizza $10–$13. AE, DC, MC, V.

Open: Sun–Thurs 5–11pm, Fri–Sat 5pm–1am.

This delightful place brings together two naturals—Italian food and opera. The restaurant is dim and cluttered, with lots of small tables, heavy antique chandeliers, bronze statuary, and hanging clusters of grapes.

The food is good and hearty. You can dine on fresh river trout in white sauce, chicken cacciatore, veal parmigiana, one of many pasta dishes, or—if you have a real appetite—a complete dinner that includes fresh vegetables, soup, salad, bread, pasta, a main dish, dessert, and coffee. Salads, sandwiches, and pizza with a variety of toppings are also available.

The fun at Sarno's begins at 7:30pm, when Alberto, staff members, and customers take turns regaling the diners with their renditions of opera arias, show tunes, and old Italian favorites. If you drink enough, it can be a lot of fun. It's more fun when you go with a large group.

SHANGHAI WINTER GARDEN, 5651 Wilshire Blvd. Tel. 213/934-0505.

Cuisine: CHINESE. **Reservations:** Accepted for parties of four or more. **Directions:** From U.S. 101, exit onto Highland Avenue, and turn right onto Sunset Boulevard. After about 1 mile, turn left onto Fairfax Avenue, and after another mile turn right onto Wilshire Boulevard. The restaurant is about 10 blocks ahead at the corner of Hauser Boulevard.

$ Prices: Appetizers $4–$11; main courses $10–$25; lunch $6–$10. AE, DC, MC, V.

Open: Lunch, Mon–Sat 11:30am–3pm; dinner, daily 4–10:30pm.

This is one of my favorite Los Angeles Chinese restaurants. An archway depicting a phoenix and dragon, set in an intricately carved teak wall, separates the dining areas; Chinese paintings and wood carvings adorn the walls; and large tasseled Chinese lamps hang overhead.

The menu features more than 150 main dishes, including diced fried chicken sautéed with spinach, shrimp with bamboo shoots and green peas in a delicious sauce with crisp sizzling rice, crispy duckling made with five spicy ingredients, and crushed white meat chicken sautéed with diced ham, pine nuts, and green peas. As you can see, this is no ordinary take-out joint.

TOM BERGIN'S TAVERN, 840 S. Fairfax Ave. Tel. 213/936-7151.

Cuisine: IRISH. **Reservations:** Accepted. **Directions:** From U.S. 101, exit onto Highland Avenue and turn right onto Sunset Boulevard. After about 1 mile, turn left onto Fairfax Avenue. The restaurant is located about 1 mile ahead, at Barrows Drive, between Wilshire and Olympic Boulevards.

$ Prices: Appetizers $5–$7; main courses $13–$20; bar lunch $4–$10. AE, DC, DISC, MC, V.

Open: Lunch, Mon–Fri 11am–4pm; dinner, daily 4–11pm; bar 11am–2am.

Tom Bergin's is L.A.'s Irish community's unofficial headquarters. Since 1936, this has also been a gathering place for sportswriters, athletes, and fans. Actors Bing Crosby and Pat O'Brien were early friends of the house. Bergin's was the first city restaurant to charter buses to pro football games—they still do, and they hold 230 seats to the games reserved five years in advance.

Mesquite-fired New York steak with onion rings, garlic cheese toast, salad, and potatoes is the specialty of the house. More traditional Irish fare like Dublin-style corned beef and cabbage with a steamed potato; or chicken Erin, simmered in cream and cider sauce, with bacon, leeks, mushrooms, and rice pilaf are also served, along with burgers and salads. For dessert you can choose from fresh fruit pies or Bailey's Irish Cream cheesecake, and wash it down with an Irish coffee.

INEXPENSIVE

PINK'S HOT DOGS, northwest corner of La Brea and Melrose Avenues. Tel. 213/931-4223.

Cuisine: AMERICAN. **Directions:** From the Santa Monica Freeway (I-10), exit north onto La Brea Avenue. The stand is about 4 miles ahead at Melrose Avenue.

$ Prices: Hot dogs $2.

Open: Daily 8am–2:30am.

Pink's is not your usual guidebook recommendation, but then again this hot dog stand, near the heart of old Hollywood, is not your usual doggery. Even health-conscious Angelenos sometimes forgo their principles to stand in line at this corner stand. The chili dogs are famous, and thousands are served daily. There are a few tables scattered around the corner, but most people stand while they down their dogs. Pray the bulldozers stay away from this little nugget of a place.

ROSCOE'S HOUSE OF CHICKEN 'N' WAFFLES, 1514 N. Gower St. Tel. 213/466-7453.

Cuisine: AMERICAN. **Reservations:** Not accepted. **Directions:** From U.S. 101, exit onto Highland Avenue and turn left onto Sunset Boulevard. The restaurant is straight ahead, at Gower Street.

$ Prices: Main courses $4–$8. No credit cards.

Open: Sun–Thurs 9am–midnight, Fri–Sat 9am–3am.

Proximity to the CBS Studios alone would probably guarantee a celebrity clientele. Roscoe's devotees have included Jane Fonda, Stevie Wonder, Flip Wilson, Eddie Murphy, Alex Haley, and the Eagles. The setting is very simple, with slanted cedar and white stucco walls, changing art exhibits, track lighting overhead, lots of plants, and good music in the background.

Only chicken and waffle dishes are served, though that includes eggs and chicken livers. A chicken-and-cheese omelet with French fries accompanied by an order of homemade biscuits makes for a unique and delicious breakfast. One specialty is a quarter chicken smothered in gravy and onions, served with waffles or grits and biscuits. You can also get chicken salad and chicken sandwiches. Homemade cornbread, sweet-potato pie, homemade potato salad, greens, and corn on the cob are all available as side orders, and wine and beer are sold.

A second Roscoe's is located at 4907 W. Washington Blvd., at La Brea Avenue (tel. 213/936-3730).

3. WEST HOLLYWOOD

EXPENSIVE

CHASEN'S, 9039 Beverly Blvd. Tel. 213/271-2168.
   Cuisine: AMERICAN. **Reservations:** Recommended. **Directions:** From Santa Monica Boulevard, exit onto Beverly Boulevard and continue straight 4 blocks to the restaurant at Doheny Drive.

 FROMMER'S COOL FOR KIDS:
RESTAURANTS

Aunt Kizzy's Back Porch   (see p. 116) This restaurant was practically invented for children. It serves fried chicken and has a down-home fun atmosphere.

Sarno's Caffè Dell'Opera   (see p. 97) Not only does this restaurant serve good Italian food, but it comes with song, supplied by the staff and patrons. Kids will have fun, even if they don't know all the words, and they can still have their pizza.

The Warehouse   (see p. 116) Kids won't have any trouble finding something they like from this extensive international menu. The atmosphere is quite leisurely, and the thousands of moored boats will hold the kids' interest.

$ Prices: Appetizers $9–$19; main courses $22–$30; lunch $5–$18. AE, DISC, MC, V.
Open: Lunch, Tues–Fri 11:30am–2pm, dinner, Tues–Sun 6pm–1am.

The original Chasen's, a chili parlor, was financed by *New Yorker* editor Harold Ross, and early patrons at this "Algonquin West" included Jimmy Durante and James Cagney. James Thurber once spent hours drawing murals on the men's room wall; unfortunately, they were immediately removed by an overly industrious janitor.

The main dining room of this enduring favorite is wood-paneled and softly lit, with beamed ceilings, brass reading lamps, and plush tufted red-leather booths. The menu has come a long way since chili (Elizabeth Taylor's favorite; she's even ordered it shipped to her), but the continental fare still retains its American simplicity. Specialties include the exceptional hobo steak (not listed on the menu), veal bone chop, and rack of lamb. You can top off your meal with the house special: banana or strawberry shortcake.

L'ERMITAGE, 730 N. La Cienega Blvd. Tel. 213/652-5840.

Cuisine: FRENCH. **Reservations:** Required. **Directions:** From U.S. 101, exit onto Highland Avenue and turn right onto Beverly Boulevard. After about 1 mile turn right onto La Cienega Boulevard and drive about 2 blocks to the restaurant, located just north of Melrose Avenue.
$ Prices: Appetizers $7–$13; main courses $15–$30; fixed-price dinners $65–$70. AE, CB, DC, MC, V.
Open: Dinner, Mon–Sat 6:30–10pm.

Created by the late Jean Bertranou, L'Ermitage is one of L.A.'s most highly acclaimed restaurants. The current owner, Dora Fourcade, has enhanced its reputation for fine cuisine and lovely interior design. From the beginning, the restaurant has maintained rigorous standards for all ingredients that go into its dishes. The wine list (all 12 pages) also reflects this pursuit of quality.

The delicate dining area is a masterpiece of understated elegance, suggestive of the private dining rooms in plush Parisian homes. Tables are set with flowers, Christofle silver, and Villeroy and Boch china. Beautifully remodeled during the summer of 1991, a wood-burning fireplace creates a warm, sparkling atmosphere. A back patio with a fountain is enclosed by a domed glass skylight.

The menu changes seasonally. You would do well to begin with the incredibly light puff filled with seasonal vegetables—perhaps tender stalks of young asparagus. Main courses might include roast squab on a bed of green cabbage; Maine lobster with green onions and julienne of mushrooms; or Viennoise of striped bass with mushrooms and fresh tomatoes.

Whatever you order, leave room for an unforgettable dessert, like poached pear in red wine and black-currant sauce with homemade vanilla ice cream, or a flaky crusted apple tart. L'Ermitage also offers one of the best cheese selections in Los Angeles.

SPAGO, 8795 Sunset Blvd. Tel. 310/652-4025.

Cuisine: CALIFORNIA. **Reservations:** Required. **Direc-**

tions: From U.S. 101, exit onto Highland Avenue and turn right onto Sunset Boulevard. The restaurant is about 3 miles ahead, at Horn Avenue.

$ Prices: Appetizers $10–$15; main courses $18–$28. AE, DC, DISC, MC, V.

Open: Dinner, daily 6–11:30pm.

Celebrity chef Wolfgang Puck has a flair for publicity and has made Spago one of the best known restaurants in America. Famous across the land as the site of Swifty Lazar's annual Oscar-night party, this noisy L.A. restaurant is popular with celebrities, wannabes, and tourists throughout the year. Designed by Barbara Lazaroff, the restaurant is elegantly decorated in clean, light shades punctuated with armfuls of flowers. A huge picture window and an open kitchen give diners an alternative view when they get tired of looking at each other.

Puck invented California-style gourmet pizza, baked in a wood-burning oven, and topped with exotic ingredients like duck sausage, shiitake mushrooms, leeks, artichokes, and even lox and sour cream. Pastas like black-pepper fettuccine with Louisiana shrimp, roasted garlic, and basil ratatouille; or angel-hair spaghetti with goat cheese and broccoli are also available, as are more substantial dishes like roast Sonoma lamb with braised shallots and herb butter, and grilled chicken with garlic and parsley. Despite all the hype, Spago is really terrific. Reservations should be made three to four weeks in advance.

MODERATE

ANTONIO'S, 7472 Melrose Ave. Tel. 213/655-0480.

Cuisine: MEXICAN. **Reservations:** Accepted. **Directions:** From U.S. 101, exit onto Highland Avenue and turn right onto Melrose Avenue. The restaurant is located about 1 mile ahead, between Fairfax and La Brea Avenues.

$ Prices: Appetizers $5–$7; main courses $11–$15. AE, MC, V.

Open: Lunch, Tues–Fri 11am–3pm; dinner, Tues–Fri 5–10:30pm.

There's "gringo food"—fiery tamales, with lots of cheese, sour cream, and refried beans—and then there's the subtle, delicate, and delicious Mexican cooking of Antonio's. For almost 25 years, this gourmet Mexican restaurant has been serving top-notch food without the bright reds, yellows, and greens of the usual taco joint. The true cuisine of Mexico City is delicious, well seasoned, high in protein, low in cholesterol, and lean on calories. A variety of fresh seafood and meats with exotic vegetables are featured, and most of the main dishes are steamed rather than fried.

The menu changes daily, but fresh fish is available at all times. Chicken is served in a variety of ways—Guadalajara style, in tamales stuffed with assorted fresh vegetables; or stewed in a delicate green sauce of tomatillos, green peppers, and exotic spices. Meat-stuffed cabbage, and spareribs with chile-and-herb sauce are both recommended.

A second Antonio's is located in Santa Monica, at 1323 Montana Ave., at 14th Street (tel. 213/395-2815).

INEXPENSIVE

THE SOURCE, 8301 W. Sunset Blvd. Tel. 213/656-6388.
Cuisine: CALIFORNIA HEALTH FOOD. **Reservations:** Not accepted. **Directions:** From U.S. 101, exit onto Highland Avenue and turn right onto Sunset Boulevard. The restaurant is located about 2 miles ahead at Sweetzer Avenue, between La Cienega and Fairfax Avenues.
$ Prices: Appetizers $3–$5; main courses $5–$11. AE, CB, DC, MC, V.
Open: Mon–Fri 8am–midnight, Sat–Sun 9am–midnight.

This is where Woody Allen met Diane Keaton for a typical L.A. lunch in *Annie Hall*—part of his New York–centric statement about southern California. Inside it's cozy, with curtained windows, tables set with fresh flowers, and a plant-filled stone fireplace in one corner. Those who want fresh air with their health food shouldn't be in L.A., but outdoor dining at umbrella-topped tables is available.

Cheese-walnut loaf, served with homemade soup or salad, and a basket of whole wheat rolls and butter comprises a typical meal. Salads and sandwiches are also available. Most menu items are vegetarian, but chicken and fish are also served. Portions are huge. Drinks include yogurt shakes, beer, and wine. The homemade date-nut cheesecake is so good it's hard to believe it's healthy.

4. BEVERLY HILLS & CENTURY CITY

EXPENSIVE

THE BISTRO, 246 N. Canon Dr., Beverly Hills. Tel. 213/273-5633.
Cuisine: CONTINENTAL. **Reservations:** Required. **Directions:** From Santa Monica Boulevard exit onto Canon Drive. The restaurant is 2 blocks ahead at Dayton Way.
$ Prices: Appetizers $8–$13; main courses $15–$27. AE, CB, DC, MC, V.
Open: Dinner, Mon–Fri 6–10:30pm, Sat 6–11pm.

Conceived more than two decades ago by film director Billy Wilder and Romanoff's maître d' Kurt Niklas, The Bistro is both elegant and charming. The restaurant is decorated in authentic Parisian Belle Epoque, with mirrored walls, hand-painted panels with classical motifs, tables set with gleaming silver, soft pink lighting, and fresh roses on every table.

Both the service and the cuisine are top-notch. The mussel soup is outstanding, and the rich lobster bisque and cream of watercress soups are excellent. Two appetizers you won't want to overlook are the salmon and the pheasant pâté. You might choose a cold main dish of duck or quail salad, or one such as linguine with raddichio, asparagus, and scallops. The rack of lamb is also recommended. All the pasta is homemade and fresh. For dessert, I recommend the sumptuous chocolate soufflé. Jackets are required at dinner, when there is live piano music.

JIMMY'S, 201 Moreno Dr., Beverly Hills. Tel. 213/879-2394.
Cuisine: CONTINENTAL. **Reservations:** Recommended. **Directions:** From Santa Monica Boulevard, exit east onto Wilshire Boulevard and immediately turn right onto Lasky Drive. The restaurant is 3 blocks ahead at Moreno Drive.
$ Prices: Appetizers $8–$20; main courses $23–$30; lunch $13–$18. AE, CB, DC, MC, V.
Open: Lunch, Mon–Fri 11:30am–3pm; dinner, Mon–Sat 5pm–1am.

Jimmy Murphy—the long-time maître d' at L.A.'s elite Bistro—struck out on his own several years ago, with backing from Johnny Carson and Bob Newhart. Jimmy's reputation has attracted a top staff, and he has created one of the prettiest and most comfortable restaurants in town. Baccarat crystal chandeliers hang from recessed ceilings, which have been painted to look like the sky. Tables are set with Limoges china, crystal glasses, and fresh flowers. One wall of windows overlooks the terrace with its small garden, fountain, shade trees, and tables under white canvas umbrellas. From the chinoiserie statues at the entrance to the considered placement of mirrors, plants, and floral arrangements, Jimmy's is perfectly lovely in every detail, including the posh bar/lounge where a pianist entertains nightly.

You could begin lunch or dinner with an hors d'oeuvre of assorted shellfish or pheasant pâté with truffles. Dinner main dishes include filet mignon with foie gras and truffles wrapped in a fluffy pastry shell, and peppered salmon with cabernet sauce. At lunch you might opt for seafood salad, cold salmon in aspic, white fish with limes, or steak tartare with fresh asparagus.

LAWRY'S THE PRIME RIB, 55 N. La Cienega Blvd., Beverly Hills. Tel. 310/652-2827.
Cuisine: AMERICAN. **Reservations:** Recommended. **Directions:** From Santa Monica Boulevard, exit onto Wilshire Boulevard and continue straight for about 2 miles. Turn left onto North La Cienega Boulevard; the restaurant is just half a block ahead.
$ Prices: Appetizers $4–$8; main courses $18–$25. AE, CB, DC, DISC, MC, V.
Open: Mon–Thurs 5–11pm, Fri–Sat 5pm–midnight, Sun 3–10pm.

A family enterprise begun in 1938, Lawry's enjoys an excellent Restaurant Row location, near Beverly Hills's eastern edge. The restaurant was created by Lawrence Frank and his brother-in-law, Walter Van de Kamp. Frank set out to offer "the greatest meal in America," serving just one main dish—the hearty prime rib he had enjoyed every Sunday for dinner as a boy (his father was in the meat business). Then the beef was showcased atop three gleaming silver carts, each costing as much as a Cadillac, and carved tableside by knowledgeable experts. Lawry's is also the home of the now famous seasoned salt invented as the perfect seasoning for prime rib.

Lawry's clubroom atmosphere begins in the homey cocktail lounge, where drinks are served from a pewter-topped wood-paneled bar. The dining room is equally opulent, decorated with original oil paintings (including one of the Duke of Windsor at age 7), Persian-carpeted oak floors, plush burned-orange-leather booths, and high-backed chairs at tables draped with orange-sherbet cloths.

There's still only one main dish—a choice of four cuts of Lawry's award-winning prime ribs of beef. With it you get Yorkshire pudding, salad, mashed potatoes, and creamed horseradish. You can also order such side dishes as creamed spinach, corn, or buttered peas, and a good wine list is available.

R.J.'S THE RIB JOINT, 252 N. Beverly Dr. (between Dayton Way and Wilshire Boulevard), Beverly Hills. Tel. 310/274-7427.
Cuisine: AMERICAN. **Reservations:** Accepted.
$ Prices: Appetizers $5–$12; main courses, dinner $12–$24, lunch $9–$14. AE, DC, MC, V.
Open: Mon–Sat 11:30am–10:30pm; Sun lunch 10:30am–3pm, dinner 5–10:30pm.

No dainty endive salads and kiwi tarts here. R.J.'s gargantuan meals include steaks; oakwood-grilled beef, pork, and ribs; clams; chili; hickory-smoked chicken; crispy duck; and lobster. All dinners begin with help-yourself servings from the most sumptuous 75-foot salad bar you're ever likely to encounter. Forty or so offerings are included in the price of your entrée along with sourdough rolls and butter. Doggy bags are available.

Heralded by a green-and-white-striped awning, R.J.'s casual and comfortable interior means sawdust on the floors, lots of plants, and exposed-brick and raw-pine walls cluttered with historic photos of Beverly Hills and of yesterday's stars. A pianist usually entertains with nostalgic American tunes.

The well-stocked bar features more than 500 brands. Only premium liquors and fresh-squeezed juices are used. The restaurant also carries more than 50 varieties of beer from all over the world.

TRADER VIC'S, at the Beverly Hilton Hotel, 9878 Wilshire Blvd., Beverly Hills. Tel. 213/274-7777.
Cuisine: POLYNESIAN. **Reservations:** Accepted. **Directions:** From I-405 north, exit onto Santa Monica Boulevard and go east for 3 miles to the hotel at Wilshire Boulevard.
$ Prices: Appetizers $7–$12; main courses $16–$30. AE, DC, DISC, MC, V.
Open: Dinner, daily 5pm–1am.

The interesting nautical interior of Trader Vic's features model ships and tropical shells. The restaurant has long been famous for its tropical rum drinks garnished with cute little umbrellas.

An eclectic South Pacific menu includes a host of puu puus (hors d'oeuvres) including absolutely delicious crisp calamari, padang prawns saté, and skewered shrimp brushed with saté-chile butter.

Two excellent main dishes are barbecued squab and the Indonesian lamb roast, completely trimmed and marinated and served with a peach chutney. The chateaubriand for two is an excellent cut of matured beef. Desserts include mud pie and Aloha ice cream—vanilla ice cream in mango sauce topped with banana chips.

MODERATE

HARRY'S BAR & GRILL, 2020 Ave. of the Stars, Century City. Tel. 213/277-2333.

Cuisine: ITALIAN. **Reservations:** Required. **Directions:** From Santa Monica Boulevard, exit south onto the Avenue of the Stars.

$ Prices: Appetizers $5–$8; main courses $9–$19; lunch $10–$24. AE, CB, DC, MC, V.

Open: Lunch, Mon–Fri 11:30am–5pm; dinner, Mon–Fri 5:30–11pm.

Located on the Plaza Level of the ABC Entertainment Center, Harry's is almost identical to its namesake in Florence, which is itself a spinoff of the Harry's in Venice, made famous by Ernest Hemingway in his novel *Across the River and Into the Trees*. The bar is European, with high walnut counters and tall wooden stools. Former owners Larry Mindel and Jerry Magnin hand-picked the paintings, tapestries, and furnishings on various trips to Italy. Artist Lazero Donati (who created an oil painting for the Florence Harry's) was commissioned to do a similar painting for this establishment.

The northern Italian menu, which changes every six months or so, features such dishes as duck prosciutto, beef pasta with Gorgonzola and pine nuts, and veal scaloppine with balsamic vinegar and mustard. You'll realize when you taste them that the pastas are homemade.

LA SCALA & BOUTIQUE RESTAURANT, 410 N. Canon Dr., Beverly Hills. Tel. 213/275-0579 or 550-8288.

Cuisine: ITALIAN. **Reservations:** Accepted at lunch for groups of six or more; required at dinner. **Directions:** From Santa Monica Boulevard, exit onto Canon Drive. The restaurant is half a block ahead, before Brighton Way.

$ Prices: Appetizers $6–$12; main courses $13–$25; lunch $7–$15. AE, CB, DC, MC, V.

Open: Mon–Sat 11:30am–11:30pm.

Now an institution, Jean Leon's Scala is a busy restaurant catering primarily to customers in The Business. Easily identified by the name "La Scala" on the white bowed awnings, the restaurant's relatively small interior features faux orange trees, red-leather booths, amber mirrors, soft spot lighting, and fresh flowers. To the rear, directly above a small bar, are a number of those Gerald Price caricatures of famous Hollywood faces.

Lunch might begin with bean soup with olive oil (fagioli alla toscana con olio santo), followed by Leon's popular chopped salad. Excellent, more substantial main courses include cannelloni Gigi and grilled shrimp marinara. There are sandwiches on the menu, as well as a selection of cold plates.

At dinner try the marinated salmon with white truffles, and then move on to a pasta dish like spaghetti alla checca, with chopped tomatoes, virgin olive oil, garlic, and basil. Beautifully prepared main courses include the grilled shrimp or langostines with white wine, duck sausage with Cannelli beans, and spring chicken with rosemary and white wine. Tiramisu and cappuccino are always available.

NATE & AL'S, 414 N. Beverly Dr., Beverly Hills. Tel. 213/274-0101.
Cuisine: JEWISH. **Reservations:** Not accepted. **Directions:** From Santa Monica Boulevard, exit onto Beverly Drive. The restaurant is half a block ahead at Brighton Way.
$ Prices: Appetizers $5–$11; main courses $8–$13. AE, DISC, MC, V.
Open: Sun–Fri 7:30am–9pm; Sat 7:30am–10pm.

Nate & Al's has been slapping pastrami on fresh-baked rye since 1945, not to mention chopped liver and schmaltz (chicken fat), kosher franks, and hot corned beef. Seating is in comfortable booths and lighting is pleasantly low. A big counter up front handles take-out orders that include everything from halvah to Brie.

This place is kosher style rather than strictly kosher; the book-sized menu encompasses both meat and dairy items. Sandwiches come in only one size—huge—and are overstuffed with meats, cheeses, and traditional favorites. Other offerings include chicken soup with matzoh balls; potato pancakes; and cheese, cherry, or blueberry blintzes with sour cream and applesauce. Wine and beer are available.

INEXPENSIVE

CHEESECAKE FACTORY, 364 N. Beverly Dr., Beverly Hills. Tel. 213/278-7270.
Cuisine: AMERICAN. **Reservations:** Not accepted. **Directions:** From the Santa Monica Boulevard, exit onto Beverly Drive. The restaurant is half a block ahead at Brighton Way.
$ Prices: Main courses $6–$16; cheesecake $4–$7. AE, CB, DC, DISC, MC, V.
Open: Mon–Thurs 11am–11pm, Fri–Sat 11am–12:30am, Sun 10am–10pm.

Serving great food and superb desserts, the Cheesecake Factory, off Brighton Way, is a dilemma of sorts. My advice: go there very hungry, when you're not counting calories.

More than 40 varieties of cheesecake are available, including the incredible white-chocolate raspberry truffle, fresh strawberry, coffee brownie chunk, and Kahlua almond fudge. Other baked goods include chocolate fudge cake, carrot cake, cookies, candies, and much, much more.

The Cheesecake Factory is also a reasonably priced restaurant with a substantial list of delicious dishes. Meals range from barbecue-style chicken and ribs, to spicy specialties like cashew chicken, shrimp Jambalaya, Louisiana-style blackened fish, and steak. Vegetarian dishes are also available, as are more than 15 pasta dishes, wonderful hot sandwiches, great omelets, salads, and burgers.

Other Cheesecake Factory locations include 4142 Via Marina, in Marina del Rey (tel. 310/306-3344); 605 North Harbor Dr., in Redondo Beach (tel. 310/376-0466); and 6324 Canoga Ave. in Woodland Hills (tel. 818/883-9900).

5. WEST LOS ANGELES

MODERATE

CASTEL, 12100 Wilshire Blvd. Tel. 310/207-4273.
   Cuisine: CALIFORNIA/FRENCH. **Reservations:** Recommended. **Directions:** From I-405, take the Wilshire Boulevard exit and head west, toward the ocean. The restaurant is about 1¼ miles ahead, on your left, just past Bundy Drive.
$ Prices: Appetizers $4–$8; main courses $11–$17; pasta $8–$12; lunch $5–$12. AE, DC, MC, V.
   Open: Mon–Fri 11:30am–10:30pm, Sat 6–10:30pm.

Located on the ground floor of a large office building, Castel's relatively modest dining room bends around a U-shaped bar, and has large windows that face busy Wilshire Boulevard. While the locally produced art that adorns the walls changes periodically, the room's main focus—an absolutely enormous flower bouquet—is freshened daily.

Chef Jean-Pierre Bosc has amassed quite a following with his contemporary preparations and innovative sauces. Lunch might include warm duck salad with honey, garlic, and soy dressing; or tagliolini pasta with smoked bacon, peas, and corn. Dinners begin with a healthy choice of starters, including smoked salmon salad with shallot dressing; mussels steamed with apple cider; and tomato, cucumber, and bell-pepper soup. Pasta dishes include shrimp ravioli with pumpkin sauce, and oven-roasted leg of lamb ravioli. Other top entrées are baked Chilean sea bass, and veal shortribs topped with a sorrel sauce.

Desserts like Belle Helene–poached pear with vanilla ice cream and hot chocolate sauce are equally imaginative and technically excellent. The restaurant has a modest wine list and a full bar.

MISHIMA, 11301 Olympic Blvd. Tel. 310/473-5297.
   Cuisine: JAPANESE. **Reservations:** Not accepted. **Directions:** From I-405, take the Tennessee Avenue exit and head south (toward the beach). Make an immediate right onto Sawtell Boulevard. The restaurant is in the shopping center on the corner of Sawtell and Olympic Boulevards.
$ Prices: Appetizers $1–$7; noodles $4–$7; combinations $5–$9. MC, V.
   Open: Tues–Sun 11:30am–9pm. Closed: Mon.

Hidden on the second floor of an unobtrusive strip mall, this small Japanese eatery is well worth finding. A carbon copy of an excellent noodle shop in downtown Tokyo, Mishima is

Asian-contemporary, complete with matte black tables and chairs, white walls decorated with Japanese style prints, and plastic food displays that let you see what you are ordering.

A loyal clientele fills the small bright dining room with noodle slurps and chopstick clacks. Udon (thick wheat noodles) or soba (narrow buckwheat linguine) are the main choices here. Both are served either hot or cold in a variety of soups and sauces. Sushi, chicken dishes, and a variety of tempuras are also available. Highly recommended.

6. PASADENA

MODERATE

MI PIACE, 25 E. Colorado Blvd., Pasadena. Tel. 818/795-3131.
 Cuisine: ITALIAN. **Reservations:** Accepted. **Directions:** From I-210 east, take the Fair Oaks Avenue exit and turn right. Turn left onto Colorado Boulevard, and the restaurant will be immediately on your left.
$ Prices: Appetizers $2–$5; main courses $6–$12; pasta $2–$8; lunch $4–$8. AE, DC, MC, V.
 Open: Sun–Thurs 11am–11:30pm, Fri–Sat 11am–1am.

High ceilings, large windows, light wood floors, and contemporary colors all contribute to the bright, open airiness of this friendly Italian eatery. The main room has about 20 square tables, all topped with white cloths and balsamic vinegar, and surrounded by blond wood chairs.

Pronounced "Me-Pee-ah-che," the restaurant serves an extensive menu that includes dozens of pastas, as well as veal, chicken, and seafood entrées. Creative, individual-size pizzas are a particular specialty, as is gnocchi (potato dumplings), and linguine with New Zealand–green lip mussels.

Many knowledgeable diners just visit Mi Piace for dessert. Their tremendous selection of elegant, homemade creations includes hazelnut cake layered with cappuccino mousse and covered with cappuccino bean cream; a variety of chocolates; traditional tiramisu; and Spaghetinni Castagne—a chestnut pasta and white chocolate cream–filled meringue, topped with vanilla sauce.

MIYAKO, in the Livingstone Hotel, 139 S. Los Robles Ave., Pasadena. Tel. 818/795-7005.
 Cuisine: JAPANESE. **Reservations:** Accepted. **Directions:** From I-210, exit Walnut Street east and turn right (south) on Los Robles Avenue. The restaurant is half a mile on your right, across from the Pasadena Hilton hotel, between Green and Cordova Streets.
$ Prices: Appetizers $5–$8; main courses $10–$23; lunch $6–$13. AE, MC, V.

Open: Lunch, Mon–Fri 11:30am–2pm; dinner, Mon–Thurs 5:30–9:30pm, Fri–Sat 5:30–10pm, Sun 4–9pm.

The Miyako is on the same street as the Hilton, but it's been around much longer—since 1959. People come here for fine Japanese cuisine in an attractive setting. You can choose to sit either on the floor (in the Japanese tradition) in the tatami room or at western-style tables, which overlook a small Japanese garden.

If you're not used to eating raw fish, begin with a sashimi appetizer, a small portion of tuna slices. A full Imperial dinner offers a combination of shrimp tempura, chicken teriyaki, and sukiyaki.

PASADENA BAKING COMPANY, 29 E. Colorado Blvd., Old Pasadena. Tel. 818/796-9966.
Cuisine: CONTINENTAL. **Reservations:** Not accepted. **Directions:** From I-210 east, take the Fair Oaks Avenue exit and turn right. Turn left onto Colorado Boulevard, and the restaurant will be immediately on your left.
$ Prices: Baked goods 50¢–$3; breakfast $3–$6; lunch $2–$6. AE, MC, V.
Open: Mon–Thurs 7am–11pm, Fri 7am–midnight, Sat 8am–midnight, Sun 8am–11pm.

Located next door to Mi Piace (see above), this little bakery with large windows overlooking the boulevard holds just a handful of small tables, which spill out onto the sidewalk during nice weather.

You can practically "see the smell" of their particularly large selection of fresh pastries, tarts, truffles, cakes, and candies, all of which are proudly displayed behind large glass cases. The bakery also makes and sells an assortment of fresh breads, including Bohemian pumpernickel, potato and dill, and even strawberry.

Breakfast foods include homemade croissants and muffins, as well as omelets, a cereal bar, and fruit stand. Fresh cut sandwiches are lunch favorites, as are fruit and cobb salads, and "vegestronni," a pie prepared with fresh seasonal vegetables.

A variety of espresso drinks, hot or iced, are always available.

INEXPENSIVE

OLD TOWN BAKERY & RESTAURANT, 166 W. Colorado Blvd., Pasadena. Tel. 818/792-7943.
Cuisine: CONTINENTAL. **Reservations:** Not accepted. **Directions:** From I-210 south, take the Pasadena Street exit and turn left. Turn right onto Colorado Boulevard. The restaurant will be on your right, between Pasadena and Miller Streets.
$ Prices: Appetizers $2–$5, breakfast $3–$7, lunch and dinner $5–$10. DISC, MC, V.
Open: Sun–Thurs 7:30am–11pm, Fri–Sat 7:30am–midnight.

Set back from the street, inside a quaint courtyard, this cheery bakery is an especially popular place to read the morning paper with a cappuccino and a croissant. The tall, glass display counters are packed with cakes, muffins, scones, and other confections; all of them have been baked expressly for this shop.

Beyond bakery items, meals include eggs, potatoes, pasta, salads, sandwiches, and pan pizza, topped with chicken sausage, mushrooms, onions, and mozzarella.

7. MALIBU & TOPANGA CANYON

EXPENSIVE

GRANITA, 23725 W. Malibu Rd., Malibu. Tel. 310/456-0488.
    Cuisine: CALIFORNIA. **Reservations:** Recommended.
$ Prices: Appetizers $9–$21; main courses $21–$29. AE, CB, DC, DISC, MC, V.
    Open: Lunch, Mon–Wed 11:30am–2:30pm; dinner, nightly 5:30–10:30pm; brunch, Sat–Sun 10:30am–2:30pm.

Granita is the latest outpost of Wolfgang Puck, one of the most successful entrepreneurial chefs in California. Together with West Hollywood's Spago and Santa Monica's Chinois on Main, Puck's Malibu restaurant consciously combines hip food and contemporary surroundings. Granita's happy interior is swirling in color. Even the wait staff is outfitted in vests or ties that explode in design and color.

Puck serves many of his own house specialties here, including a salmon and caviar pizza and grilled chicken with roasted garlic sauce. Several new dishes have been introduced such as a sturgeon pizza and fresh sea urchin topping saffron tagliatelli.

LA SCALA MALIBU, 3874 Cross Creek Rd. (off Pacific Coast Highway), Malibu. Tel. 310/456-1979.
    Cuisine: ITALIAN. **Reservations:** Recommended.
$ Prices: Appetizers $6–$10; main courses $17–$28. Lunch about half price. AE, CB, DC, MC, V.
    Open: Lunch, Tues–Fri 11:30am–2:30pm; dinner, Tues–Fri 5:30–10pm, Sat–Sun 5:30–10:30pm.

This restaurant is the venture of Jean Leon, who made a name for himself with several ultra-chic Beverly Hills restaurants. But this eatery differs from the others; La Scala is known for its relaxed atmosphere and friendly, leisurely dining. Architectural highlights include an Italian marble entry, terra-cotta tile floors, and etched-glass area dividers. There's an impressive wood-paneled 1,800-bottle wine room and an exhibition kitchen. Solarium windows overlook the wilds of Malibu Creek with a view of the Pacific.

Lunch at La Scala might begin with a fresh turkey salad, smoked salmon with onions and capers, or a hot entrée such as veal and peppers, swordfish, or the daily fresh pasta. For dessert, try the homemade ice cream with fresh raspberries. Dinner begins with antipasti such as mozzarella marinara, seafood salad, carpaccio, or a Caesar salad and continues with entrées such as baked sea bass, veal with pepperoni, or the nightly fresh pasta.

MODERATE

ALICE'S, 23000 Pacific Coast Hwy., Malibu. Tel. 213/456-6646.

Cuisine: CALIFORNIA. **Reservations:** Recommended. **Directions:** From Santa Monica, take Calif. 1 north to Malibu. The restaurant is located directly on Calif. 1 about a quarter mile before the Malibu Pier.

$ Prices: Appetizers $6–$11; lunch main courses $6–$16; dinner main courses $8–$19. AE, MC, V.

Open: Mon–Fri 11:30am–10pm, Sat–Sun 10am–11pm.

Alice's has a 20-year history as one of the liveliest restaurants in Malibu. Facing the Malibu Pier, the dining area is glassed in on three sides; rear tables are on a raised platform so that everyone can view the ocean. It's light and airy, and the menu is mostly seafood—as always, beautifully fresh.

Among the tempting luncheon main courses are yellowtail tuna with spinach, lemon, and tarragon butter; and grilled chicken breast marinated in garlic, soy, and spices, served with a tomato-cilantro relish. But don't overlook the pasta choices, especially the spaghetti with hot Creole sausage, zucchini, and a sweet red-pepper sauce. Alice's also has a good selection of salads, warm and cold. Consider also the Malibu sausage burger with sautéed onions and peppers, and mustard dressing.

For dinner, you might begin with the smoked Norwegian salmon served with caviar cream. Of the salads, my choice is the hot roasted goat cheese salad with mixed greens, fresh herbs, walnuts, and a sherry vinaigrette. Great main dishes include grilled swordfish with herb butter and the stir-fried scallops with black-bean sauce and sweet peppers over pan-fried angel hair pasta.

INN OF THE SEVENTH RAY, 128 Old Topanga Canyon Rd., Topanga Canyon. Tel. 213/455-1311.

Cuisine: CALIFORNIA HEALTH FOOD. **Reservations:** Required at dinner. **Directions:** From Santa Monica, take Calif. 1 north to Malibu, then turn right onto Calif. 27 (Topanga Canyon Boulevard), which, after about 2 miles, turns into Topanga Canyon Road.

$ Prices: Appetizers $6–$10; main courses $14–$28; lunch and brunch $7–$13. MC, V.

Open: Lunch, Mon–Fri 11:30am–3pm, Sat 10:30am–3pm; brunch, Sun 9:30am–3pm; dinner, daily 6–10pm.

Located about 4 miles from Pacific Coast Calif. 1, this unusual and lovely creekside inn offers tranquil dining under the shade of an ancient canyon. About half of the seating is outdoors, at tables that overlook the creek and endless untamed foliage. Inside, tables are neatly arranged beneath a sloped shingle-and-stucco roof; a glass wall provides mountain views.

Although it is not vegetarian, the Inn of the Seventh Ray is the most orthodox, and the most beautiful, of L.A.'s natural-food restaurants. It was opened about 20 years ago by Ralph and Lucille Yaney as a place to practice and share their ideas about the relationship of food and energy. Main dishes are listed on the menu in order of their "esoteric vibrational value"; the lightest and least dense—hence, more purifying—items get top billing. Everything is prepared from scratch on the premises. Since top priority is given to serving chemical- and preservative-free foods, even the fish are caught in deep water far offshore and served the same day. Lunch options include sandwiches (such as avocado, cheese, and sprouts), salads, omelets, quiche, and waffles. The dinner menu offers 10 main dishes, all served with soup or salad, complimentary hors d'oeuvres, steamed vegetables, baked potato or herbed brown rice, and stone-ground homemade bread. The lightest item is called Five Secret Rays: lightly steamed vegetables served with lemon-tahini and caraway cheese sauces; the densest—vibrationally speaking—is a 10-ounce New York steak cut from naturally fed beef. A glass of fruit wine is suggested as an apéritif, and delicious desserts are also available. Even if you're not especially enthusiastic about natural foods, all the dishes are excellent and the setting is enjoyable.

SAND CASTLE, 28128 W. Pacific Coast Hwy., Malibu. Tel. 213/457-2503.

    Cuisine: AMERICAN. **Reservations:** Accepted. **Directions:** From Santa Monica, take Calif. 1 north to Malibu. The restaurant is located on Calif. 1 at the Malibu Pier.

$ **Prices:** Appetizers $5–$9; main courses $12–$30. AE, MC, V.

    Open: Breakfast, daily 6am–noon; lunch, daily 11:30am–4pm; dinner, Mon–Thurs 5–10pm, Fri–Sat 5–11pm, Sun 4–10pm.

Leisurely breakfasts and lunches are the best meals to eat in this gray New England–style shingled house, complete with weather vane and widow's walk. The restaurant is located right on the beach, and has a wall of windows overlooking the ocean. The rustic interior sports a nautical theme, with ship-light chandeliers, rigging decor, and the like. A giant fireplace separates the dining room from the lounge, which sees a lot of action on weekend nights.

Hearty egg breakfasts give way to lunches that can be anything from a Monte Cristo sandwich to scallops sautéed in white wine. Dinners are often meat-and-potato affairs, and include steak, fish, chicken, and the like.

INEXPENSIVE

CARLOS AND PEPE'S, 22706 Pacific Coast Hwy., Malibu. Tel. 213/456-3105.

    Cuisine: MEXICAN. **Reservations:** Not accepted. **Directions:** From Santa Monica, take Calif. 1 north to Malibu. The restaurant is located on Calif. 1 about ¼ mile before the Malibu Pier.

$ **Prices:** Appetizers $3–$6; main courses $8–$12. AE, CB, MC, V.

    Open: Sun–Thurs 11:30am–11pm, Fri–Sat 11:30am–midnight.

Carlos and Pepe's is a delightful weathered-wood seacoast structure. Inside you'll find a few touches from south of the border, including, at the bar, papier-mâché banana trees with tropical birds. The interior is designed so that each table has an ocean view. An immense aquarium filled with tropical fish separates the bar and dining areas. The best place to sit is on the plant-filled, glass-enclosed deck that directly overlooks the ocean.

The restaurant should be best known for its 16-ounce margaritas, made with freshly squeezed juices. But the sizable menu, which includes the usual enchiladas, chimichangas (a burrito fried crisp), and tacos, isn't too bad either. The fajitas are the restaurant's top ticket: grilled steak or chicken, served sizzling with peppers, onions, and tomatoes. Roll and fill your own tortillas with guacamole, salsa, lettuce, and beans. Hamburgers, omelets, and steaks are also available.

8. SANTA MONICA & VENICE

EXPENSIVE

BIKINI, 1413 5th Ave., Santa Monica. Tel. 310/395-8611.
Cuisine: INTERNATIONAL. **Reservations:** Essential. **Directions:** From the Santa Monica Freeway west, take the 4th Street exit and turn right. Turn right again onto Colorado Avenue, then left onto 5th Street. The restaurant is on your right, between Broadway and Santa Monica Boulevard.
$ Prices: Appetizers $6–$30; main courses $16–$26; lunch $6–$15.
Open: Lunch, Mon–Fri 11:30am–2:30pm; dinner, Mon–Thurs 6–10pm, Fri–Sun 6–10:30pm; brunch, Sun 11:30am–2pm.

If you needed just one morsel of proof that Los Angeles remains on the culinary edge, Bikini would provide it. Enter through huge glass doors, with handles that resemble breaking waves, into a small reception area, where a fire-engine red hostess desk contrasts against curvaceous black and gray simulated stone.

A dramatic free-standing green wood stairway separates the reception area from the restaurant's ultra-colorful, multi-million dollar dining room. Bikini's 15 main dining room tables are dwarfed by huge, two-story, floor-to-ceiling windows, and surrounded by curved walls and primary colors. The less coveted upstairs dining room is backed by a large mural of an ocean nymph, created by the artist Muramasa Kudo and commissioned especially for this restaurant.

Chef/owner John Sedlar's flair for style doesn't stop in the kitchen, where he combines French techniques with flavors and spices from Japan, China, Thailand, Greece, and the American Southwest. You won't find Bikini's salmon-mousse-filled corn husk tamale at any Mexican taco stand. But, along with a duck sandwich, cooked medium-rare, with wild mushrooms and orange-mint mayonnaise on potato bread, it's typical of the lunch entrées. Dinners include vanilla poached Pacific prawns, and grilled saddle of lamb with green Indian curry sauce.

CHINOIS ON MAIN, 2709 Main St., Santa Monica. Tel. 310/392-9025.
Cuisine: CALIFORNIA/CHINESE. **Reservations:** Required.
Directions: From the Santa Monica Freeway, take the 4th Street exit and turn left. Turn right onto Pico Boulevard and after 2 blocks turn left onto Main Street. The restaurant is on your left.

$ Prices: Appetizers $9–$21; main courses $21–$29. AE, DC, MC, V.

Open: Lunch, Wed–Fri 11:30am–2pm; dinner, daily 6–10:30pm.

Created by Wolfgang Puck, this is one of the trendiest spots in Santa Monica for moneyed diners. Decorated in a colorful Asian-tech, the stunning restaurant is as much an extravaganza for the eye as it is for the palate. It's loud and lively and perpetually packed.

"Chinois," means Chinese in French, and that's sort of what you get; a delicious combination of Asian, French, and California cooking. The seasonal menu might offer stir-fried garlic chicken, whole sizzling catfish, or charcoal-grilled Szechuan beef, thinly sliced, with hot chili oil and cilantro sauce.

MICHAEL'S, 1147 3rd St., Santa Monica. Tel. 213/451-0843.

Cuisine: CONTINENTAL. **Reservations:** Essential. **Directions:** From the Santa Monica Freeway west, exit at 4th Street and turn right. Turn left on Wilshire Boulevard and then right onto 3rd Street; the restaurant is on the right.

$ Prices: Appetizers $6–$14; main courses $18–$27; lunch $13–$23. AE, CB, DC, DISC, MC, V.

Open: Lunch, Wed–Fri noon–2pm; dinner, Tues–Sat 6:30–10pm.

Hidden behind an intimidating white facade, Michael's opens up into a friendly, airy interior that cascades back to a light indoor patio. Original art and a working fountain give the dining room an upscale bistro feel—a sensation that is confirmed by simple and elegant meals.

For starters, mix and match a variety of pastas with a plethora of toppings; try fettucine with salmon, or spaghetti with scallops or lobster. Salads are composed of Hawaiian tuna, capers, and grilled onions; or papaya, avocado, and Maine lobster. Top entrée choices include grilled duck with Grand Marnier and oranges, and pork tenderloin with cream sauce and apples.

WEST BEACH CAFE, 60 N. Venice Blvd., Venice. Tel. 213/823-5396.

Cuisine: CALIFORNIA. **Reservations:** Recommended. **Directions:** From the Santa Monica Freeway, take the 4th Street exit and turn left. Turn right onto Pico Boulevard and after 2 blocks, turn left onto Neilson, which becomes Pacific Avenue. After about 1 mile, turn right onto Venice Boulevard. The restaurant is near the corner, ½ block from the beach.

$ Prices: Appetizers $6–$8; main courses $8–$22; lunch $8–$22; weekend brunch $12–$18; late-night pizzas $13–$17. AE, CB, DC, MC, V.

Open: Lunch, Tues–Fri 11:30am–2:45pm; dinner, daily 6–10:45pm; brunch, Sat–Sun 10am–2:45pm; late-night snacks 11:30pm–1am.

This trendy, boxy eatery is minimally decorated with white cinder-block walls, track lighting, and simple black chairs and white-clothed tables. The walls of the café serve as a gallery for an ever changing variety of works by local artists, and the room features unobstructed views for easy table-hopping.

Lunch means fancy hamburgers, Caesar salads, pastas, and seafood main dishes. Dinners are more elaborate: Favorites on the changing weekly menu are Chilean seabass lasagne, and oxtails with mashed potatoes and roasted vegetables. A special brunch served on weekends includes eggs Benedict, Belgian waffles, huevos rancheros, and do-it-yourself tacos (you pick the ingredients). There's a fine wine list, and good late-night pizzas, made with whatever's left in the kitchen, are also available.

INEXPENSIVE

SIDEWALK CAFE, 8 Horizon Ave. (at Oceanfront), Venice. Tel. 310/399-5547.
  Cuisine: AMERICAN. **Reservations:** Not accepted.
$ Prices: Appetizers $3–$5; main courses $6–$12. MC, V.
  Open: Sun–Thurs 7am–10:30pm, Fri–Sat 7am–midnight.
Venice is the home and hangout of L.A.'s most eclectic creative community, and few places in Venice offer you a better view of the local action than Sidewalk Cafe. The constantly bustling restaurant is ensconced in one of the city's few remaining original early 20th-century buildings. The best seats are out front, around overcrowded open-air tables, all with a perfect view of the skaters, bikers, joggers, skateboarders, breakdancers, and sidewalk performers who provide nonstop free entertainment. If you have to sit inside, try the small bar in the back.

The extensive menu features overstuffed sandwiches and healthy portions of other American favorites such as: omelets, salads, and burgers.

9. MARINA DEL REY, REDONDO BEACH & LONG BEACH

EXPENSIVE

555 EAST, 555 East Ocean Blvd., Long Beach. Tel. 310/437-0626.
  Cuisine: CONTINENTAL. **Reservations:** Accepted. **Directions:** From I-710 south, take the Broadway exit and turn right onto Lime Avenue. The restaurant will be on your left, at the corner of Ocean Boulevard and Lime Avenue.
$ Prices: Appetizers $3–$10; main courses $15–$35; lunch $5–$15. AE, DC, DISC, MC, V.
  Open: Lunch, daily 11:30am–3pm; dinner, daily 5:30–10pm; bar, until midnight.
This restaurant's East-Coast steakhouse looks are accentuated by a dark wood bar, pressed tin ceiling, and black-and-white marble chessboard floor. Except for the grand piano, around which the

dining areas are arranged, the restaurant looks somewhat like an upscale TGI Fridays.

The restaurant's foot-long menu changes weekly, but usually includes chicken and steaks grilled over mesquite, citrus, apple, and cherry woods, and a variety of sandwiches and seafood melts. Dinner means grilled meats and poultry, as well as a good selection of seasonal seafood. Look for softshell crab, Maine lobster, seared scallops, and tuna. A spectacular wine list encompasses hundreds of selections from California and Europe.

THE WAREHOUSE, 4499 Admiralty Way, Marina del Rey. Tel. 213/823-5451.
   Cuisine: INTERNATIONAL. **Reservations:** Not accepted. **Directions:** From I-405, exit onto Calif. 90, which ends at Lincoln Boulevard. Turn left onto Lincoln Boulevard, right on Bali Way, and then right onto Admiralty Way to the restaurant.

$ Prices: Appetizers $4–$10; main courses $14–$23; lunch $8–$15. AE, MC, V.
   Open: Lunch, Mon–Fri 11:30am–3pm; dinner, Mon–Thurs 4–10pm, Fri–Sat 4–11pm, Sun 5–10pm; brunch, Sat 11am–3pm, Sun 10am–3pm.

Admittedly, the leisurely ambience and terrific views are better than the food, but this is still a good place to eat. The owner, photographer Burt Hixson, traveled 23,000 tax-free miles, ostensibly to find the perfect decor for his dream restaurant. The result is a two-level dockside eatery with cask-and-barrel seating; burlap coffee bag wall hangings; and a hodgepodge of nettings, ropes, peacock chairs, and the like. Hixson's photos line the walls, but the best views are in the other direction, toward the marina. During warm weather, the best tables are outside.

The cuisine is influenced by as many nations as the beer menu, and includes chicken Dijon, Malaysian shrimp, and steak teriyaki. There's also a raw bar serving oysters, and snacks like garlic bread, nachos, and quesadillas.

MODERATE

AUNT KIZZY'S BACK PORCH, in the Villa Marina Shopping Center, 4325 Glencove Ave., Marina del Rey. Tel. 213/578-1005.
   Cuisine: AMERICAN. **Reservations:** Not accepted. **Directions:** From I-405, exit onto Calif. 90, which ends at Lincoln Boulevard. Turn right onto Lincoln Boulevard and right again onto Maxella Avenue. The Villa Marina Shopping Center is just ahead, on the corner of Glencove Avenue.

$ Prices: Appetizers $3–$6; main courses $8–$13; Sun brunch $12. No credit cards.
   Open: Lunch, Mon–Sat 11am–4pm; dinner, Sun–Thurs 4–11pm, Fri–Sat 4pm–midnight; brunch, Sun 11am–3pm.

Authentic Southern (American) home-cooked meals are prepared from time-honed recipes by a chef from Cleveland, Mississippi.

Menu options include fried chicken, chicken Creole, jambalaya, catfish with hush puppies, and some of the best smothered pork chops you've ever tasted. Almost everything comes with two vegetables, cornbread, or rice and gravy. Whitebread desserts include peach cobbler and sweet-potato pie.

Sunday brunches are really special. Served buffet style, dishes include meat and cheese omelets, grilled potatoes, smothered pork chops, barbecued beef ribs, fried chicken, and a choice of five vegetables.

Nothing is easy to find in the shopping center, though. Aunt Kizzy's is located to the right of Vons supermarket, across a small driveway.

MUMS, 144 Pine Ave., Long Beach. Tel. 310/437-7700.

Cuisine: ITALIAN. **Reservations:** Accepted. **Directions:** From I-710 south, take the Broadway exit and turn right on Pine Avenue. The restaurant will be on your left, between Broadway and 1st Street.

$ Prices: Appetizers $7–$9; main courses $9–$19; lunch $7–$12. AE, CB, DC, DISC, MC, V.

Open: Mon 11:30am–9pm, Tues–Thurs 11:30am–10pm, Fri 11:30am–midnight, Sat 5pm–midnight, Sun 5–9pm.

Mums has jumped on the haute California bandwagon, serving contemporary Italian foods in bright wood-and-glass surroundings. The restaurant is comfortable, fun, unpretentious, and good.

Salads are good lunch choices, and include goat cheese, tomatoes, pinenuts, and a sun-dried tomato vinaigrette; or grilled vegetables with a lime-ginger vinaigrette. An assortment of pizzas, pastas, and calzones are served for dinner, as are blackened shrimp, and barbecued chicken topped with creamy pesto, peppers, and sun-dried tomatoes.

The upstairs roof garden opens on weekend nights for dining and dancing. Bring a sweater.

RED ONION, 655 N. Harbor Dr., Redondo Beach. Tel. 310/376-8813.

Cuisine: MEXICAN. **Reservations:** Accepted.

$ Prices: Appetizers $3–$6; main courses $9–$15. AE, CB, DC, DISC, MC, V.

Open: Daily 11am–2am; food served until 10pm.

Part of a small Mexican restaurant chain, The Red Onion is zany in concept, with south-of-the-border decor that is overdone to the extreme. Slow moving paddle fans are suspended from bamboo ceilings, and the white stucco walls are hung with hundreds of photos of Mexico. An eclectic selection of chairs, many of them rattan and bamboo mix with an open brick-and-tile fireplace, Persian-style carpets, and a forest of plants.

You get the feeling that they serve more margaritas than meals here, but the food is both good and plentiful. The extensive menu covers all the hits such as tacos, enchiladas, and fajitas, as well as fancier dishes like sea bass sautéed in lemon butter and arroz con pollo—a chicken-and-rice casserole. The best deal is offered during happy hour—weekdays between 4 and 8pm—when a free buffet of salads, rice, beans, enchiladas, tacos, and chips is available for the price of a drink. The bar becomes lively after the kitchen closes.

10. SPECIALTY DINING

A DINING COMPLEX

**FARMER'S MARKET, Fairfax and 3rd Avenues. Tel. 213/
933-9211.**
Open: Mon–Sat 9am–6:30pm, Sun 10am–5pm.

Located near West Hollywood, the fun Farmer's Market is one of
America's best prepared food malls. In addition to endless isles of
food stalls, the covered outdoor market is jam-packed with local
produce and international goodies like pickled Georgia freestone
peaches, Norwegian cod roe, beef-blood pudding, and Japanese
pin-head gunpowder—a type of green tea.

The market dates from 1934, when 18 *Grapes of Wrath*-era
farmers began selling fresh produce here, right from the backs of their
trucks. Who knows when the first Jane Darwell predecessor decided
to fry a chicken, bake some raisin bread, and whip up an old-
fashioned potato salad the way the folks back home in Oklahoma like
it. Eventually, tables were set up under olive trees, where customers
could consume the prepared food.

Today, dining is still al fresco, at one of the many outdoor tables.
The variety of foods is staggering. Your selections might include fresh
fruit juices; barbecued beef, chicken, ribs, or Texas chili; tacos,
tamales, enchiladas; waffles; hundreds of cheeses; smoked fish;
blintzes; hot roasted chestnuts; fruit salads, vegetable salads, seafood
salads; roast meats; seafood entrées; pizza; fish and chips; burgers;
stuffed cabbage; falafel; or Italian fare, from eggplant parmigiana to
lasagna.

BRUNCH

**AUNT KIZZY'S BACK PORCH, in the Villa Marina Shop-
ping Center, 4325 Glencove Ave., Marina del Rey. Tel.
213/578-1005.**
Cuisine: AMERICAN. **Reservations:** Not accepted. **Directions:** From I-405, exit onto Calif. 90, which ends at Lincoln
Boulevard. Turn right onto Lincoln Boulevard and right again onto
Maxella Avenue. The Villa Marina Shopping Center is just ahead,
on the corner of Glencove Avenue.
$ Prices: Sun brunch $12. No credit cards.
Open: Brunch, Sun 11am–3pm.

Authentic Southern (American) home-cooked meals are prepared
from time-honed recipes by a chef from Cleveland, Mississippi.
Sunday brunches are really special. Served buffet style, dishes include
meat and cheese omelets, grilled potatoes, smothered pork chops,
barbecued beef ribs, fried chicken, and a choice of five vegetables.

**THE BEACON, in the Hyatt Regency, 200 S. Pine Ave.,
Long Beach. Tel. 310/491-1234.**
Cuisine: CALIFORNIA. **Reservations:** Recommended. **Di-
rections:** From the Long Beach Freeway (I-710) south, take the
Shoreline Drive exit and turn left onto Pine Avenue.

$ Prices: Sunday brunch $19.50.
   Open: Brunch, Sun 11am–3pm.
They serve other meals here, but Sunday brunch is what makes The Beacon special. Themed around a large glass lighthouse, the long and narrow dining room offers terrific views of the Long Beach Marina as well as the large ponds and walkways of the Hyatt Regency Hotel.
   The buffet is an all-you-can-eat affair, and the offerings seem endless. There is an omelet bar, a ham and roast beef carving station, Belgian waffles, eggs Benedict, breakfast meats, and a huge selection of salads and seafood, including smoked salmon and peel-and-eat shrimp. Champagne and fresh juices are also bottomless. Did I mention the dessert station, which has at least seven different cakes and pies to choose from, as well as pastries and fresh fruit with hot chocolate fondue for dipping?

WEST BEACH CAFE, 60 N. Venice Blvd., Venice. Tel. 213/823-5396.

   Cuisine: CALIFORNIA. **Reservations:** Recommended. **Directions:** From the Santa Monica Freeway, take the 4th Street exit and turn left. Turn right onto Pico Boulevard and after 2 blocks, turn left onto Neilson, which becomes Pacific Avenue. After about 1 mile, turn right onto Venice Boulevard. The restaurant is near the corner, ½ block from the beach.
$ Prices: Weekend brunch $12–$18. AE, CB, DC, MC, V.
   Open: Brunch, Sat–Sun 10am–2:45pm.
This trendy, boxy eatery is an excellent choice for any meal, but brunches are really special. Served only on weekends, the brunch menu includes eggs Benedict, Belgian waffles, huevos rancheros, and do-it-yourself tacos (you choose the ingredients).

LATE-NIGHT EATING

CANTOR'S FAIRFAX RESTAURANT, DELICATESSEN & BAKERY, 419 N. Fairfax Ave., Los Angeles. Tel. 213/651-2030.

   Cuisine: JEWISH. **Reservations:** Not accepted.
$ Prices: Appetizers $3–$7, main courses $4–$10. AE, MC, V.
   Open: Daily, 24 hours.
Popular with rock stars and other celebs, Cantor's has also been a hit with late-nighters since it opened 65 years ago. In addition to a full range of sandwiches, diners can get matzoh ball soup, knishes, and other Jewish specialties. There's live music in the restaurant's Kibitz Room every Tuesday.

DENNY'S, 7373 W. Sunset Blvd., West Hollywood. Tel. 213/876-6660.

   Cuisine: AMERICAN. **Reservations:** Not accepted.
$ Prices: Appetizers $2–$4, main courses $4–$7. AE, MC, V.
   Open: Daily, 24 hours.
When someone says "let's go to Rock and Roll Denny's," they don't mean just any restaurant in this nationwide chain; they're referring to the one at the corner of Sunset and Vista. On weekends between 2am and 4am a half-hour wait should be expected. You can get the same

food at a dozen other Denny's citywide, but the crowd makes this one the best.

LARRY PARKER'S 24-HOUR DINER, 206 S. Beverly Dr., Beverly Hills. Tel. 310/724-5655.
   Cuisine: AMERICAN. **Reservations:** Not accepted.
$ Prices: Appetizers $3–$6, main courses $4–$8. AE, MC, V.
   Open: Daily, 24 hours.

On the weekend, don't be surprised to find a 45-minute wait at 4am. This is the most popular of the after-bar eateries; it blasts high-decibel hip-hop, sports a spinning disco ball, and attracts a flashy crowd. Patrons line up behind a doorman-watched velvet rope.

CHAPTER 7

WHAT TO SEE & DO IN LOS ANGELES

There's plenty to do in L.A.; the only problem is that you have to drive everywhere to do it. Traffic makes it impossible to see everything in a day; order your priorities and don't plan on seeing everything in a short time or you'll end up not seeing much of anything. Be sure to get a good map; any accordion foldout, sold in gas stations and drugstores all around town, will do. If you can, pick up a copy of the Sunday *Los Angeles Times* and check the "Calendar" for a good list of the week's events.

SUGGESTED ITINERARIES

IF YOU HAVE 1 DAY After spending the morning in Hollywood, visiting the Walk of Fame and Mann's Chinese Theatre, cruise along Sunset Boulevard or stop in at the Rancho La Brea Tar Pits. Spend the afternoon in Beverly Hills. Window-shop along Rodeo Drive and drive by famous homes.

IF YOU HAVE 2 DAYS Spend the first day as above, then tour a television or film studio, or go shopping along Melrose Avenue and visit the world-famous Farmer's Market. In the evening, go to a baseball or football game, see a play, or visit the Griffith Observatory.

IF YOU HAVE 3 DAYS Spend your third day exploring the city's beach communities, especially Santa Monica, Venice, and Malibu. Don't miss the scene along the Venice Beach Walk.

IF YOU HAVE 5 DAYS OR MORE Visit a theme park— Universal Studios, Disneyland, or Knott's Berry Farm—or try out as a contestant on a TV game show. Perhaps join a studio audience and watch your favorite show being taped. Museum-lovers should visit the J. Paul Getty Museum or explore Forest Lawn Cemetery.

1. THE TOP ATTRACTIONS

GRIFFITH OBSERVATORY, 2800 E. Observatory Rd., Los Angeles. Tel. 213/664-1191.

Almost 50 million people have visited Griffith Observatory since its doors opened in 1935. Located on the south slope of Mt. Hollywood, the observatory is still one of L.A.'s best evening attractions. Visitors are invited to look through the observatory's 12-inch telescope, one of the largest in California for use by the public. On a clear night, you can see the moon, planets, and other celestial objects. Phone 213/663-8171 for the Sky Report—a recorded message on current planet positions and celestial events.

Admission: Free.

Viewing Times: Winter, Tues–Sun 7–9:45pm; summer, daily dark–9:45pm. **Directions:** From U.S. 101, take the Vermont Avenue exit north to its end in Griffith Park.

HOLLYWOOD SIGN, Hollywood.

The 50-foot-high white sheet-metal letters of the world-famous HOLLYWOOD sign have long been a symbol of the movie industry city. But it wasn't always that way. Erected in 1923, the sign was originally intended as an advertisement for an area real estate development, and the full text read "Hollywoodland" until 1949. Unfortunately, laws prohibit visitors from climbing up to the base, but that's okay since the best view is from down below in Hollywood.

WALK OF FAME, Hollywood Boulevard and Vine Street, Hollywood.

Nearly 2,000 stars are honored on the world's most famous sidewalk. Bronze medallions set into the center of each star pay tribute to famous television, film, radio, and record personalities, from nickelodeon days to the present. Some of the most popular include: Marilyn Monroe, 6744 Hollywood Blvd.; James Dean, 1719 Vine St.; John Lennon, 1750 Vine St.; and Elvis Presley, 6777 Hollywood Blvd. Each month another celebrity is awarded a star on the Walk of Fame, and the public is invited to attend. For dates and times, contact the Hollywood Chamber of Commerce, 6255 Sunset Blvd., Suite 911, Hollywood, CA 90028 (tel. 213/469-8311).

Directions: From U.S. 101, exit onto Highland Boulevard and turn left onto Hollywood Boulevard.

J. PAUL GETTY MUSEUM, 17985 Pacific Coast Hwy., Malibu. Tel. 310/458-2003.

Waggishly dubbed "Pompeii-by-the-Pacific," the J. Paul Getty Museum is a spectacular reconstruction of the Roman Villa dei Papiri, which was buried in volcanic mud when Mount Vesuvius erupted in A.D. 79, destroying Pompeii and Herculaneum. Completed in 1974, this 10-acre museum is believed to have the largest endowment of any museum worldwide.

The magnificent Italian-style museum is, fittingly, particularly strong in Greek and Roman antiquities. One of the most notable pieces in the collection is a 4th-century B.C. Greek sculpture, *The Victorious Athlete* (known as the Getty bronze), possibly crafted by Lysippus, court sculptor to Alexander the Great.

A second strength is pre-20th-century European paintings and decorative arts, major examples of which include 17th- and 18th-century French furniture, tapestries, silver, and porcelain. The painting galleries accommodate an extensive Italian Renaissance collection (including the only documented painting in the country by Masaccio), a Flemish baroque collection, and important paintings by such French artists as Georges de la Tour, Nicolas Poussin, Jacques-Louis David, and Jean-François Millet.

In March 1990, the museum announced that it had acquired *Irises,* painted in 1889 by Vincent van Gogh. It is the Getty's most famous 19th-century painting and is among the most important works of art in the western United States. *Irises* can be seen in the museum's second-floor galleries together with a growing collection of important 19th-century works, such as Pierre-Auguste Renoir's *La Promenade,* Edouard Manet's *Rue Mosnier with Flags,* Edvard Munch's *Starry Night,* and James Ensor's *Christ's Entry into Brussels in 1889.* Among other recent acquisitions is a watercolor by Honoré Daumier, *A Criminal Case (Une Cause Criminelle),* illustrating one aspect of Daumier's fascination with the French judicial system. The museum also has major examples of styles of French silver that were fashionable in the late 17th and 18th centuries.

If that's not enough, the museum displays medieval and Renaissance illuminated manuscripts, sculpture, and drawings; as well as 19th- and 20th-century European and American photographs.

Two incredible educational interactive videodiscs allow visitors to guide themselves through the rich and complex worlds of Greek vases and illuminated manuscripts with the touch of a finger. This new technology enables you to study these subjects in depth, depending on your level of interest, and have the otherwise forbidden luxury of leafing through a medieval manuscript or handling an ancient Greek vase.

Moderately priced snacks, salads, and sandwiches are sold in the Garden Tea Room, a cafeteria-style eatery. Picnics are not permitted on the premises.

Docent orientation lectures are given at the ocean end of the main garden every 15 minutes from 9:30am to 3:15pm.

Important: Parking is free, but visitors are required to phone for a parking reservation 7 to 10 days in advance. Due to an agreement with local homeowners, walk-in visitors are not permitted. Carless visitors may enter the grounds by bicycle, motorcycle, taxi, or RTD

bus no. 434 (phone the museum for information and request a museum pass from the driver).

Admission: Free.

Open: Tues–Sun 10am–5pm (last entrance 4:30pm). **Directions:** From Santa Monica, take Calif. 1 (Pacific Coast Highway) north about 5 miles to the museum entrance.

MANN'S CHINESE THEATRE, 6925 Hollywood Blvd., Hollywood. Tel. 213/461-3331.

★ One of Hollywood's greatest landmarks, Grauman's Chinese Theatre was opened in 1927 by impresario Sid Grauman. Opulent both inside and out, the theater combines authentic and simulated Chinese decor. Original Chinese heaven doves top the facade, and two of the theater's columns actually come from a Ming Dynasty temple. Despite its architectural flamboyance, the theater is most famous for its entry court, in which movie stars' signatures, and hand- and footprints are set in concrete. Sid Grauman, who was credited with originating the idea of the spectacular movie "premiere," was an excellent promoter. To this day countless visitors continue to match their hands and feet with those of Elizabeth Taylor, Paul Newman, Ginger Rogers, Humphrey Bogart, Frank Sinatra, and others. It's not always hands and feet, though; Betty Grable made an impression with her shapely leg; Gene Autry with the hoofprints of Champion, his horse; and Jimmy Durante and Bob Hope used (what else?) their noses. The theater's name was changed to Mann's in the 1970s. Movie tickets cost $8.

Open: Call for showtimes. **Directions:** From U.S. 101, exit onto Highland Boulevard and turn right onto Hollywood Boulevard. The Theatre is located 3 blocks ahead on your right.

RANCHO LA BREA TAR PITS/GEORGE C. PAGE MUSE-UM, Hancock Park, 5801 Wilshire Blvd., Los Angeles. Tel. 213/857-6311.

Even today a bubbling, odorous, murky swamp of congealed oil still oozes to the earth's surface in the middle of L.A. It's not pollution; it's the La Brea Tar Pits, an incredible, primal attraction right on the Miracle Mile in the Wilshire district. The pits date back some 40,000 years, when they formed a deceptively attractive drinking area for mammals, birds, amphibians, and insects, many of which are now extinct. Thousands of prehistoric animals crawled into the sticky sludge and stayed forever. Although the existence of the pits was known as early as the 18th century, it wasn't until 1906 that scientists began a systematic removal and classification of the fossils. Disengorged specimens have included ground sloths, huge vultures, mastodons (early elephants), camels, and prehistoric relatives of many of today's rodents, bears, lizards, and birds, as well as plants and freshwater shells.

There are currently six pits here, in which asphalt seeps to the surface to form sticky pools. Tar Pit tours are offered on Saturdays and Sundays at 1pm, starting from the Observation Pit at the west end of Hancock Park.

More than two dozen specimens have been mounted and are exhibited in the George C. Page Museum of La Brea Discoveries, at the eastern end of Hancock Park. Skeletons of trapped birds and animals are also on display. A 15-minute film documents the Tar Pit discoveries. In the adjacent Paleontology Laboratory, you can watch scientists as they clean, identify, and catalog new fossils.

Admission: $5 adults, $2.50 seniors (62 and older) and students with I.D., $1 children ages 5–12; kids 4 and under, free. Admission is free the second Tues of every month.

Open: Museum, Tues–Sun 10am–5pm; Paleontology Laboratory, Wed–Sun 10am–5pm; Observation Pit, Sat–Sun 10am–5pm. **Directions:** From the Santa Monica Freeway (I-10), exit onto La Brea Avenue north, continue for 3 miles, and then turn left onto Wilshire Boulevard. The museum and tar pits are about 10 blocks ahead, between Fairfax and La Brea Avenues.

VENICE BEACH WALK, Venice oceanfront.

Nestled against the ocean, between Santa Monica and Marina del Rey, the city of Venice is one of the trendiest sections of Los Angeles, and a unique tourist destination. The character of Venice has undergone a remarkable change since the turn of the century, when it was founded with the idea that it would resemble its namesake in Italy. The streets, graced with canals, were connected by quaint one-lane bridges; and authentic imported gondolas plied the inland waterways. The area became fashionable when self-enchanted silent-screen star Mae Murray *(The Merry Widow)* built a pistachio-colored, Venetian-style palazzo here, near the St. Mark's hotel, an Italian-style rococo hostelry.

But then oil was discovered. Block after block of residences gave way to the profitable derricks, and the canals became slimy sewers. As a beach resort (not to mention a harbinger of Disneyland) Venice died a miserable death. The area began to revive in the '50s, when Venice attracted southern California's beatniks. And in the '60s, Venice became the hippies' primary place for turning on and dropping out.

Today, Venice is quickly becoming a chic seaside community; developers are renovating, and gentrification is in full swing. Soaring real estate is bringing in scores of new restaurants and boutiques. Venice's beach walk is one of the city's greatest cultural treasures; a "Coney Island west" circus of skaters, hipsters, and posers of all ages and shapes. You go there just to stroll and watch the carnival of humanity that is attracted to this ever so L.A. meeting ground.

UNIVERSAL STUDIOS HOLLYWOOD, Hollywood Freeway, Lankershim Boulevard exit, Universal City. Tel. 818/777-3750.

The largest and busiest movie studio in the world, Universal began offering tours to the public in 1964. Now a full-fledged amusement park, the "studio" attracts more than 5 million visitors a year who want to experience the rides and get a behind-the-scenes look at the movies.

Visitors board a tram for the one-hour guided tour of the studio's 420 acres. You'll pass stars' dressing rooms and countless departments involved in film production. Backlot sets are the most interesting; they include Six Point, Texas, a western town that has been used since the days of Tom Mix; and a typical New York City street. A stop at Stage 32 focuses on special effects.

The tram encounters several disasters along the way, including an attack by the deadly 24-foot *Jaws* shark, a laser battle with Cyclon robots, an alpine avalanche, a bridge collapse, a flash flood, earthquake, and more.

After the ride, visitors can wander around the Entertainment Center, where several times each day skilled stuntpeople fall off buildings, dodge knife blows, and ride trick horses. In addition, you can perform as a "guest star" in the *Star Trek Adventure,* then watch yourself perform with spliced-in pictures of Leonard Nimoy and William Shatner. Terrific special effects shows based on the movies *An American Tail* and *Back to the Future* showcase spectacular moviemaking techniques. On Universal's newest ride, *E.T. Adventure,* visitors take a ride on simulated bicycles and relive key parts of the film. Almost any day you can be part of a live audience for the taping of a television show.

Open: Summer, daily 8:30am–5pm; the rest of the year, daily 9:30am–3:30pm.

Admission: $25 adults; $19 seniors (65 and older) and children aged 3 to 11; under 3, free. **Parking:** $4. **Directions:** From U.S. 101 (Hollywood Freeway), take the Lankershim Boulevard exit to the park entrance.

WARNER BROTHERS STUDIOS, Olive Avenue at Hollywood Way, Burbank. Tel. 818/954-1744.

Home to Warner Brothers and Lorimar Television, the Warner Brothers Studios offer the most comprehensive and the least Disneyesque of studio tours. They call it the VIP tour, because it's created for no more than 12 people per group.

The tours are flexible, since they look in on whatever is being filmed at the time. Whether it's an orchestra scoring a film or a TV program being taped or edited, you'll get a glimpse of how it's done. Whenever possible, guests visit working sets to watch actors filming actual productions. Possible stops may include the wardrobe department or the mills where sets are made.

Because you're seeing people at work—people who mustn't be disturbed—there are usually only two tours a day, and children under 10 are not admitted. It is recommended that you make a reservation at least one week in advance.

Admission: $24 per person.

Tours: Mon–Fri 10am and 2pm.

TELEVISION TAPINGS

Television producers need enthusiastic audiences for their game and talk shows. It can be fun, too. To gain admission to a taping, you must be willing to be seen on camera, and there is often a minimum age. T.V. Ticket Hotline (tel. 818/894-7777) will arrange for you to be part of a live audience for a television taping. They help assemble audiences for many popular game and talk shows, and their service is free. You can reserve tickets over the phone.

UNIVERSAL STUDIOS, 100 Universal City Plaza, Universal City, CA 91608. Tel. 818/777-3750.

To see a television show being taped at Universal Studios without going to the theme park, write or call the ticket office. Be sure to give them your preferred dates; they will supply you with a taping schedule. Tickets are free.

Ticket Office Hours: Mon–Fri 8am–5pm, Sat–Sun 9:30am–4pm.

NBC STUDIOS, 3000 W. Alameda Ave., Burbank, CA 91523. Tel. 818/840-3537.

For tickets to any of the shows taped at NBC Studios (including the "Tonight Show"), write to the address above. You'll receive a "guest letter," which can be exchanged for free tickets on your arrival in Los Angeles. It does not guarantee entrance to a specific taping. Tickets are distributed on a first-come, first-served basis. Tickets for the "Tonight Show" are available on the day of the show only; tickets for other shows may be picked up in advance. Minimum age limits vary from 8 to 18; it's 16 for the "Tonight Show."

Ticket Office Hours: Mon–Fri 8am–5pm.

TELEVISION GAME SHOWS

Have you ever dreamed of being a contestant on a television game show? Producers are choosy, but if you have the "looks" they are searching for, you may be selected. Since most contestants are from California, coordinators are especially pleased to see out-of-towners. If they like you, they will do everything within reason to accommodate you. The average audition lasts about an hour, and usually consists of a written test. Callbacks are held anywhere from a few hours to a few days later.

With proper planning, you can audition for three or four shows in a single week, and still have plenty of time to tour the city. Shows looking for contestants advertise daily on the front page of *The Los Angeles Times* classified section. You can also contact production companies directly to see if they're currently auditioning. Below is a short list of major companies, together with the game shows they produce.

Merv Griffin Enterprises, 1541 North Vine St., Hollywood, CA 90028 (tel. 213/859-0188). "Wheel of Fortune" and "Jeopardy!"

Mark Goodson Productions, 5757 Wilshire Blvd., Suite 206, Los Angeles, CA 90036 (tel. 213/965-6500). "Match Game," "The Price Is Right," and "Family Feud."

Dick Clark Productions, 3003 West Olive Ave., Burbank, CA 91510 (tel. 818/841-3003). "The Challengers" and "Let's Make a Deal."

2. MORE ATTRACTIONS

CEMETERIES & CHURCHES

HOLLYWOOD MEMORIAL PARK CEMETERY, 6000 Santa Monica Blvd., Hollywood. Tel. 213/469-1181.

This centrally located cemetery is a popular, if morbid, sightseeing excursion. Dedicated movie buffs can visit the graves of Valentino, Peter Lorre, Douglas Fairbanks, Sr., Norma Talmadge, Tyrone Power, Cecil B. DeMille, Marion Davies, and others. Almost every day a mysterious lady in black pays homage at the crypt of Valentino.

Admission: Free.

Open: Daily 8am–5pm. **Directions:** From U.S. 101, exit onto Sunset Boulevard west. After 5 blocks, turn left onto Gower Street, then left at the cemetery to the entrance on Santa Monica Boulevard.

FOREST LAWN CEMETERY, 1712 S. Glendale Ave., Glendale. Tel. 213/254-3131.

There are five Forest Lawns in L.A., but this is the one you've

FROMMER'S FAVORITE
LOS ANGELES EXPERIENCES

A Visit to a Film or TV Studio Nothing is more common to L.A. than a backstage tour of a film or television production facility. It's a lot of fun to see how your favorite TV show or a movie is actually made.

Dining at a Top Restaurant Splurge for an expensive dinner in a trendy restaurant. L.A. is one of America's great restaurant cities. Don't just go for the food—do as the locals do and make it an evening to see and be seen.

A Day at the Beaches Stroll along the Venice Beach Walk, cruise the Santa Monica Pier, and sunbathe in Malibu.

A Shopping Tour of the City You might want to just window-shop along Rodeo Drive, but then seriously consider the stores on Melrose Avenue and in trendy Santa Monica. Don't miss an excursion to the Beverly Center, the city's most famous shopping mall.

A Day at a Theme Park Whether it's Disneyland, Knott's Berry Farm, or Universal Studios Hollywood, these attractions can be fun for the entire family.

heard about. Comic Lenny Bruce called this place "Disneyland for the dead," but to founder Dr. Hubert Eaton, Forest Lawn was the cemetery of his dreams—a symbol of the joys of eternal life. It's quite a place. Thousands of southern Californians are entombed in the Great Mausoleum, including Jean Harlow, Clark Gable, Carole Lombard, and W. C. Fields. The Mausoleum's Memorial Court of Honor features a stunning stained-glass re-creation of da Vinci's *The Last Supper,* created by Rosa Caselli Moretti, the last member of a Perugia, Italy, family known for their secret process of making stained glass. There are special crypts in the Court that money cannot buy—they're reserved for men and women whose service to humanity has been outstanding. Those already so entombed include Gutzon Borglum, creator of Mount Rushmore, and composer Rudolph Friml.

The cemetery's biggest draws are two paintings: *The Crucifixion* (called "deeply inspiring" by Pope John Paul II), and *The Resurrection* (the Pope had no comment). The artworks are part of a narrated show, presented daily every hour from 10am to 4pm in a special theater specifically built for this purpose.

There are a number of cemetery churches, including Wee Kirk o' the Heather, modeled after the 14th-century Scottish church where Annie Laurie worshipped; and the Church of the Recessional, a memorial to the sentiments expressed by Rudyard Kipling. More than 30,000 marriages have been performed here, including that of Ronald Reagan and Jane Wyman.

Other attractions at the Forest Lawn Museum include 14th-century European cathedral stained glass from the William Randolph Hearst collection, and reproductions of famous artworks, including Ghiberti's *Paradise Doors* and Michelangelo's *Sotterraneo* and *David*. Pick up a map at the Information Booth at the entrance to the cemetery.

Admission: Free.

Open: Daily 9am–5pm. **Directions:** From U.S. 101, exit onto Barham Boulevard, which turns into Forest Lawn Drive. The cemetery entrance is straight ahead.

WAYFARERS CHAPEL, 5755 Palos Verdes Drive South, Rancho Palos Verdes. Tel. 213/377-1650.

Built on a cliff with a broad, steep face, the Wayfarers Chapel sits serenely in a quiet spot above the lashing waves of the Pacific. Built by Lloyd Wright, the celebrated architect Frank Lloyd Wright's son, the church is constructed of glass, redwood, and native stone, and surrounded by pretty gardens.

The "glass church" is a memorial to Emanuel Swedenborg, the Swedish 18th-century philosopher and theologian who claimed to have conversed with spirits and heavenly hosts in his visions.

Rare plants, some of which are native to the Holy Land, surround the building. Phone in advance to arrange a free escorted tour.

Admission: Free.

Open: Daily 9am–5pm.

HISTORICAL SIGHTS

CASA DE ADOBE, 4605 N. Figueroa St., Highland Park. Tel. 213/225-8653.

Casa de Adobe is a re-creation of an early 19th-century Mexican California rancho. Latino art and artifacts are on exhibit from the Southwest Museum's permanent collection, together with Spanish Colonial-period furnishings.

Admission: Free; donations accepted.

Open: Tues–Sat 11am–5pm, Sun 11am–1pm.

EL ALISAL, 200 E. Avenue 43, Highland Park. Tel. 213/222-0546.

Charles F. Lummis, founder of the Southwest Museum, built this rugged two-story "castle" himself, using rocks from a nearby arroyo and telephone poles purchased from the Santa Fe Railroad. His home became a cultural center for many famous people in the literary, theatrical, political, and art worlds. Himself an author, editor (he coined the slogan "See America First"), archeologist, and librarian, Lummis was equally at home with Will Rogers, Teddy Roosevelt, singer Mary Garden, Madame Schumann-Heink, and writers such as Blasco Ibanez.

One of the particularly interesting aspects of El Alisal is its new and most attractive water-conserving garden. The primary plants are those that thrive in a Mediterranean climate. The experimental section, the yarrow meadow, is a substitute for a water-consuming lawn.

Admission: Free.

Open: Sat–Sun 1–4pm.

MISSIONS

On July 16, 1769, a Franciscan padre, Junípero Serra established the first in a string of missions that were to stretch along El Camino Real (the Royal Road) from San Diego to Sonoma. Eventually, the total number of missions reached 21, each one spaced a day's walk from the next. These controversial buildings were the first European structures on the West Coast; they represented the beginning of the end for the region's Native Americans. Today, California's missions are the oldest structures in the state. Most are still owned by the church, and can be visited for a small fee.

MISSION SAN FERNANDO, 15151 Mission Blvd., San Fernando. Tel. 818/361-0186.

Near the junction of the Golden State–Santa Ana (I-5) Freeway and San Diego Freeway (I-405) in San Fernando, the Mission San Fernando, established in 1747, occupies 7 acres of beautiful grounds. With an arcade of 21 classic arches and adobe walls 4 feet thick, it was a familiar stop for wayfarers along El Camino Real. The museum and the adjoining cemetery (where half a dozen padres and hundreds of Shoshone Indians are buried) are also of interest.

Admission: $3 adults, $1.50 children under 13.

Open: Daily 9am–5pm. **Directions:** From I-5, exit at San Fernando Mission Boulevard east, and drive 5 blocks to the mission.

MISSION SAN GABRIEL ARCANGEL, 537 West Mission Dr., San Gabriel. Tel. 818/282-5191.

San Gabriel's completely self-contained compound encompasses an aqueduct, a cemetery, a winery, a tannery, a mission church, and a famous set of bells. Construction on the church—distinguished by its buttresses—was begun in 1790. Glittering, hand-carved polychrome statues surround the altar, while a copper font in the rear has the dubious distinction of being the first one used to baptize a California Indian in 1771.

The most notable contents of the mission's museum are Native American paintings depicting the Stations of the Cross. They're painted on sailcloth, with colors made from crushing the petals of desert flowers.

The mission itself was constructed with walls that are about 5 feet thick—erected to withstand the ravages of time. But even they were no match for two earthquakes in 1987, which have necessitated massive renovations.

Admission: Free; donations accepted.

Open: Daily Mon–Fri 9:30am–4pm. **Closed:** Christmas, Thanksgiving, and Easter.

MUSEUMS/GALLERIES

HUNTINGTON LIBRARY, ART COLLECTIONS, AND BO-TANICAL GARDENS, 1151 Oxford Rd., San Marino. Tel. 818/405-2100, or 405-2141.

The 207-acre estate of the pioneer industrialist, Henry E. Huntington (1850–1927)—complete with gardens and mansion—has been converted into an educational and cultural center for scholars, art devotees, and the general public. Mr. Huntington's thirst for original manuscripts, rare books, great paintings, and skillfully planned gardens led to the formation of what many consider to be one of the greatest attractions in southern California.

Huntington's house is now an art gallery, containing an extraordinary collection of paintings, tapestries, furniture, and other decorative arts. Works are mainly of English and French origin and date from the 18th century. The most celebrated painting here is Gainsborough's *The Blue Boy. Pinkie,* by Sir Thomas Lawrence, is a famous portrait of the youthful aunt of Elizabeth Barrett Browning. Equally well known are Sir Joshua Reynolds's *Sarah Siddons as the Tragic Muse;* Rembrandt's *Lady with the Plume,* and Romney's *Lady Hamilton in a Straw Hat.* You'll also find a collection of Beauvais and Gobelin tapestries.

The adjacent Virginia Steele Scott Gallery for American Art contains an eclectic variety of paintings spanning more than 200 years. Some of the better known works are Gilbert Stuart's portrait of George Washington, John Singleton Copley's *Sarah Jackson,* George Caleb Bingham's *In a Quandary,* Mary Cassatt's *Breakfast in Bed,* and Frederic Church's *Chimborazo.*

The Library Exhibition Hall displays a rotating selection of great treasures drawn from its remarkable collection of English and American first editions, letters, and manuscripts. They include a copy of the Gutenberg Bible printed in Mainz in the 1450s, a 1410 copy of Chaucer's *Canterbury Tales,* a First Folio of Shakespeare, and Benjamin Franklin's handwritten manuscript for his *Autobiography.*

It's worth a trip just to see the Botanical Gardens, which are studded with rare shrubs, trees, and 17th-century statuary from Padua. Strolling paths wend their way through a variety of flora, including the Desert Garden, with extensive cacti in all shapes; the Camellia Garden with 1,500 varieties; and the Japanese Garden, with dwarf maples, reflection pools, Zen Garden, and bonsai court.

The Huntington Library is located about 12 miles from downtown Los Angeles.

Admission: Free; $5 donation suggested.

Open: Tues–Fri 1–4:30pm, Sat–Sun 10:30am–4:30pm. **Closed:** Mon and major hols.

NORTON SIMON MUSEUM OF ART, 411 Colorado Blvd., Pasadena. Tel. 818/449-6840.

One of the most important museums in California, the Norton Simon Museum of Art features old masters from the Italian, Dutch, Spanish, Flemish, and French schools; Impressionist paintings; Franco-Flemish tapestries; and 20th-century painting and sculpture. Highlights of the collections include works by Raphael, Rubens, Rembrandt, Rousseau, Courbet, Matisse, Picasso, Corot, Monet, and van Gogh. A superb collection of Southeast Asian and Indian sculpture is also displayed.

The museum itself sits among broad plazas, sculpture gardens, a reflection pool, and semitropical plantings.

Admission: $4 adults, $2 students and seniors; children under 12, free.

Open: Thurs–Sun noon–6pm; bookshop Thurs–Sun noon–5:30pm.

THE SOUTHWEST MUSEUM, 234 Museum Dr., Highland Park. Tel. 213/221-2164, or 213/221-2163 for a recording.

At the top of a steep hill overlooking Arroyo Seco, the Southwest Museum is Los Angeles' oldest art museum. Founded in 1907 by amateur historian and Native American expert Charles F. Lummis, the privately funded museum contains one of the finest collections of Native American art and artifacts in the United States.

Inside the two-story structure, the whole world of the original Americans opens onto a panoramic exhibition, complete with a Cheyenne summer tepee, rare paintings, weapons, moccasins, and other artifacts of Plains life. A separate two-level hall presents the culture of the native people of southeastern Alaska, Canada's west coast, and the northern United States. A major exhibition interprets 10,000 years of history of the people of the American Southwest, featuring art and artifacts of the native peoples of Arizona, New Mexico, Colorado, and Utah. The California Hall offers insights into the lifestyles of the first Californians. The Caroline Boeing Poole Memorial Wing exhibits a changing display of more than 400 examples of native North American basketry from the museum's 11,000-plus collection.

An exceptionally interesting calendar of events includes a Native American Film Festival; lectures on the sacred art of the Huichols; Mexican songs, dance, and costumes; and Native American masks—to name just a few.

Admission: $5 adults; $3 seniors (over 55) and students; $2 children 7–18; children under 7, free.

Open: Tues–Sun 11am–5pm. **Directions:** From the Pasadena Freeway (Calif. 110), exit onto Avenue 43. Turn right onto Figueroa and follow the signs zigzagging up the hill to the museum at Museum Drive.

NATURAL HISTORY MUSEUM OF LOS ANGELES COUNTY, Exposition Park, 900 Exposition Blvd., Los Angeles. Tel. 213/744-3466.

The largest natural history museum in the West houses seemingly endless exhibits of fossils, minerals, birds, mammals, and the like. It's a warehouse of history, chronicling the earth and its environment from 600 million years ago to the present day. Other permanent displays include the world's rarest shark, a walk-through vault containing priceless gems, a Children's Discovery Center, Insect Zoo, and state-of-the-art Bird Hall. Dioramas depict animals in their natural habitats, and other exhibits detail human cultures, including one on American history from 1660 to 1914.

Free docent-led tours are offered daily at 1pm.

Admission: $5 adults; $2.50 children 12–17, seniors, and students with I.D.; $1 children 5–12; children under 5, free. Free admission first Tues of every month.

Open: Tues–Sun 10am–5pm, and some Mons and hols. **Directions:** From the Pasadena Freeway (Calif. 110), exit onto

Exposition Boulevard east. The museum is located 3 blocks ahead, 1 block west of Hoover Street.

LOS ANGELES COUNTY MUSEUM OF ART, 5905 Wilshire Blvd., Los Angeles. Tel. 213/857-6111, or 857-6000 for a recording.

A complex of five modern buildings around a spacious central plaza, the Los Angeles County Museum of Art in Hancock Park is probably one of the finest art museums in the United States.

The Ahmanson Building, with a central atrium, contains the permanent collection, which encompasses everything from prehistoric to 19th-century art. The museum's holdings include Chinese and Korean pieces; pre-Columbian Mexican art; American and European painting, sculpture, and decorative arts; ancient and Islamic art; a unique glass collection from Roman times to the 19th century; and the renowned Gilbert collection of mosaics and monumental silver. The museum also has one of the nation's largest holdings of costumes and textiles, and an important Indian and Southeast Asian art collection.

Major special loan exhibitions, as well as galleries for prints, drawings, and photographs, are in the adjacent Hammer Building.

The Robert O. Anderson Building features 20th-century painting and sculpture, as well as special exhibits. The Leo S. Bing Center has a 600-seat theater and a 116-seat auditorium where lectures, films, and concerts are held.

The Pavilion for Japanese Art was opened in September 1988. It was designed by the late Bruce Goff specifically to accommodate Japanese art, though certain elements of the museum resemble New York's Frank Lloyd Wright–designed Guggenheim Museum—the curved rising ramp, the central treatment of light, the structure of the displays. An extraordinary touch was Goff's use of Kalwall (a translucent material) for the exterior walls; besides blocking out ultraviolet light, these walls, like shoji screens, permit the soft, delicate entry of natural light. The museum now houses the internationally renowned Shin'enkan collection of Edo Period (1615–1865) Japanese painting, rivaled only by the holdings of the former emperor of Japan. It also displays Japanese sculpture, ceramics, lacquerware, screens, scrolls, and prints.

Two sculpture gardens contain a dozen large-scale outdoor sculptures, as well as works by the 19th-century French master Auguste Rodin, and the German artist George Kolbe.

Free guided tours covering the highlights of the permanent collections are given daily on a regular basis.

Admission: $5 adults; $3.50 students and seniors (62 and over); $1 children 6–17 years; children 5 and under, free. Free admission for regular exhibitions second Tues of every month.

Open: Tues–Thurs 10am–5pm, Fri 10am–9pm, Sat–Sun 11am–6pm. **Directions:** From the Hollywood Freeway (U.S. 101), take the Santa Monica Boulevard exit west to Fairfax Avenue. Turn left onto Wilshire Boulevard to the museum.

THE GENE AUTRY WESTERN HERITAGE MUSEUM, 4700 Zoo Dr., Los Angeles. Tel. 213/667-2000.

A life-size bronze sculpture of Gene Autry (once called "the singing cowboy") and his horse Champion greet visitors to this museum of American nostalgia.

Opened in 1988, this remarkable repository is undoubtedly one of the most comprehensive historical museums in the world. More than 16,000 artifacts and art pieces, including 100 of Gene Autry's personal treasures, illustrate the everyday lives and occupations of the early pioneers who helped settle the West. There are antique firearms, common tools, saddles (some intricately tooled), stagecoaches, and many hands-on exhibits. As the tour progresses, visitors enter the West of romance and imagination, as seen by artists, authors, filmmakers, and in TV and radio productions. Show business is illustrated with items from Buffalo Bill's Wild West Show, movie clips from the silent days, contemporary films, and memorabilia from TV-western series. Many exhibits, including a Hollywood-type set with viewer-activated videos, were capably designed by Walt Disney Imagineering.

Recorded Acoustaguide tours, narrated by Willie Nelson, are available for $4.

The museum shop is worth a visit in itself. Gifts include cowboy hats, western posters, books, shirts, bolo ties, and silver and turquoise jewelry.

Admission: $6 adults; $4.50 seniors (60 and over) and students 13–18; $2.50 children 2–12; children under 2, free.

Open: Tues–Sun 10am–5pm. **Directions:** From I-5, exit at Zoo Drive and follow signs to Griffith Park. The museum is located opposite the zoo.

PARKS & GARDENS

DESCANSO GARDENS, 1418 Descanso Dr., La Cañada. Tel. 818/952-4402, or 952-4400 for a recording.

E. Manchester Boddy began planting camellias in 1941 as a hobby. Today the Rancho del Descanso (Ranch of Rest) contains thousands of camellias, with more than 600 varieties and more than 100,000 plants—making it the world's largest camellia garden. The County of Los Angeles purchased the gardens in 1953.

In addition to the camellias, there is a 4-acre rose garden, which includes some varieties dating back to the time of Christ. Paths and streams wind through a towering oak forest and untended native chaparral. Each season features different plants: daffodils, azaleas, and lilacs in the spring; chrysanthemums in the fall; and so on. Monthly art exhibitions are also held in the gardens.

A Japanese-style teahouse is located in the camellia forest. Landscaped with money donated by the Japanese-American community, it features pools, waterfalls, and a rock garden, as well as a gift shop built in the style of a Japanese farmhouse. The teahouse serves tea and cookies Tuesday through Sunday from 11am to 4pm. Free docent-guided walking tours are offered every Sunday at 1pm; guided tram tours, which cost $3, run Tuesday through Friday at 1, 2, and 3pm, and on Saturday and Sunday at 11am. Picnicking is allowed in specified areas.

Open: Daily 9am–4:30pm.
Admission: $3 adults; $1.50 students and seniors (over 62); 75¢

children 5–12; children under 12, free. **Parking:** Free. **Directions:** From downtown L.A., take Calif 2 north and exit onto Verdugo Boulevard. Turn right; after 1 mile turn right again onto Descanso Drive.

GRIFFITH PARK, Los Angeles. Tel. 213/665-5188.

Encompassing more than 4,000 acres of trees and hills, verdant Griffith Park claims to be the largest municipal park in the United States. Home of the Los Angeles Zoo and the Griffith Observatory, the park's facilities include golf courses, a bird sanctuary, tennis courts, a huge swimming pool, picnic areas, an old-fashioned merry-go-round, and large expanses of wilderness.

The park is located just northeast of Hollywood. Enter via Western Avenue for the beautiful Ferndell and children's playground. Vermont Avenue is the best entrance for the observatory, bird sanctuary, and Mount Hollywood.

WILL ROGERS STATE HISTORIC PARK, 14253 Sunset Blvd., Pacific Palisades. Tel. 310/454-8212.

The 31-room ranch house and grounds of the "cracker-barrel philosopher" was willed to the state of California in 1944. The estate is now supervised as a historic site by the Department of Parks and Recreation. Visitors may explore the grounds, seeing the former Rogers stables, even watching polo games, usually on Saturday afternoon and Sunday mornings, weather permitting. The house is filled with the original comfortable furnishings, including a porch swing in the living room and many Indian rugs and baskets.

Will Rogers began in show business as a trick roper in traveling rodeos, an act he later brought to the Ziegfeld Follies in New York. Eventually he settled in Hollywood, buying his own ranch and making films, which led one movie critic to write: "Will Rogers upheld the homely virtues against the tide of sophistication and sex." He was killed in an air crash with his friend, Wiley Post, in Alaska in mid-August 1935.

The park is open from 8am to 7pm during the summer, till 6pm the rest of the year. The house is open from 10am to 5pm daily, except on Christmas, Thanksgiving, and New Year's Day. There is a $4-per-vehicle fee for entry, including all passengers. The fee includes a guided tour of the Will Rogers home, an audio tour, and a film on Will Rogers shown in the Visitor Center. There are picnic tables, although no food is sold, and a small gift shop in the Center. Incidentally, Charles Lindbergh and his wife hid out here in the '30s during part of the kidnap craze that followed the murder of their first son.

3. COOL FOR KIDS

GRIFFITH PLANETARIUM AND HALL OF SCIENCE, 2800 E. Observatory Rd., Los Angeles. Tel. 213/664-1181, or 213/664-1191 for a recording.

Griffith's "great Zeiss projector" flashes five different shows a year across a 75-foot dome. Excursions into interplanetary space might range from a search for extraterrestrial life to a quest into the causes of earthquakes, moonquakes, and starquakes. The shows last about an hour, but showtimes vary; call for information.

The Hall of Science, with many fascinating exhibits on galaxies, meteorites, and other cosmic subjects, includes a solar telescope that's trained on the sun; a Foucault Pendulum, which demonstrates the earth's rotation; 6-foot earth and moon globes; meteorites; a Cosmic Ray Cloud chamber; and more.

Admission: Hall of Science, free; Planetarium, $3.50 adults; $2.50 seniors (65 and older); $2 children 5–12. Those under 5 are admitted to the children's programs only at 1:30pm on Saturday and Sunday.

Open: Summer, daily 12:30–10pm; the rest of the year, Tues–Fri 2–10pm, Sat–Sun 12:30–10pm. **Closed:** Mon. **Directions:** From U.S. 101, take the Vermont Avenue exit north to its end in Griffith Park.

THE HOLLYWOOD WAX MUSEUM, 6767 Hollywood Blvd., Hollywood. Tel. 462-8860.

Cast in the Madame Tussaud mold, The Hollywood Wax Museum features dozens of life-like figures of famous movie stars and events.

The "museum" is not great, but it is entertaining. A "Chamber of Horrors" exhibit includes the coffin used in *The Raven,* as well as a scene from Vincent Price's old hit, *The House of Wax.*

The "Movie Awards Theatre" exhibit is a short film highlighting Academy Award presentations from the last four decades.

Admission: $8 adults; $6.50 seniors; $5 children 6–12; children under 6, free.

Open: Sun–Thurs 10am–midnight, Fri–Sat 10am–2am.

THE LOS ANGELES ZOO, 5333 Zoo Dr., in Griffith Park, Los Angeles. Tel. 213/666-4090.

Only in southern California would a zoo advertise its "cast of thousands." Here the stars include more than 2,000 mammals, birds, and reptiles walking, flying, and slithering over 113 acres. Habitats are divided by continent: North America, South America, Africa, Eurasia, and Australia. Active in wildlife conservation, the zoo is also home to an intense research facility, and it houses about 50 endangered species. There's also an aviary with a walk-in flight cage, a reptile house, an aquatic section, and Adventure Island.

Adventure Island, the revamped children's zoo, is an unusual addition that looks nothing like a zoo. Four distinct habitats blend into one another in a space of about 2½ acres, where mountains, meadows, deserts, and shorelines are re-created. Especially popular with children, Adventure Island houses an aviary, tidepool, petting zoo, animal nursery, and outdoor theater for animal performances.

Admission: $6 adults; $5 seniors; $2.75 children 2–12; children under 2, free.

Open: Summer, daily 10am–6pm; the rest of the year, daily 10am–5pm. **Directions:** From I-5, exit at Zoo Drive and follow the signs to the zoo in Griffith Park.

LOS ANGELES CHILDREN'S MUSEUM, 310 N. Main St., Los Angeles. Tel. 213/687-8800.

This delightful museum is a place where children learn by doing. Everyday experiences are demystified in an interactive, playlike atmosphere; children are encouraged to imagine, invent, create, pretend, and work together. In the Art Studio they can make everything from Mylar rockets to finger puppets. There's a City Street where kids can sit on a policeman's motorcycle, play at driving a bus or at being a firefighter. Young visitors can become "stars" in the recording or TV studio; learn about health in a doctor's and dentist's office and about X-rays in an emergency room; see their shadows frozen on walls in the Shadow Box; and play with giant foam-filled Velcro-edged building blocks in Sticky City.

In addition to the regular exhibits, there are all kinds of special activities and workshops, from cultural celebrations to T-shirt decorating and making musical instruments. There is a 99-seat theater for children where live performances or special productions are scheduled every weekend. Call the museum for upcoming events.

Admission: $5; children under 2, free.

Open: Summer, Mon–Fri 11:30am–5pm, Sat–Sun 10am–5pm; the rest of the year, Wed–Thurs 2–4pm, Sat–Sun 10am–5pm.

Directions: The Museum is located just north of downtown. From U.S. 101 south, exit onto Los Angeles Street, turn right and the museum will be on the right-hand side. Northbound 101 traffic should exit at Alameda, proceed straight past Alameda and turn left on Los Angeles Street.

WELLS FARGO HISTORY MUSEUM, 333 S. Grand Ave., Downtown. Tel. 213/253-7166.

Owned by the bank of the same name, this museum highlights the history of Wells Fargo and its impact on California and the American West. It's a delightful place. Among the exhibits are an authentic 19th-century Concord stagecoach; a coach under construction (where you can sit inside and listen to taped excerpts from the diary of a young Englishman who made the arduous trip to California by coach); tools used by coachmakers; the Challenge nugget—a 2-pound gold lump of 76% purity found in 1975; mining entrepreneur and Wells Fargo agent Sam Dorsey's gold collection; and a fascinating selection of mining and Wells Fargo artifacts.

Admission: Free.

Open: Mon–Fri 9am–5pm. **Closed:** Bank hols.

4. ORGANIZED TOURS

GRAY LINE TOURS, 6541 Hollywood Blvd., Hollywood. Tel. 213/856-5900.

Offering the largest selection of organized city tours, Gray Line runs several daily itineraries throughout the city. Via air-conditioned motorcoaches, visitors are taken to Sunset Strip, the movie studios, the Farmer's Market, Hollywood, and homes of the stars. Other tours visit Disneyland, Knott's Berry Farm, and Catalina Island. Phone for itineraries, times, and prices.

5. SPORTS & RECREATION

SPECTATOR SPORTS

BASEBALL

Los Angeles has two major-league baseball teams. The Los Angeles Dodgers (tel. 213/224-1500) play at Dodger Stadium, 1000 Elysian Park, near Sunset Boulevard. The California Angels (tel. 714/634-2000) call Anaheim Stadium home at 2000 S. State College Blvd., near Katella Avenue in Anaheim. The regular season runs from about mid-April to early October.

BASKETBALL

The two Los Angeles National Basketball Association franchises are the L.A. Lakers (tel. 213/419-3100), who play in Great Western Forum, 3900 W. Manchester Blvd., at Prairie Avenue, in Inglewood; and the L.A. Clippers (tel. 213/748-8000), who hold court in the L.A. Sports Arena, 3939 S. Figueroa Ave. The regular season runs from April to September.

FOOTBALL

The two Los Angeles–area NFL football teams are the L.A. Raiders (tel. 213/322-5901), playing at the L.A. Memorial Coliseum, 3911 S. Figueroa Ave.; and the L.A. Rams (tel. 714/937-6767), playing in 70,000-seat Anaheim Stadium, 2000 S. State College Blvd., near Katella Avenue in Anaheim. The regular season runs from August to December.

HORSE RACING

HOLLYWOOD PARK RACETRACK, 1050 S. Prairie Ave., Inglewood. Tel. 213/419-1500.

Frequented by Hollywood personalities, the scenic track, with its lakes and flowers, features thoroughbred racing from early April through July as well as November and December. The $1-million Hollywood Gold Cup is also run here. Well-placed monitors project views of the back stretch as well as stop-action replays of photo finishes. Races are usually held Wednesday through Sunday. Post times are 1pm in the summer (Fridays at 7:30pm), 12:30pm in the fall. Admission is $6 general, $9 clubhouse.

SANTA ANITA RACETRACK, 285 W. Huntington Dr., Arcadia. Tel. 818/574-7223.

One of the most beautiful tracks in the country, Santa Anita offers thoroughbred racing from October through mid-November and December through late April. On weekdays, the public is invited to watch morning workouts from 7:30 to 9:30am. Post time is 12:30 or 1pm. Admission is $3.

ICE HOCKEY

The NHL L.A. Kings (tel. 310/673-6003) play at the Great Western Forum at 3900 W. Manchester Blvd., at Prairie Avenue in Inglewood. The regular season runs from September to March.

RECREATION

BEACHES

There are more than 75 miles of beach along the L.A. coast.

Zuma Beach, on the Pacific Coast Highway in Malibu (tel. 310/457-9701 for surf conditions) is one of the largest and most popular, especially among surfers.

Santa Monica Beach (tel. 310/451-8761), at the west end of Wilshire Boulevard, is crowded with Angelenos who live inland. The beach is fronted by an 18-mile bike path that runs to Palos Verdes.

Manhattan, Hermosa, and **Redondo State beaches** (tel. 310/379-8471), located south of LAX, are also good for swimming and sunning.

Note: There are privately operated bathhouses at most of the public beaches, where you can rent a locker, shower, and towel. State beaches provide lifeguards, and I'd strongly advise staying within the areas supervised by them. The surf in many rocky places is only for the highly experienced, if at all. Swimming in much of southern California is possible all year round if you're accustomed to very cold water. Many swimmers wear wet suits on winter days.

BICYCLING

The best place to bike (or skate) is on the 22-mile auto-free beach path that runs along Santa Monica and Venice beaches. You can rent 10-speeds from **Sea Mist Rental,** 1619 Ocean Front, Santa Monica (tel. 310/395-7076).

BILLIARDS

HOLLYWOOD BILLIARDS, 5504 Hollywood Blvd., Hollywood. Tel. 213/465-0115.

Perhaps the oldest pool hall in the city, this 24-hour games emporium has dozens of pool tables, as well as backgammon, darts, and video games. It's located at the corner of Hollywood Boulevard and Western Avenue.

Cost: Pool, $8 per hour.

GOLF

Most L.A. area golf courses are privately owned. Some of the prettiest ones, however, allow public access—for a fee.

INDUSTRY HILLS GOLF CLUB, 1 Industry Hills Parkway, City of Industry. Tel. 818/810-4455.

Two 18-hole courses encompass 8 lakes, 160 bunkers, and long fairways, planned by William Bell. An adjacent driving range is lighted for night use.

Greens fees: $45 weekdays, $60 weekends.

MONARCH BELL, 33080 Niguel Rd., Laguna Niguel. Tel. 714/240-8247.

Located about an hour from Los Angeles, this Robert Trent Jones, Jr., course is one of the most beautiful in the area since it fronts the Pacific Ocean. Beautiful elevated greens and rolling fairways make this a popular course year round.

Greens fees: Mon–Thurs $50, Fri–Sun $75, including required cart rental.

HORSEBACK RIDING

The **Griffith Park Livery Stables,** 480 Riverside Dr., Burbank (tel. 818/840-8401) rents horses by the hour for Western or English riding. There's a 200-pound weight limit, and children under 12 are not permitted to ride. Horses cost $13 per hour, and there's a two-hour rental limit maximum. The stables are open Monday through Friday from 8am to 7pm, Saturday and Sunday from 8am to 4pm.

ROLLER SKATING

Who would even think of going to an indoor rink when they are so near the Venice Beach Walk. Roller skating was practically invented here, and Los Angeles is certainly the world's center for in-line skating.

SPOKES 'N STUFF, 36B Washington Blvd., Venice. Tel. 310/306-3332.

Renting both in-line Rollerblades and conventional skates, this is just one of the many places to find wheels near the Venice Beach Walk. Knee pads and wrist guards come with every rental.

Cost: $5 per hour.

TENNIS

Public courts, administered by the City of Los Angeles Department of Recreation and Parks (tel. 213/485-4825), are located all around the city.

The Griffith Park tennis courts are some of the best municipal courts in the country. All 12 of its outdoor courts are lighted for night play. Call the Department of Recreation and Parks (see above) for reservations.

WINDSURFING

LONG BEACH WINDSURFING CENTER, 3850 E. Ocean Ave., Long Beach. Tel. 310/433-1014.

Surfing meets sailing in this fun sport which is much more difficult than it looks. The Long Beach Windsurfing Center, rents boards by the hour. They're open daily from 10am to 6pm.

CHAPTER 8

WALKING & DRIVING AROUND LOS ANGELES

1. DOWNTOWN & CHINATOWN
2. HOLLYWOOD
3. BEVERLY HILLS

All too often, it seems as though the sights in Los Angeles are so far apart from one another that you can spend an entire afternoon just traveling on the freeway. There are, however, some special areas in the city where many sights are grouped together, enabling you to leave your car and spend the day strolling. The following itineraries are ideal for such a venture.

WALKING TOUR 1 — DOWNTOWN & CHINATOWN

Start: Los Angeles City Hall, 200 N. Spring St.
Finish: Chinatown.
Time: About 2 hours, not including food stops.
Best Times: During the day, and on weekends, when everything's open.
Worst Times: After dark.

This ever expanding sprawl of a city did have an origination point: the downtown area, in and around the Old Plaza and Olvera Street. Due to concern about earthquakes, city-planning authorities originally prohibited the construction of buildings over 13 stories high. This limitation led many companies to locate in outlying areas, leaving the original downtown to fall into relative disrepair. In 1957 new construction technology permitted tall buildings to be constructed safely; therefore, the downtown experienced a renaissance that included tall office buildings, fancy hotels, good restaurants, and a newfound tourist industry.

Los Angeles' downtown area is surprisingly accessible to walkers. In one easy stroll you can familiarize yourself with both the city's historic past and its bustling present. You can see a piece of city government, and immerse yourself in the cultural heritage that has become an integral part of Los Angeles life. To reach the starting point of our downtown tour from U.S. 101 South, exit onto Los Angeles Street, turn right on 1st Street, and right again on Spring Street. Northbound 101 traffic should exit onto Alameda Street, turn right on 1st Street, and right again on Spring Street. Park near:

1. Los Angeles City Hall, the only structure to surpass the

150-foot-height limit prior to 1957. This much-photographed, beautifully angular building is famous for the roles it has played in "Superman," "Dragnet," and many other television shows. If you make an advance reservation, you can ascend to the observation tower on the top floor, where you will be treated to great views of the city (depending on smog conditions). Tours are offered Monday through Friday at 10 and 11am only.

Turn right onto Temple Street, and walk 1 block to the:

2. Los Angeles Children's Museum, 310 N. Main St. (tel. 213/687-8800). This delightful museum is great for travelers with kids in tow. It's a place where children learn by doing; they are encouraged to imagine, invent, create, pretend, and work together. There's a City Street where kids can sit on a policeman's motorcycle, or play at driving a bus or at being a firefighter. Young visitors can become "stars" in the recording or TV studio, and more. See Chapter 7 for complete information.

Continue north on Main Street, under U.S. 101, and enter the park. You are now in:

3. El Pueblo de Los Angeles, an historical complex of 27 Mexican-style buildings ranging in date from 1818 to 1927. Covering more than 44 acres, the site centers around bustling Olvera Street, an outdoor, cobblestoned marketplace that has the feel of old Mexico. During a stroll along Olvera Street, you will encounter a variety of shops and eateries, and be entertained by street performers and ethnic bands.

Olvera Street cuts straight through the park, and is the area's central attraction. The city's oldest structures line the street, which cuts through:

4. The Old Plaza, a pretty Spanish Mediterranean–style park that makes up the center of El Pueblo. The directory and map, located near the gazebo in the middle of the park, is a good place to get your bearings.

The first place to stop in the Pueblo is:

5. Sepulveda House, 22 N. Main St. Built by Eliosa Martinez de Sepulveda in 1887, this was one of California's first hotels. Today the structure houses the Visitor Information Center (tel. 213/628-1274). It's open Monday through Friday from 10am to 3pm, and Saturdays from 10am to 4:30pm. You can pick up a brochure and map here that includes a good self-guided tour. The best time to arrive at El Pueblo is between 10am and 1pm Tuesday through Saturday, when free guided tours of the historical site are offered. To take part, meet in front of Firehouse No. 1, next to the Information Center.

Continue walking along Olvera Street where you will pass:

6. The Old Plaza Church. Completed in 1818, it's Los Angeles' oldest extant Catholic church. Today, its primarily Hispanic congregation is one of the largest in the United States.

Further along you will see:

7. Firehouse No. 1, dating from 1884; it has not been a working firehouse for more than 100 years. The firehouse has served as a hotel, a store, and a saloon. Today it is a museum, where you can see some of the finest examples of American turn-of-the-century fire-extinguishing equipment.

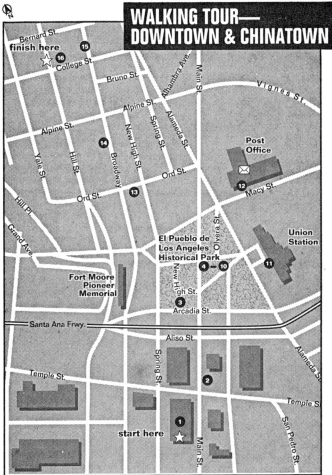

**WALKING TOUR—
DOWNTOWN & CHINATOWN**

Bernard St.
finish here 15
College St.
Bruno St.
Alpine St.
Alpine St.
Yale St.
Hill St.
Broadway
New High St.
Spring St.
Alhambra Ave.
Main St.
Vignes St.
14
Ord St.
Ord St.
13
Ord St.

Post Office ✉ 12 Macy St.

Hill Pl.
Grand Ave.

El Pueblo de Los Angeles Historical Park
4 — 10
Olvera St.
Union Station 11

Fort Moore Pioneer Memorial
New High St.
3
Arcadia St.

Santa Ana Frwy.

Aliso St.
Spring St.
Alameda St.
Temple St.
2
Temple St.
1
start here ⭐
Main St.
San Pedro St.

❶ Los Angeles City Hall
❷ Los Angeles Children's Museum
❸ El Pueblo de Los Angeles
❹ The Old Plaza
❺ Sepulveda House
❻ The Old Plaza Church
❼ Firehouse No. 1
❽ Victorian Garnier Building
❾ The Avila Adobe
❿ The Pelanconi House
⓫ Union Station
⓬ Main Post Office– Terminal Annex
⓭ Chinatown
⓮ North Broadway
⓯ Chinatown Arches and Pagoda Buildings
⓰ Bamboo Plaza

Directly behind the firehouse is the:

8. Victorian Garnier Building. This is one of the few remaining structures from L.A.'s first Chinatown; most of the buildings were leveled in 1939 to make way for Union Station, the western terminus for the Union Pacific, Santa Fe, and Southern Pacific rail lines.

Back on Olvera, you'll encounter:

9. The Avila Adobe, 10 Olvera St. Recognized as the oldest private house in Los Angeles, this was the home of Don Francisco Avila, the Pueblo's first mayor. The simple interior is outfitted with period furnishings from the mid-19th century.

A few doors down you will see:

10. The Pelanconi House, 17 W. Olvera St. Built in 1855, it's one of the city's oldest brick buildings.

Exit on the park's east side and visit:

11. Union Station, 800 N. Alameda St., one of America's last grand-scale train stations. Commuters and long-distance travelers continue to tread over the marble floors, beneath 50-foot cathedral ceilings. Built in 1939, the Spanish mission–style structure is still awesome and well worth a look.

Turn north, up Alameda Street, and step inside the:

12. Main Post Office–Terminal Annex, 900 Alameda St., to see the large Works Progress Administration (WPA) murals. These Depression-era paintings, commissioned by the Roosevelt administration in the 1930s, depict human communications throughout history.

REFUELING STOP   Take a break from your tour and get a bite to eat at **Philippe the Original,** 1001 N. Alameda St. (tel. 213/628-3781). It was founded in 1908 and claims to have created the French dip sandwich. While there's nothing stylish about the place, it's full of good old-fashioned value; great beef, pork, ham, turkey, or lamb French-dip sandwiches are served on the lightest, crunchiest French rolls.

Turn left onto Macy Street, walk 3 blocks, and turn right onto North Broadway. You are now looking toward:

13. Chinatown. Although this "little Asia" lacks the exotic excitement of its larger counterparts in San Francisco, New York, and Vancouver, L.A.'s Chinese section is a great place to shop, eat, and explore. Walk along:

14. North Broadway, Chinatown's primary thoroughfare. You are now heading into the heart of Chinatown, which flourishes primarily between College and Bernard streets.

REFUELING STOP   Turn left onto Sun Mun Way and visit **Grand Star,** 943 Sun Mun Way (tel. 213/626-2285)—an excellent Chinese eatery. Owned and operated by the Quon family since 1967, Grand Star offers an unusual selection of top-notch Chinese dishes, including spicy chicken wings, Mongolian beef with mushrooms, and lobster Cantonese.

Just north of College Street, at Gin Ling Way, you will see the:

15. Chinatown Arches and Pagoda Buildings. As the word "Chinatown," inscribed on the arches will attest, this is the area's formal entrance.

One block ahead, between North Hill and Bernard streets is:

16. Bamboo Plaza, a small shopping mall filled with both oriental and occidental shops and restaurants. In the plaza, and on nearby streets you will find many shops and restaurants that may interest you.

FINAL REFUELING STOP   **Little Joe's,** 900 N. Broadway (tel. 213/489-4900), is one of the last holdouts from the days when this used to be primarily an Italian neighborhood. Opened as a grocery in 1927, Joe's has grown steadily over the years; now it encompasses several bars and six dining rooms. You can get a full pasta dinner, eggplant parmigiana, sausage and peppers, and a variety of other excellent foods. Without doubt, Little Joe's is the best occidental restaurant in Chinatown.

WALKING TOUR 2 — HOLLYWOOD

Start: Mann's Chinese Theater, 6925 Hollywood Blvd.
Finish: Capitol Records Building, 1756 N. Vine St.
Time: About 1½ hours, not including shopping.
Best Times: During the day, when shops are open, and you can see the buildings.
Worst Times: At night, when the area becomes even more seedy.

The legend of Hollywood as the movie capital of the world still persists, though many of its former studios have moved to less-expensive and more spacious venues. The famous city where actresses once posed with leashed leopards is certainly on everyone's must-see list. And although the glamour is badly tarnished, and Hollywood Boulevard has been accurately labeled "the Times Square of the West" (the city itself seems to be unaware of its decline), there is still plenty to see. Shopping is good here, too. Between the T-shirt shops and frenzied pizza places, you'll find some excellent poster shops, film souvenir stores, and assorted Hollywood memorabilia outfits. See Chapter 9, "Savvy Shopping," for specifics.

From U.S. 101, exit onto Highland Boulevard and turn right onto Hollywood Boulevard. Park as soon as you can and go 3 blocks ahead on your right to:

1. **Mann's Chinese Theatre,** one of Hollywood's greatest landmarks. Opened in 1927 as Grauman's Chinese Theatre, the imposing structure was the brainchild of impresario Sid Grauman. Opulent both inside and out, the theater combines authentic and simulated Chinese decor. Original Chinese heaven doves top the facade, and two of the theater's columns actually come from a Ming Dynasty temple. Despite its architectural flamboyance, the theater is most famous for its entry court, in which movie stars' signatures, and hand- and footprints are set in concrete. Sid Grauman, who was credited with originating the idea of the spectacular movie "premiere," was an excellent promoter. To this day countless visitors continue to match their hands and feet with those of Elizabeth Taylor, Paul Newman, Ginger Rogers, Humphrey Bogart, Frank Sinatra, and others. It's not always hands and

feet, though; Betty Grable made an impression with her shapely leg; Gene Autry with the hoofprints of Champion, his horse; and Jimmy Durante and Bob Hope used (what else?) their noses. The theater's name was changed to Mann's in the 1970s. Movie tickets cost $8.

Walk east on Hollywood Boulevard. You are now trodding along the famous:

2. Walk of Fame, where nearly 2,000 stars are honored in the world's most famous sidewalk. Bronze medallions set into the center of each star pay tribute to famous television, film, radio, and record personalities, from nickelodeon days to the present. Some of the most popular include: Marilyn Monroe, 6744 Hollywood Blvd.; James Dean, 1719 Vine St.; John Lennon, 1750 Vine St.; and Elvis Presley, 6777 Hollywood Blvd. Each month another celebrity is awarded a star on the Walk of Fame, and the public is invited to attend. For dates and times, contact the Hollywood Chamber of Commerce, 6255 Sunset Blvd., Suite 911, Hollywood, CA 90028 (tel. 213/469-8311).

As soon as you cross Highland Avenue you will encounter:

3. The Hollywood Wax Museum, 6767 Hollywood Blvd. (tel. 462-8860). Cast in the Madame Tussaud mold, this museum features dozens of life-like figures of famous movie stars and events. One of the most talked-about images pairs John F. Kennedy with Marilyn Monroe—dress blowing and all. A tableau of Leonardo da Vinci's *Last Supper,* as well as scenes depicting Queen Victoria and Martin Luther King, Jr., are on display. A "Chamber of Horrors" exhibit includes the coffin used in *The Raven,* as well as a scene from Vincent Price's old hit, *The House of Wax.* It's open Sunday through Thursday from 10am to midnight, and Friday and Saturday from 10am to 2am.

Further along the block you will see:

4. The Hollywood Egyptian Theater, 6712 Hollywood Blvd., one of the area's top theaters and the site of Hollywood's first premiere: *Robin Hood,* starring Douglas Fairbanks.

REFUELING STOP   Musso & Frank Grill, 6667 Hollywood Blvd. (tel. 213/467-7788) may be Hollywood's oldest extant eatery. Established in 1919, the restaurant was a hangout for Faulkner and Hemingway during their screenwriting days. The setting is richly traditional, and the extensive menu features everything from salads to seafood.

Just down the block you will reach the beautiful art deco building that is the headquarters of:

5. Frederick's of Hollywood, 6606 Hollywood Blvd. (tel. 213/466-8506). Easily one of the most famous panty shops in the world, Frederick's is also one of Hollywood's top tourist attractions. Everything from overtly tight spandex suits to skimpy bikini bras, to sophisticated nighties are sold here. A small "museum" displays the undergarments of the stars. Even if you're not buying, stop in and pick up one of their informative catalogs.

Continue straight ahead, along several more tourist-oriented

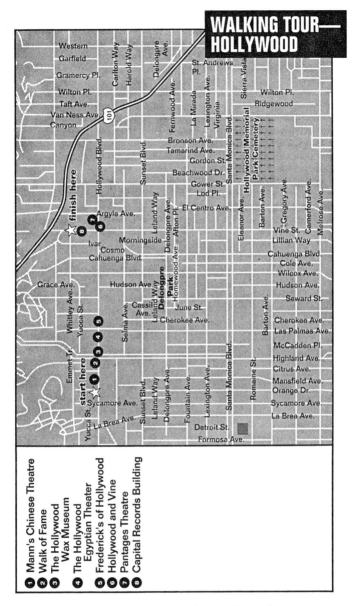

Western
Garfield
Gramercy Pl.
Wilton Pl.
Taft Ave.
Van Ness Ave.
Canyon

Carlton Way
Harold Way
Delongpre Ave.
St. Andrews Pl.

Fernwood Ave.
La Mirada
Lexington Ave.
Virginia
Ridgewood
Wilton Pl.
Sierra Vista

Hollywood Blvd.
Sunset Blvd.
Bronson Ave.
Tamarind Ave.
Gordon St.
Beachwood Dr.
Gower St.
Lod Pl.
El Centro Ave.
Santa Monica Blvd
Eleanor Ave.
Hollywood Memorial Park Cemetery

finish here
Argyle Ave.
Morningside
Ivar
Cosmo
Cahuenga Blvd.
Leland Way
Delongpre Ave.
Afton Pl.
Homewood Ave.
Barton Ave.
Gregory Ave.
Camerford Ave.
Vine St.
Lillian Way
Cahuenga Blvd.
Cole Ave.
Wilcox Ave.
Hudson Ave.
Seward St.

Grace Ave.
Whitley Ave.
Yucca St.
Hudson Ave.
Cassil Ave.
Selma Ave.
June St.
Cherokee Ave.
Leland Way
Delongpre Park
Cherokee Ave.
Las Palmas Ave.
McCadden Pl.
Highland Ave.
Citrus Ave.
Mansfield Ave.
Orange Dr.
Sycamore Ave.
La Brea Ave.

start here
Emmet Tr.
Sycamore Ave.
Yucca St.
La Brea Ave.
Sunset Blvd.
Leland Way
Delongpre Ave.
Fountain Ave.
Lexington Ave.
Santa Monica Blvd
Romaine St.
Barton Ave.

Detroit St.
Formosa Ave.

1. Mann's Chinese Theatre
2. Walk of Fame
3. The Hollywood Wax Museum
4. The Hollywood Egyptian Theater
5. Frederick's of Hollywood
6. Hollywood and Vine
7. Pantages Theatre
8. Capital Records Building

schlock shop blocks, and you will be standing at the intersection of:

6. **Hollywood and Vine.** Once considered the heart of Hollywood, this corner is legendary, not for its uneventful architecture, but for the big-name stars who crossed the intersection. When Greta Garbo walked down the street in trousers, and was widely photographed, the pictures shocked women all over America.

After recovering from their horror and the headlines—"Garbo Wears Pants"—women rushed to their astonished dressmakers (or, in some cases, their husbands' tailors) to have the slacks duplicated.

Just east of Vine Street you will see:

7. Pantages Theatre, 6233 Hollywood Blvd. (tel. 213/468-1700). Built in 1930, this luxurious theater was opened at the very height of Hollywood's heyday. For 10 years this art deco beauty was the setting for the presentation of the Academy Awards, including the first televised Oscar ceremony. Since that time, the theater has been through several incarnations, and is now one of the city's leading legitimate theaters. Recent productions have included *Me and My Girl* and *Starlight Express,* as well as the Julie Andrews/Carol Burnett TV special, the Grammy "Living Legend" Awards, and the televised Country/Western Music Awards.

Turn north on Vine Street and walk half a block to the:

8. Capitol Records Building, 1756 N. Vine St. The building's design, shaped like a stack of records and topped by a stylus, is said to have been conceived by songwriter Johnny Mercer and singer Nat "King" Cole. The round structure has been a Hollywood landmark since its opening in 1956.

FINAL REFUELING STOP   Roscoe's House of Chicken 'N' Waffles, 1514 N. Gower St. (tel. 213/466-7453), is really just a dive, but its devotees have included Jane Fonda, Stevie Wonder, the Eagles, and many other stars. It seems like a joke, but only chicken and waffle dishes are served. To reach the restaurant, continue east on Hollywood Boulevard for about 5 blocks and turn right onto Gower Street. Roscoe's will be about 5 blocks ahead.

WALKING AND DRIVING
TOUR — BEVERLY HILLS

Start: Regent Beverly Wilshire Hotel, 9500 Wilshire Blvd.
Finish: Beverly Hills Hotel & Bungalows, 9641 Sunset Blvd.
Time: About 2 hours, if you don't stop to follow stars.
Best Times: Monday to Saturday from 10am to 6pm, when the stores are open.
Worst Times: At night, when shops are closed, and you can't see the view.

The aura of Beverly Hills is unique. Beneath its veneer of wealth, it's a curious blend of small-town neighborliness and cosmopolitan worldliness. Many of southern California's most prestigious hotels, restaurants, high-fashion boutiques, and department stores are located here. Don't miss that remarkable assemblage of European-based super-upscale stores along Rodeo Drive. A shopping guide is available from the Beverly Hills Chamber of Commerce and Visitors Bureau (see "Tourist Information," in Chapter 4). Beverly Hills is also the

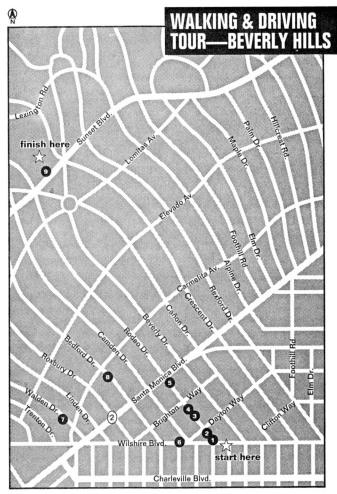

finish here

⑨

Lexington Rd.

Sunset Blvd.

Lomitas Av.

Palm Dr.

Hillcrest Rd.

Maple Dr.

Elevado Av.

Foothill Rd.

Elm Dr.

Carmelita Av.

Alpine Dr.

Rexford Dr.

Crescent Dr.

Cañon Dr.

Beverly Dr.

Rodeo Dr.

Camden Dr.

Bedford Dr.

Roxbury Dr.

⑧

Santa Monica Blvd.

⑤

Foothill Rd.

Walden Dr.

Linden Dr.

Trenton Dr.

⑦

②

Brighton Way

④③

Dayton Way

②①

Clifton Way

Elm Dr.

Wilshire Blvd.

⑥

start here ☆

Charleville Blvd.

① Regent Beverly Wilshire Hotel
② Rodeo Drive
③ Anderson Court
④ Via Rodeo
⑤ Artists and Writers Building
⑥ Department Store Row
⑦ Witch's House
⑧ The Church of the Good Shepherd
⑨ Beverly Hills Hotel & Bungalows

adopted hometown of such motion-picture and TV stars as George Burns, Warren Beatty, James Stewart, Kirk Douglas, Linda Evans, Harrison Ford, Jacqueline Bisset, Frank Sinatra, and Jack Nicholson. Its first mayor was the homespun philosopher/comedian/star Will Rogers. Douglas Fairbanks and Mary Pickford led the migration of stars to the area when they built their famous home, Pickfair, atop the ridge at 1143 Summit Drive; today a drive through the glens, canyons, and hillsides of Beverly Hills will reveal one palatial home after another. Nowhere else in the world are you likely to find such an assemblage of luxury homes—each one a virtual candidate for inclusion in *House Beautiful*. Beware of hawkers selling "Maps of Stars' Homes," though. Many of the occupants pinpointed have moved elsewhere (and some even to Forest Lawn—a cemetery).

From Santa Monica Boulevard, exit onto Wilshire Boulevard and continue east for 8 blocks until you reach the:

1. **Regent Beverly Wilshire Hotel,** 9500 Wilshire Blvd., one of the priciest hotels in the city. This grand Beverly Hills hotel has long attracted international royalty, media celebrities, stage personalities, presidents, and the usual smattering of rich and famous. Parts of the movie *Pretty Woman,* with Richard Gere and Julia Roberts, were filmed here. The spacious lobby contains French Empire furnishings, French and Italian marble flooring, restored bronze and crystal chandeliers, hand-wrought sconces, and two paintings by Verhoven. If you are lucky enough to stay here, you will be greeted by a guest-relations officer who will personally escort you to your room, and have the service of a steward, stationed on every floor.

REFUELING STOP **The Lobby Lounge,** inside the Regent Beverly Wilshire, is an elegant European-style salon serving light meals and cocktails. It's best at teatime, daily from 3 to 5pm, and is surely a place to see and be seen.

The hotel is located at the bottom of:
2. **Rodeo Drive,** Beverly Hills's most famous street, known for its haute couture boutiques, expensive jewelry shops, top restaurants, and major department stores. World-class names on the drive include: Tiffany & Co. (210 N. Rodeo Dr.), Van Cleef & Arpels (300 N. Rodeo Dr.), Chanel (301 N. Rodeo Dr.), Bally of Switzerland (340 N. Rodeo Dr.), Gucci (347 N. Rodeo Dr.), and Cartier (370 N. Rodeo Dr.).

Stroll along Rodeo Drive and poke into interesting shops while rubbing shoulders with T-shirted tourists and snazzy jet-setters.

Halfway between Dayton Way and Brighton Way, you will see:
3. **Anderson Court,** 332 N. Rodeo Dr., a Frank Lloyd Wright–designed art deco–style shopping complex. Built in 1953, it is located right next to:
4. **Via Rodeo,** a pretty cobblestone shopping street that feels like a little bit of Europe in the sun.

On the next block, at the corner of Little Santa Monica Boulevard, you'll find the:
5. **Artists and Writers Building,** 9507 Little Santa Monica Blvd., a squat Spanish-style structure that once housed the offices of Will Rogers, Billy Wilder, Ray Bradbury, and Jack Nicholson, among others.

REFUELING STOP **Nate & Al's,** 414 N. Beverly Dr. (tel. 310/274-0101), is the best-known Jewish deli around. Try a pastrami on fresh-baked rye, chopped liver, a kosher frank, or hot corned beef. It's not fancy; food can be ordered to go.

After a long stroll on Rodeo Drive, get into your car and drive west from the Regent Beverly Wilshire Hotel along Wilshire Boulevard. Here you'll pass:

6. Department Store Row, a fancy cluster of blocks that house some of the country's top names, including Neiman Marcus (9700 Wilshire Blvd.), I. Magnin (9634 Wilshire Blvd.), and Saks Fifth Avenue (9600 Wilshire Blvd.).

After about 8 blocks, cross Santa Monica Boulevard and turn right onto Carmelita Avenue. On your left, at the corner of Walden Drive, you'll see the:

7. Witch's House, 516 N. Walden Dr., a gingerbread-style cottage famous for its storybook look. Since it's a private residence, you won't be able to go inside.

After 3 blocks, turn right on Bedford Drive, and take a look at:

8. The Church of the Good Shepherd, 505 N. Bedford Dr., the oldest house of worship in Beverly Hills. Built in 1924, the church has seen its share of the rich and famous. In 1950, Elizabeth Taylor and first husband, Nicholas Hilton, were married here. Good Shepherd funerals included those of Alfred Hitchcock, Gary Cooper, and Jimmy Durante, among others.

Return to Carmelita Avenue, and turn left onto Beverly Drive. Turn left onto Sunset Boulevard, and on your left you will see the Will Rogers Park (not to be confused with the Will Rogers State Historic Park in Pacific Palisades). Just opposite the park is the:

9. Beverly Hills Hotel & Bungalows, 9641 Sunset Blvd. (tel. 310/276-2251), one of the most famous stomping grounds of millionaires and maharajahs, jet-setters and movie stars. There are hundreds of anecdotes about this famous place, most of which took place in the hotel's Polo Lounge, one of the world's most glamorous bars (closed for renovations until 1994). For years Howard Hughes maintained a complex of bungalows, suites, and rooms here, using some of the facilities for an elaborate electronic-communications security system, and a separate room for his personal food-taster. Years ago Katharine Hepburn did a flawless dive into the pool—fully clad in her tennis outfit, shoes and all. Dean Martin and Frank Sinatra once got into a big fistfight with other Polo Lounge habitués. And in 1969 John Lennon and Yoko Ono checked into the most secluded bungalow under assumed names, then stationed so many armed guards around their little hideaway that discovery was inevitable. So it goes. The stories are endless and concern everyone from Charlie Chaplin to Madame Chiang Kai-shek.

What attracts them all? For one thing, each other. And of course, you can't beat the service—not just the catering to such eccentricities as a preference for bear steak, but little things like being greeted by your name every time you pick up the phone. It doesn't hurt that the Beverly Hills Hotel is a beauty; its green-and-pink stucco buildings are set on 12 carefully landscaped and lushly planted acres. There are winding paths lined with giant palm trees throughout, and the privacy of each veranda is protected by flowering and leafy foliage.

CHAPTER 9

SAVVY SHOPPING

1. THE SHOPPING SCENE

2. SHOPPING A TO Z

One of the biggest cities in the United States, Los Angeles is well known for its plethora of top shops, trendy boutiques, and gaggle of shopping malls. Although the city is quite spread out, the shopping areas are distinct; each is oriented to a particular market.

1. THE SHOPPING SCENE

HOLLYWOOD BOULEVARD   One of Los Angeles' most famous streets is, for the most part, a sleazy strip. But between the T-shirt shops and frenzied pizza places you'll find some excellent poster shops, film souvenir stores, and assorted Hollywood memorabilia outfits.

MELROSE AVENUE   The area between Fairfax and La Brea Avenues is one of the best shopping streets in the country for young, trendy fashions. Hundreds of stores sell the latest in clothes, gifts, jewelry, and accessories.

VENICE BEACH WALK   Stalls and shops sell youth-oriented street fashions to beachgoers and tourists who come here to see and be seen. Even if you're not shopping, come here for the carnival of people showing off their unique talents and fashions.

RODEO DRIVE   Beverly Hills's most famous street is known for its haute couture boutiques, expensive jewelry shops, top restaurants, and major department stores.

DOWNTOWN GARMENT DISTRICT   The blocks close to 9th Street are known for the many shops that sell clothes, luggage, and assorted goods at significantly discounted prices.

HOURS, TAXES & SHIPPING

Store hours are generally Monday through Saturday from 10am to 6pm, and Sunday from noon to 5pm. Most department stores and malls stay open later—usually Monday through Friday from 10am to 9pm, Saturday from 10am to 6pm, and Sunday from 11am to 6pm.

The sales tax in Los Angeles is 7.75%; it is added on at the register for all goods and services purchased.

15 • **SHOPPING A TO Z**

Most of the city's shops can wrap your purchase and ship it anywhere in the world via United Parcel Service (UPS). If they can't, you can send it yourself, either through UPS, at 10690 Santa Monica Blvd. (tel. 213/626-1551), and other locations; or through the U.S. Mail (see "Fast Facts: Los Angeles" in Chapter 4).

2. SHOPPING A TO Z

ANTIQUES

THE ANTIQUE GUILD, 8800 Venice Blvd., near Culver City. Tel. 310/838-3131.
Billing itself as "the world's largest antique outlet," the Guild is a veritable warehouse of history, with more than 3 acres of antiques under one roof. Their buyers are constantly checking-out, and purchasing, the entire contents of European castles, beer halls, estates, and mansions. New shipments arrive weekly, so the merchandise is constantly changing.
Look for everything from old armoires to chandeliers to stained glass, crystal, china, clocks, washstands, tables, and mirrors, and much more.
Open: Mon–Fri 10am–7pm, Sat 10am–6pm, Sun 11am–6pm.

ARTE DE MEXICO, 5356 Riverton Ave., North Hollywood. Tel. 818/769-5090.
Seven warehouses full of carved furniture and wrought iron reportedly once sold only to moviemakers and restaurants. One of the most fascinating places in North Hollywood.
Open: Mon–Sat 8:30am–5:30pm, Sun 10am–5:30pm.

BEACHWEAR

THE BIKINI SHOP, 245 S. Beverly Dr., Beverly Hills. Tel. 310/550-9954.
Top names in two-pieces are sold at this bathing suit shop in the heart of Beverly Hills. The store carries a large variety of styles and sizes.
Open: Mon–Sat 10am–6pm, Sun closed.

BOOKS

There are hundreds of bookshops in Los Angeles; below are some of the more specialized shops.

ARTWORKS, 170 S. La Brea Ave., Los Angeles. Tel. 213/487-7220.
Commercial artists' books, one-of-a-kind editions, periodicals, trade books, and other art-oriented literature are featured.
Open: Mon–Sat 12–5pm.

C. G. JUNG BOOKSTORE & LIBRARY, 10349 W. Pico Blvd., Los Angeles. Tel. 310/556-1196.
Specializes in folklore, fairy tales, alchemy, dream studies, myths,

symbolism, and other related books. Tapes and videocassettes are also sold.

Open: Mon–Sat 12–5pm.

MANDALA BOOKSTORE, 616 Santa Monica Blvd., Santa Monica. Tel. 310/393-1953.

In addition to crystals and Southeast Asian music, this store stocks many hard-to-find books on Buddhism and religion from Nepal, Tibet, and India.

Open: Mon–Sat 10am–10pm, Sun 11am–8pm.

DEPARTMENT STORES

Most L.A. department stores have their flagship store or a large branch either downtown or in Beverly Hills. Many stores also serve as anchors in L.A.'s largest shopping malls; here are some of the best known.

THE BROADWAY, Beverly Center, West Hollywood. Tel. 310/854-7200.

Based in southern California, The Broadway sells moderately priced designer clothes, sportswear, and casual clothing; it also has excellent cosmetics and cookware departments.

Open: Mon–Fri 10am–9:30pm, Sat 10am–9pm, Sun 11am–7pm.

BULLOCK'S, 10861 Weyburn Ave. (near Westwood Boulevard), Westwood. Tel. 310/208-4211.

Upper-middle-class fashion-conscious customers shop here for imported designer fashions and good-quality private label merchandise in all departments.

Open: Mon–Fri 10am–9pm, Sat 10am–7pm, Sun 12–6pm.

I. MAGNIN, 3050 Wilshire Blvd. (near Westmoreland Avenue), Los Angeles. Tel. 213/382-6161.

Operated by a separate division of the same company that owns Bullock's (above), the Wilshire Boulevard flagship store is the mother of all L.A. department stores and a designated historical landmark. High fashions by Chanel, Ungaro, Krizia, and others are so exclusive that they are kept out of sight for viewing on request. Top quality men's fashions are also shown, as are real and costume jewelry.

Open: Mon, Thurs–Fri 9:30am–8pm; Tues–Wed, Sat 9:30am–6pm; Sun noon–6pm.

NORDSTROM, Westside Pavilion, West Los Angeles. Tel. 213/470-6155.

Emphasis on customer service has won this Seattle-based store a loyal following. Equally devoted to women's and men's fashions, the store has one of the best shoe selections in the city, and thousands of suits in stock. The Nordstrom Cafe, on the top floor, is a great place for an inexpensive lunch or light snack.

Open: Mon–Fri 9:30am–8pm, Sat 9:30am–7pm, Sun 11am–6pm.

ROBINSON'S, 600 W. 7th St. (near Hope Street), Downtown. Tel. 213/488-5522.

Home accessories, furniture, and household supplies are featured here, along with sportswear for women and large selections of costume jewelry.

Open: Mon–Sat 10am–6pm, Sun closed.

SAKS FIFTH AVENUE, 9600 Wilshire Blvd., Beverly Hills. Tel. 310/275-4211

Los Angeles' oldest branch of this famous New York–based shop is as opulent as any. Saks sells fashions and gifts for men, women, and children, and has a well-respected restaurant on the top floor.

Open: Mon, Thurs–Fri 10am–8pm; Tues–Wed, Sat 10am–6pm; Sun noon–5pm.

FASHIONS

GUCCI, 347 N. Rodeo Dr., Beverly Hills. Tel. 310/278-3451.

An elegant selection of apparel for men and women is offered by one of the best-known and most prestigious names in international fashion. In addition to shoes, leather goods, and scarfs beautiful enough for framing, the shop offers pricey accessories like a $7,000 handmade crocodile bag.

Open: Mon–Sat 9:30am–6pm.

JERRY MAGNIN/POLO, 323 N. Rodeo Dr., Beverly Hills. Tel. 310/273-8044.

This beautifully assembled store between Brighton Way and Dayton Way is a tribute to the elegance and taste of Ralph Lauren, Armani, Matsuda, and other top designers. An adjacent shop features the entire collection of Polo apparel, from casual and roughwear to couture clothing, footwear, and accessories.

Open: Mon–Sat 10am–6pm.

RETAIL SLUT, 7264 Melrose Ave., Los Angeles. Tel. 213/934-1339.

New and vintage clothing, shoes, and accessories for hip guys and girls are offered at this famous psychedelic shop. Unique designs are sold to a select crowd.

Open: Daily noon–7pm.

MEN'S FASHIONS

BOY LONDON, 7519 Melrose Ave., Los Angeles. Tel. 213/655-0302.

Once on the cutting edge of London's King's Road, Boy has toned down a bit, now selling shirts and other clothes emblazoned with its own logo. It's still cool, though.

Open: Daily 11am–7pm.

BROOKS BROTHERS, 604 S. Figueroa St., Downtown. Tel. 213/629-4200.

Brooks Brothers introduced the button-down collar, and single-handedly changed the standard of the well-dressed businessman. The multilevel shop also sells traditional casual wear, including sportswear, sweaters, and shirts.

Open: Mon–Sat 9:30am–6pm.

KANJI, 7547 Melrose Ave., Los Angeles. Tel. 213/655-7244.

Japanese and European clothes for men are sold at this industrial-looking store in the heart of the Melrose shopping district. Well-made tops and trousers are predominantly black and white, though colorful vests and accessories are also available.

Open: Daily 10am–7pm.

WOMEN'S FASHIONS

BETSEY JOHNSON BOUTIQUE, 7311 Melrose Ave., Los Angeles. Tel. 213/931-4490.

The New York–based designer came to L.A. with this trendy, cutesy shop known for colorful prints and faddy fabrics.

Open: Sun–Fri noon–7pm, Sat noon–9pm.

CHANEL, 301 N. Rodeo Dr., Beverly Hills. Tel. 310/278-5500.

The entire elegant Chanel line is under one roof, and includes clothing, accessories, scents, cosmetics, and jewelry.

Open: Mon–Sat 10am–6pm.

SECOND-HAND

AARDVARK'S ODD ARK, 1516 Pacific Ave., Venice. Tel. 310/392-2996.

This large storefront near the Venice Beach Walk is crammed with racks of antique and used clothes from the '60s, '70s, and '80s. They stock everything from suits and dresses to neckties, hats, handbags, and jewelry. Aardvark's anticipates some of the hottest new street fashions.

Open: Daily 10am–7pm.

FILM MEMORABILIA

BOOK CITY COLLECTIBLES, 6631 Hollywood Blvd., Hollywood. Tel. 213/466-0120.

More than 70,000 color prints of stars past and present are available, together with a good selection of autographs, including those of Lucille Ball ($175), Anthony Hopkins ($35), and Grace Kelly ($750).

Open: Mon–Sat 10am–10pm, Sun 10am–6pm.

CINEMA COLLECTORS, 1507 Wilcox Ave. (at Sunset Boulevard), Hollywood. Tel. 213/461-6516.

Original movie posters, magazines, stills, head shots, and associated memorabilia are cross-referenced on computer. Helpful, uniformed employees can answer your questions and help you find your way around.

Open: Mon–Sat 10am–7pm, Sun noon–5pm.

HOLLYWOOD BOOK AND POSTER COMPANY, 6349 Hollywood Blvd., Hollywood. Tel. 213/465-8764.

Owner Eric Caidin's excellent collection of movie posters is particularly strong in horror and exploitation flicks (about $20). Photocopies of about 5,000 movie and television scripts are also sold for $10 to $15 each.

Open: Mon–Sat 11am–7pm, Sun noon–5pm.

THE LAST MOVING PICTURE SHOW, 6307 Hollywood Blvd., Hollywood. Tel. 213/467-0838.

Movie-related merchandise of all kinds is sold here, including stills from the 1950s and authentic production notes from a variety of films.

Open: Mon–Sat 10am–6pm, Sun closed.

STAR WARES ON MAIN, 2817 Main St., Santa Monica. Tel. 310/399-0224.

Owner Marcia Tysseling was governess to Joan Rivers's daughter and sometimes house-sits for Cher. Now she is the proprietor of a unique resale boutique carrying celebrity clothes and memorabilia. Threads include Joan Rivers's Bob Mackie beaded letterman jacket, Michael Jackson's leather jacket worn in the Pepsi commercial, a pair of Bette Midler's autographed shoes worn in the movie *Beaches,* and various items from Cher, Lionel Richie, Charlton Heston, and others. Ten percent of every sale of celebrity-owned merchandise goes to charity.

Open: Daily 10am–6pm.

GIFTS

THE SHARPER IMAGE, 601 Wilshire Blvd., Downtown. Tel. 213/622-2351.

This is a great place for hard-to-find presents for adults who never grew up. Many state-of-the-art electronics and other sleekly designed toys are unique items.

Open: Mon–Sat 10am–6pm.

Z GALLERIE, 2728 Main St., Santa Monica. Tel. 310/392-5879.

This California-based chain, offers a good selection of poster art, together with unusual gifts, matte black furnishings, and kitchenware.

Open: Mon–Sat 10:30am–7pm, Sun 10am–6pm.

JEWELRY

CARTIER, 370 N. Rodeo Dr., Beverly Hills. Tel. 310/275-4272.

One of the most respected names in jewelry and luxury goods has its Los Angeles shop near Brighton Way. The boutique's setting is as elegant as the beautifully designed jewelry, watches, crystal, and accessories on sale.

Open: Mon–Sat 10am–5:30pm.

TIFFANY & CO., 210 N. Rodeo Dr., Beverly Hills. Tel. 310/273-8880.

Amid sporadic pieces of crystal and china, shoppers will find an exquisite collection of fine jewelry known the world over for classic styles. Top designers include Elsa Peretti and Paloma Picasso.

Open: Mon–Sat 10am–5:30pm, Sun closed.

VAN CLEEF & ARPELS, 300 N. Rodeo Dr., Beverly Hills. Tel. 310/276-1161.

There are three rooms of breathtakingly beautiful gems and jewelry at this shop. Pieces are expensive, but of the highest quality. Some creative fashions highlight an otherwise conservative collection.

Open: Mon–Sat 10am–5pm.

LINGERIE

FREDERICK'S OF HOLLYWOOD, 6606 Hollywood Blvd., Hollywood. 213/466-8506.

Behind the purple facade lies one of the most famous panty shops in the world. Everything from overtly tight spandex suits to skimpy bikini bras and sophisticated nighties are sold here. Even if you're not buying, stop in and pick up one of their famous catalogs.

Open: Mon–Thurs, Sat 10am–6pm; Fri 10am–9pm; Sun noon–6pm.

TRASHY LINGERIE, 402 N. La Cienega Blvd., Hollywood. Tel. 213/652-4543.

Everything here is house-designed. They tailor-fit clothes ranging from tacky patent leather bondage wear to elegant bridal underthings. There's a $2 "membership" fee to enter the store, but even for browsers, it's worth it.

Open: Mon–Sat 10am–7pm.

LEATHER

LEATHERS & TREASURES, 7511 Melrose Ave., Los Angeles. Tel. 213/655-7541.

Amid rows of cowboy boots, skin lovers will find an abundance of bomber jackets, pants, vests, accessories, and hats. It's a crowded little shop with a good, unusual selection of goods.

Open: Daily 11am–7pm.

NORTH BEACH LEATHER, 8500 W. Sunset Blvd., West Hollywood. Tel. 310/652-3224.

Primarily selling leather jackets and dresses, this San Francisco-based shop has up-to-the-minute fashions at high prices. Other leather items from casual to elegant are also available.

Open: Mon–Sat 10am–6pm.

MALLS/SHOPPING CENTERS

Like any city, Los Angeles' malls are filled with carbon copy chain stores, but they also have a good selection of local specialty shops, and a taste of the avant garde.

ARCO PLAZA, 505 S. Flower St., Downtown.

ARCO Plaza offers convenient shopping and elegant dining in a unique subterranean mall. Located beneath the Atlantic Richfield/Bank of America's Twin Towers is a labyrinth of corridors leading to shops and restaurants. Stores and boutiques can be found on the second and third underground levels. The Greater Los Angeles Visitors and Convention Bureau is within ARCO Plaza's precincts. And, of course, there are the shops—selling everything from needle-point patterns to insurance.

Open: Most shops open Mon–Fri 8am–6pm, Sat 10am–7pm.

BEVERLY CENTER, 8500 Beverly Blvd. (at La Cienega), Los Angeles. Tel. 310/854-0070.

One of the city's best-known malls also has one of the best locations. The 1991 film *Scenes from a Mall,* starring Woody Allen and Bette Midler, was shot here. About 170 shops occupy the huge, eight-story building, constructed with interesting exterior glass-covered escalators. Both The Broadway and Bullock's department stores are anchored here, sandwiching dozens of shops, restaurants, and movie theaters. The Warner Brothers Studio Store and Aveda Esthetique are two of the mall's newest additions. Despite the mall's immense size, it's actually quite a pleasant place to shop.

Open: Most shops open Mon–Fri 10am–9pm, Sat 10am–8pm, Sun 11am–6pm. Most restaurants stay open later.

THE BROADWAY PLAZA, 7th Street and Flower Street, Downtown. Tel. 213/624-2891.

Anchored by the Hyatt Regency Los Angeles Hotel and The Broadway department store, the one-square-block Plaza encompasses more than 25 shops and 17 restaurants. Most of the shops are middle-class-oriented clothing chain stores.

FARMER'S MARKET, 6333 W. 3rd St. (near Fairfax), Los Angeles. Tel. 213/933-9211.

Since 1934, this city market has been attracting locals and tourists with more than 100 restaurants, shops, and grocers. It has since become one of the area's top tourist draws. More than 150 retailers sell souvenirs, pet supplies, clothes, books, art, and anything else you can imagine. The best part of the market is the food stands—at least 25 in all—which sell fast foods from almost every international cuisine.

Open: Mon–Sat 9am–6:30pm, Sun 10am–5pm.

FISHERMAN'S VILLAGE, 13763 Fiji Way, Marina del Rey. Tel. 310/823-5411.

Containing about 30 specialty shops built in the style of an Old English whaling village, Marina del Rey's waterfront village is one of the city's most pleasant strolling malls. International imports are available in shops that line cobblestoned walks. The stores and restaurants surround an authentic 60-foot lighthouse.

Open: Sun–Thurs 10am–9pm, Fri–Sat 10am–10pm.

GLENDALE GALLERIA, Central Avenue (at Hawthorne Avenue), Glendale. Tel. 818/240-9481.

Located in the eastern San Fernando Valley, the Glendale Galleria is one of the largest malls in the nation, occupying two levels on two wings, and housing about 250 retailers. Five department stores compete for business here, along with well-known name-brand shops like Benetton, Ann Taylor, and ACA Joe.

Open: Mon–Fri 10am–9pm, Sat 10am–7pm, Sun 11am–6pm.

PORTS O' CALL VILLAGE, Berth 77, Samson Way (between 6th and 22nd Streets), San Pedro. Tel. 310/831-0287.

This collection of shops sells crafts and clothing from around the world. More than 80 international specialty shops offer such goods as hand-blown glass, Philippine jewelry, and Japanese gun-powder tea; while several restaurants provide myriad cuisines. You can watch a steady stream of yachts, luxury liners, tankers, freighters, schooners, and sailboats cruise by as you browse along the mall's winding cobblestoned streets. To reach Ports o' Call, take the Harbor Freeway to the Harbor Boulevard off-ramp and turn right.

Open: Daily 11am–9pm.

SANTA MONICA PLACE, Colorado Avenue (at 2nd Street), Santa Monica. Tel. 310/394-5451.

About 100 shops occupy three bright stories anchored by Robinson's and The Broadway department stores. Eats, the mall's food pavilion, sells every kind of fast food imaginable.

Open: Mon–Sat 10am–9pm, Sun 11am–6pm.

SHERMAN OAKS GALLERIA, 15301 Ventura Blvd. (at Sepulveda Boulevard), Sherman Oaks. Tel. 818/783-7100.

This famous western San Fernando Valley mall is the hangout for dedicated valley girls, popularized by the movie *Fast Times at Ridgemont High.* Trendy, mainstream clothes are in abundance, sold from about 60 storefronts.

Open: Mon–Sat 10am–9pm, Sun 11am–6pm.

SHOES

BALLY OF SWITZERLAND, 340 N. Rodeo Dr., Beverly Hills. Tel. 310/271-0666.

This is one of the world's best names for both casual and dress men's shoes. They're stylish, sturdy, expensive, and worth it.

Open: Mon–Sat 10am–6pm.

NA NA, 756 S. Broadway, Santa Monica. Tel. 310/450-8817.

Trendy new-wave styles are what Na Na is all about. Shoes that make a fashion statement start at about $100.

Open: Daily 11am–7pm.

SURF EQUIPMENT

HORIZONS WEST, 2011 Main St., Santa Monica. Tel. 310/392-1122.

Brand-name surfboards, wet suits, leashes, magazines, waxes, lotions, and everything else you need to catch the perfect wave are found here. Stop in and say "hi" to Randy, and pick up a free tide table.

Open: Mon–Sat 11am–6pm.

CHAPTER 10

EVENING ENTERTAINMENT

1. THE PERFORMING ARTS

• **THE MAJOR CONCERT/PERFORMANCE HALLS**

2. THE CLUB & MUSIC SCENE

3. THE BAR SCENE

Once criticized as a cultural wasteland, Los Angeles has increasingly attracted serious arts houses worthy of its size. The city has more than 150 active theaters, large and small, with plays, revues, and concerts. There are more than 100 rock and jazz clubs, and a number of major concert halls that regularly feature top-name performers. Without a doubt, the entertainment business—film, television, records, theater—is still the most important industry in Los Angeles. Check the "Calendar" section of the Sunday *Los Angeles Times* for good, if not comprehensive, listings of the upcoming week's events. *L.A. Weekly,* a free, alternative weekly tabloid available at sidewalk stands, shops, and restaurants, should also be consulted.

1. THE PERFORMING ARTS

There are two major charge-by-phone ticket agencies in the city: TicketMaster (tel. 213/480-3232) and Ticketron (tel. 213/642-4242). Both sell computer-generated tickets to concerts, sporting events, plays, and special events.

MAJOR PERFORMING ARTS COMPANIES

Los Angeles' most prestigious performing arts companies all call The Music Center of Los Angeles County "home."

CLASSICAL MUSIC & OPERA

THE LOS ANGELES PHILHARMONIC, Dorothy Chandler Pavilion, the Music Center, 135 N. Grand Ave., Downtown. Tel. 213/972-7211.

The city's top symphony is the only really major "serious music" name in Los Angeles. In addition to regular performances at the Music Center, it offers a popular summer season at the Hollywood Bowl. The season runs from October to May.

Tickets: $5–$45.

LOS ANGELES MASTER CHORALE, the Music Center, 135 N. Grand Ave., Downtown. Tel. 213/972-7211.

The Chorale sings both heavy classical works and lighter contemporary compositions by internationally known musicians. World premieres and guest choirs sometimes perform. The season runs from October to June.

Tickets: $7–$44.

LOS ANGELES MUSIC CENTER OPERA, the Music Center, 135 N. Grand Ave., Downtown. Tel. 213/972-7211.

Locally renowned, the Music Center Opera stages classic operas with a variety of guest stars.

Tickets: $5–$45.

DANCE

Although the best dance companies in the world are not located here, most—including the American Ballet Theatre, the Joffrey Ballet, Martha Graham, and Paul Taylor—perform on an annual basis at one of the major concert halls listed below. Check the Sunday "Calendar" section of *The Los Angeles Times,* or contact the Dance Resource Center of Greater Los Angeles' Hotline (tel. 310/281-1918) to find out what's on during your stay.

MAJOR CONCERT HALLS & ALL-PURPOSE AUDITORIUMS

DOROTHY CHANDLER PAVILION, the Music Center, 135 N. Grand Ave., Downtown. Tel. 213/972-7211.

Home of the Los Angeles Philharmonic, Master Chorale, Los Angeles Opera, and the Joffrey Ballet, this 3,197-seat multipurpose theater hosts regular concerts, recitals, opera, and dance performances. The American premiere of the London hit musical *Me and My Girl* was presented here, as are regular televised ceremonies. Ticket prices vary, depending on performance.

GREEK THEATRE, 2700 N. Vermont Ave., Griffith Park. Tel. 213/665-1927.

The Greek Theatre is a place where the entertainment ranges from performances by the Dance Theatre of Harlem to rock artists like Elvis Costello and the B-52s. The theater was designed in the style of the classical outdoor theaters of ancient Greece. Dance groups and national theater societies also perform here. Tickets run from $25 to $60, depending on the performance.

HOLLYWOOD BOWL, 2301 N. Highland Ave. (at Odin Street), Hollywood. Tel. 213/850-2000.

According to legend, the Bowl was created in the early 1920s when a musician—hiking in the hills—was startled to discover its perfect natural acoustics. Launching into song, he heard his voice carried virtually to the ridges of the mountains. Music lovers banded together, financing tiers of seats to be dug, Greek fashion, out of the mountainside. Box seats were installed in the front, and since many were reserved for film stars, intermission time at the Bowl became an extra added attraction.

THE MAJOR CONCERT/PERFORMANCE HALLS

Ahmanson Theatre, the Music Center, 135 N. Grand Ave. (at 1st Street), Downtown. Tel. 213/972-7211.

Dorothy Chandler Pavilion, the Music Center, 135 N. Grand Ave., Downtown. Tel. 213/972-7211.

Greek Theatre, 2700 N. Vermont Ave., Griffith Park. Tel. 213/665-1927.

Hollywood Bowl, 2301 N. Highland Ave. (at Odin Street), Hollywood. Tel. 213/850-2000.

James A. Doolittle Theatre, 1615 N. Vine St., Hollywood. Tel. 213/972-7372.

L.A. Sports Arena, 3939 S. Figueroa St., Los Angeles. Tel. 213/748-6136.

Mark Taper Forum, the Music Center, 135 N. Grand Ave. (at 1st Street), Downtown. Tel. 213/972-7373.

Pantages Theatre, 6233 Hollywood Blvd., Hollywood. Tel. 213/468-1700.

The Shrine Auditorium, 665 W. Jefferson Blvd., Los Angeles. Tel. 213/749-5123.

Shubert Theatre, 2020 Ave. of the Stars, ABC Entertainment Center, Century City. Tel. toll free 800/233-3123.

Universal Amphitheatre, 100 Universal City Plaza, Universal City. Tel. 818/777-3931.

Wilshire Theatre, 8440 Wilshire Blvd., Beverly Hills. Tel. 213/653-4490.

Now one of America's most famous outdoor amphitheaters, the Bowl is known for its outstanding natural acoustics. This is the summer home of the Los Angeles Philharmonic Orchestra, as well as the resident Hollywood Bowl Orchestra. Their seasons begin July 1 and end around mid-September.

Internationally known conductors and soloists often join the L.A. Philharmonic in classical programs on Tuesday and Thursday nights. Friday and Saturday concerts are often "pops" shows that feature orchestrated contemporary music.

Something is happening almost every night during the summer. The season also includes a jazz series, a Virtuoso series, and a Sunday Sunset series. Several weekend concerts throughout the season feature fireworks, including the traditional July 4th Family Fireworks picnic concert.

Picnicking at the Bowl is an established part of the classical concert ritual. You can order a picnic basket with a choice of hot and cold entrées, and a selection of wines and desserts from the Hollywood Bowl (call 213/851-3588 the day before), which you can pick up on Pepper Tree Lane on your way in and enjoy on the picnic grounds before the concert. If you're sitting in a box, you can have your picnic delivered to you there! It's cheaper, of course, to bring your own. For evening performances, be sure to bring a sweater or jacket—it gets chilly in those hills.

Prices: Classical concerts $1 lawn, $22.50 bench, $25–$71 box. Other events vary. Parking: $7–$20, subject to availability and reserved in advance; free in off-site lots, but $2 per person for parking shuttle.

Box Office Hours: May–June, Mon–Sat 10am–6pm; July–Sept, Mon–Sat 10am–9pm, Sun noon–6pm.

THE MUSIC CENTER OF LOS ANGELES COUNTY, 135 N. Grand Ave., Downtown. Tel. 213/972-7211.

Los Angeles' largest and most prestigious performing arts facility encompasses three distinct theaters: the Dorothy Chandler Pavilion (see listing under this same heading), the Ahmanson Theatre, and the Mark Taper Forum (see "Theaters," below). Free tours are scheduled on a regular basis. Call 213/972-7483 for information and reservations. All theaters are handicapped-accessible. The Music Center Shop, on the Plaza level, specializes in performing-arts merchandise. Ticket discounts are available for students and senior citizens for most performances in each theater.

THE SHRINE AUDITORIUM, 665 W. Jefferson Blvd., Los Angeles. Tel. 213/749-5123.

Once the Al Malaikah Temple, the 1920s-era Shrine stands out for its unusual Middle Eastern decor. The auditorium's 6,200 seats offer good sightlines for both local and international acts. Ticket prices vary, depending on the performance.

UNIVERSAL AMPHITHEATRE, 100 Universal City Plaza, Universal City. Tel. 818/777-3931.

This 6,251-seat enclosed theater is adjacent to the Visitors Entertainment Center at Universal Studios. It's well designed—no seat is more than 140 feet from the stage—and only top names perform here, usually for 3 to 5 days. Tickets are often sold out well before the concert dates, so check the box office as soon as possible. Tickets range from $25 to $75.

WILSHIRE THEATRE, 8440 Wilshire Blvd., Beverly Hills. Tel. 213/653-4490.

The Wilshire opened in 1980 with *The Oldest Living Graduate,* starring Henry Fonda. More recent productions have included blockbuster musicals like *A Chorus Line.* Rock and jazz concerts are held here, too. Call to see what's on. Tickets run from $25 to $50.

THEATERS

MAJOR PLAYHOUSES

AHMANSON THEATRE, the Music Center, 135 N. Grand Ave. (at 1st Street), Downtown. Tel. 213/972-7211.

L.A.'s top legitimate playhouse has 2,071 seats, and is the home base of the Center Theater Group, which stages a full season of plays each year—usually from mid-October to early May. Offerings have included Christopher Reeve in *Summer and Smoke,* Daniel J. Travanti in *I Never Sang for My Father,* and the West Coast premiere of Neil Simon's *Broadway Bound.* Visiting productions are also offered here, including a special long run of *The Phantom of the*

Opera. A variety of international dance companies and concert attractions round out the season. Tickets vary in price from $20 to $50; reductions for specified performances are available for students and seniors.

JAMES A. DOOLITTLE THEATRE, 1615 N. Vine St., Hollywood. Tel. 213/972-7372.

The Doolittle Theatre offers a wide spectrum of live theater productions, such as Amy Irving in the Pulitzer-Prize- and Tony-Award-winning *The Heidi Chronicles,* Neil Simon's Pulitzer Prize-winning *Lost in Yonkers,* and August Wilson's *Two Trains Running.* Tickets range from $20 to $42.

MARK TAPER FORUM, the Music Center, 135 N. Grand Ave. (at 1st Street), Downtown. Tel. 213/972-7373.

Adjacent to the Ahmanson Theater, this 747-seat circular theater is the Music Center's intimate playhouse. The emphasis here is on new and contemporary works, since the theater specializes in world and West Coast premieres. Recent productions have included the New York Shakespeare Festival production of *Spunk,* and *Fire in the Rain . . . Singer in the Storm,* with Holly Near. Ticket prices vary from $20 to $32; reductions are available for students and seniors.

PANTAGES THEATRE, 6233 Hollywood Blvd., Hollywood. Tel. 213/468-1700.

This luxurious Hollywood landmark dates from 1930. For 10 years it was the setting for the presentation of the Academy Awards, including the first televised Oscar ceremony. It's been through several incarnations, including one as a fine movie house. In 1977 the Pantages returned as a leading legitimate theater with a production of *Bubbling Brown Sugar.* Recent productions have included *Me and My Girl* and *Starlight Express,* as well as the Julie Andrews/Carol Burnett TV special, the Grammy "Living Legend" Awards, and the televised Country/Western Music Awards. Ticket prices range from $25 to $60.

SHUBERT THEATRE, 2020 Ave. of the Stars, ABC Entertainment Center, Century City. Tel. toll free 800/233-3123.

This opulent theater presents big-time musicals—like *Cats* and *Les Misérables.* It's located directly across from the Century Plaza Hotel. Tickets are priced from $30 to $65.

SMALLER THEATERS

Akin to New York's off-Broadway, or London's "Fringe," Los Angeles' small-scale theaters often outdo the slick, high-budget shows. Here, talented performers entertain for the love of their craft. Tickets usually cost from $10 to $20. Call the theaters and check newspaper listings for current performances.

ACTORS FORUM, 3365½ Cahuenga Blvd., Hollywood. Tel. 213/850-9016.

Opened in 1975, this intimate, 49-seat theater often presents world premieres by local playwrights. They also offer Tuesday night workshops.

STELLA ADLER THEATER, 1653 Argyle Ave., Hollywood. Tel. 213/456-4446.

One of the city's prettiest small theaters, the Adler is situated just across from the Pantages (see above). One-acts and other small plays are featured.

ATTIC THEATRE, 6562 Santa Monica Blvd., Hollywood. Tel. 213/462-9720.

Everything from Shakespeare to modern musicals are performed in this intimate 50-seat theater. The Attic is located in a former World War II parachute factory.

CAST THEATRE, 804 N. El Centro, Hollywood. Tel. 213/462-0265.

The oldest small theater in Hollywood is also widely recognized as one of the best. The Cast Theatre is a recipient of The Hollywood Arts Council's Theatre Arts Award.

COLONY STUDIO THEATRE, 1944 Riverside Dr., Los Angeles. Tel. 213/665-3011.

The theater's resident company has played in this air-conditioned, 100-seat, converted silent movie house for almost 20 years. Recent productions include *The Last Metro,* a musical adaptation of Truffaut's award-winning film.

THE COMPLEX, 6476 Santa Monica Blvd., Hollywood. Tel. 213/465-0383, or 213/464-2124.

There's always something happening on at least one of The Complex's five stages. Call for the latest information.

HENRY FONDA THEATRE, 6126 Hollywood Blvd., Hollywood. Tel. 213/480-3232, or 213/468-1700.

Formerly called the Music Box, this is one of Hollywood's oldest theaters. For a while it was a movie house, but has now been restored as a legitimate theater.

JOHN ANSON FORD THEATRE, 2580 Cahuenga Blvd. East, Hollywood. Tel. 213/489-1121.

This beautiful, historic, outdoor amphitheater is open only in summer for the Shakespeare Festival/L.A.'s acclaimed productions.

GLOBE PLAYHOUSE, 1107 N. Kings Rd., West Hollywood. Tel. 213/654-5623.

Headquarters of Thad Taylor's Shakespeare Society of America, the Globe features plays by and about the Bard. The playhouse also houses a Shakespeare exhibit, with more than 1,000 collector's items and memorabilia.

IL VITTORIALE, 2035 N. Highland Ave., Hollywood. Tel. 213/480-3232.

Once an historic American Legion Post, the space has been transformed into an elaborate three-story, 10-room Italian country "villa." This is the setting for *Tamara,* a unique environmental theater show, where audience members follow the character of their choice from room to room. Intermission buffet is included with admission.

MELROSE THEATER, 733 N. Seward St., Los Angeles. Tel. 213/465-1885.
The theater's award-winning company performs dramas and musicals in this beautifully restored art deco building.

THEATRE RAPPORT, 1277 N. Wilton Pl., Hollywood. Tel. 213/660-0433.
Established in 1967, and home of the Hollywood Theater Club, the Rapport stages both contemporary works and revivals. The theater is also noted for attracting West Coast premieres.

2. THE CLUB & MUSIC SCENE

Los Angeles' jaded music consumers are forever looking for something new and different. Always a pioneer when it comes to pop culture, the city's club and music scene offers every kind of entertainment available, from classic to cutting-edge. Los Angeles just might be the best place on earth to hear up-and-coming bands, as the world's wannabes gravitate here in hopes of landing a coveted recording contract.

COMEDY CLUBS

Each of the following venues claim to have launched the careers of the same well-known comics—and it's probably true. Emerging funny men and women strive to get as many "gigs" as possible, playing all the clubs; so choose your club by location.

COMEDY STORE, 8433 Sunset Blvd., West Hollywood. Tel. 213/656-6225.
Owner Mitzi Shore (Pauly's mother) has created a setting in which new comics can develop and established performers can work out the kinks in new material. It's always vastly entertaining. There are three showrooms.

The Best of the Comedy Store Room, which seats 400, features professional stand-ups continuously through the night on Mondays, and during two separate shows on the weekends. Several comedians are always featured, each doing about 15-minute stints. The talent here is always first rate, and includes regulars on the "Tonight Show," and other television programs.

The Original Room features a dozen or so comedians back-to-back nightly. Monday night is amateur night when anyone with enough guts can take the stage for three to five minutes.

The Belly Room alternates between comedy stage and piano bar, with Sunday nights reserved as a singer showcase.

Admission: "Best" room, $6 Mon, $12–$14 Fri–Sat; "Original" room, Mon free with 2-drink minimum, $6 Tues–Fri and Sun, $8 Sat; "Belly" room, free–$3 plus 2-drink minimum. Drinks: $3.75–$7.

Open: "Best" room, Mon 8pm–1am, Fri–Sat 2 shows 8pm and 10:30pm; "Original" and "Belly" rooms nightly 8pm–1am.

GROUNDLING THEATRE, 7307 Melrose Ave., Los Angeles. Tel. 213/934-9700, or 213/934-4747.

Los Angeles' most celebrated improvisational theater group is a must-see for anyone who likes to laugh and be entertained by a top acting troupe. Call for showtimes.

IMPROVISATION, 8162 Melrose Ave., West Hollywood. Tel. 213/651-2583.

Improvisation offers something different each night. The club's own television show, "Evening at the Improv," is now filmed at the Santa Monica location for national distribution. Although there used to be a fairly active music schedule, the Improv is now mostly doing what it does best—showcasing comedy. Major stars often appear here, for example, Jay Leno, Billy Crystal, and Robin Williams.

Admission: Sun–Thurs $8 plus 2-drink minimum; Fri–Sat $10–$11 plus 2-drink minimum.

Open: Mon–Wed 8:30pm and 10:45pm; Thurs and Sun 8pm and 10:45pm; Fri–Sat 7:30pm, 9:45pm, and 11:45pm.

IMPROVISATION, 321 Santa Monica Blvd., Santa Monica. Tel. 310/394-8664.

The Improv's second, and larger, stage is located in trendy Santa Monica. Acts, which change nightly, are often the same comedians who play the West Hollywood showroom.

Admission: Mon $5 plus 2-drink minimum; Tues free with 2-drink minimum; Sun, Wed, and Thurs $8 plus 2-drink minimum; Fri–Sat $10 plus 2-drink minimum.

Open: Sun–Thurs 8pm–midnight, Fri–Sat performances 8pm and 10:30pm.

ROCK CLUBS

DOUG WESTON'S TROUBADOR, 9081 Santa Monica Blvd., West Hollywood. Tel. 213/276-6168.

Located at the edge of Beverly Hills, local rock bands are usually served back-to-back by the half dozen. An adventurous booking policy ensures a good mix, and so many bands each night usually means there will be at least one you'll like.

Admission: $5–$15.

Open: Usually nightly 8pm–2am.

8121 CLUB, 8121 Sunset Blvd., Hollywood. Tel. 213/654-4887.

An underground all-acoustic club for locals in-the-know, they feature three to five acts per night.

Admission: Free–$7.

Open: Nightly 8pm–2am.

CHINA CLUB, 1600 North Argyle Ave., Hollywood. Tel. 213/469-1600.

Now almost five years old, this New York transplant alternates dance disks with live rock 'n' roll bands nightly.

Admission: $5–$10.
Open: Nightly 8pm–2am.

CLUB LINGERIE, 6507 W. Sunset Blvd., Hollywood. Tel. 213/466-8557.

Emerging rock 'n' roll bands and other contemporary styles play every night at Hollywood's oldest continuously operating club. When the bands stop, DJs start, and feet keep moving to the beat.

Admission: $6–$12.
Open: Nightly 8pm–2am.

GAZZARRI'S ON THE STRIP, 9039 Sunset Blvd. (near Doheny Drive), Hollywood. Tel. 310/273-6606.

Once self-described as "Hollywood's oldest disco," Gazzarri's has now changed to a live-music format, offering rock 'n' roll bands almost nightly. Sometimes it's hip hop and other nights it's rap. The age group is early 20s; dress is casual. Credit cards are not accepted and you must be at least 18 to get in.

Admission: $10–$14.
Open: Usually Wed–Sat 8pm–2am.

THE ROXY, 9009 Sunset Blvd., Hollywood. Tel. 213/276-2229, or 213/276-2222 for a recording.

Probably the top venue in L.A., the medium-sized Roxy specializes in showcasing the music industry's new signings, as well as smaller established bands, and occasionally even superstars such as David Bowie and Bon Jovi. The roster is usually packed with Los Angeles bands you've never heard of, often three or four per night. There is no age limit for entry, but only those over 21 may legally purchase alcohol.

Admission: $5–$20.
Open: Usually nightly 8pm–2am.

WHISKEY A-GO-GO, 8901 Sunset Blvd., Hollywood. Tel. 213/652-4202.

One of Hollywood's legendary clubs, the Whiskey packs 'em in with hard rock and alternative rock double and triple bills. All ages are welcome.

Admission: $5–$15.
Open: Nightly 8pm–2am.

JAZZ & LATIN CLUBS

Like the bands that play in them, jazz clubs come and go. Check the newspapers, and contact the L.A. Jazz Society (tel. 213/469-6800)—a nonprofit organization formed to promote jazz and its artists—to see what's on.

CANDILEJAS, 5060 Sunset Blvd., Hollywood. Tel. 213/665-8822.

This medium-sized club is one of the premiere places to hear hot salsa. Puerto Rican and African-Cuban bands perform almost every night.

Admission: $5–$10.
Open: Sun–Thurs 9pm–2am, Fri–Sat 9pm–4am.

CATALINA'S BAR & GRILL, 1640 North Cahuenga Blvd., Hollywood. Tel. 213/466-2210.

International and local jazz musicians perform here most nights, and food is always available.

Admission: $7–$15.

Open: Nightly 5pm–2am.

VINE STREET BAR & GRILL, 1610 Vine St., Hollywood. Tel. 213/463-4375.

Famous name jazz celebrities perform almost nightly in this intimate, art deco restaurant. Call for the latest information.

Admission: $7–$15.

Open: Nightly 5pm–2am.

DANCE CLUBS

Hollywood in general, and the down-and-dirty Sunset Strip, in particular, continue to be at the center of Los Angeles' nightlife scene.

The very nature of the club scene demands frequent fresh faces, thus making recommendations outdated before the ink can even dry on the page. Most of the venues below are promoted as different clubs on various nights of the week, each with its own look, sound, and style. Many of the rock clubs listed above are also dedicated to dance disks on different nights of the week. The weekly listings magazine *L.A. Weekly* contains the latest, but it's not comprehensive. Discount passes and club announcements are often available at trendy clothing stores along Melrose Avenue.

PALLADIUM HOLLYWOOD, 6215 Sunset Blvd., Hollywood. Tel. 213/962-7600.

Lawrence Welk used to do his famous New Year's Eve show from here. Today the huge club is one of the best venues in town, featuring everything from rock to salsa. Call to see what's on.

Admission: $15–$20.

Open: Wed–Sat 9pm–2am.

ROXBURY, 8225 Sunset Blvd., Hollywood. Tel. 213/656-1750.

A labyrinthine dance club, the Roxbury attracts a trendy crowd that dresses to impress. There are four full bars and DJ dancing almost nightly.

Admission: $10.

Open: Tues–Sat 6pm–2am.

3. THE BAR SCENE

HOTEL BARS

BEL AIR HOTEL BAR, 701 Stone Canyon Rd., Bel Air. Tel. 213/472-1211.

One of the mellower places for a quiet, romantic evening, the ritzy Bel Air bar offers good piano music in an upscale setting.

Open: Daily 10am–midnight.

THE GRAND AVENUE BAR, in the Biltmore Hotel, 506 S. Grand Ave., Los Angeles. Tel. 213/624-1011.

During the day, the bar offers a cold lunch buffet. At night the drinkery becomes popular for its showcases of top-name jazz performers.

Open: Daily 5pm–midnight.

THE BRASSERIE BAR, in the Bel Age Hotel De Grande Classe, 1020 North San Vicente Blvd., West Hollywood. Tel. 310/854-1111.

One of the classiest and prettiest bars in the city regularly features top-notch jazz performers.

Open: Sun–Wed 10:30am–9:30pm, Thurs–Sat 10:30am–1am.

GAY BARS & CLUBS

BASGO'S, 3909 Sunset Blvd., Hollywood. Tel. 213/664-1929.

Looking very much like a neighborhood bar, this small club attracts a mixed gay/straight crowd. Live bands sometimes perform. There's a pool table and a full bar.

Open: Daily 2pm–2am.

CATCH ONE, 4067 W. Pico Blvd., Hollywood. Tel. 213/734-8849.

This is one of the best dance clubs in the city for both gays and lesbians. Big crowds are attracted by a good sound system. There are four bars on two floors. Theme nights vary, so you have to call to see what's on.

Open: Wed–Thurs 9pm–2am, Fri–Sat 9pm–5am.

CIRCUS DISCO, 6655 Santa Monica Blvd., Hollywood. Tel. 213/462-1291.

It's not always gay night, but when it is, the club is packed with a predominantly young, Latino crowd. Hip hop and house music are the preferred sounds.

Cover: $8–$12.

Open: Nightly 9pm–2am.

THE MOTHER LODE, 8944 Santa Monica Blvd., West Hollywood. Tel. 310/659-9700.

Frequented by a young, upwardly mobile crowd, this collegiate-looking bar is made for drinking, and there is often a line to get in.

Open: Daily noon–2am.

THE PALMS, 8527 Santa Monica Blvd., West Hollywood. Tel. 310/652-6188.

Reputedly the oldest lesbian bar in the city, this busy hangout is becoming more popular with gay men as well.

Open: Daily noon–2am.

CHAPTER 11

EASY EXCURSIONS FROM LOS ANGELES

1. SANTA CATALINA ISLAND

2. ORANGE COUNTY: DISNEYLAND, KNOTT'S BERRY FARM & ENVIRONS

3. NEWPORT BEACH

4. PALM SPRINGS

5. SANTA BARBARA

Los Angeles is situated within the most fascinating and diverse area of southern California. And the contrasts of the region are even more spellbinding than its beauties. There are arid deserts and smartly sophisticated seaside resorts. Humming industrial cities and serene, sun-drenched Spanish missions contrast with rolling hillsides, wildly rugged mountain ranges, a plethora of theme parks, and an off-shore island that has been transformed into the ultimate close getaway.

Using Los Angeles as either your travel base or your springboard, you can reach any of these points within a few hours or less by car or public transport. The purpose of this chapter is to give you a glimpse of some of the attractions beckoning beyond Coit Tower . . . how to get there and what to expect.

1. SANTA CATALINA ISLAND

22 miles W of mainland Los Angeles

GETTING THERE   By Plane   Pacific Coast Airlines (tel. toll free 800/426-5400) flies from the Imperial Terminal at Los Angeles International Airport (LAX) to Catalina's Airport in the Sky (tel. 213/510-0143), 1,600 feet above the sea-level town of Avalon. Tickets are $55 to $70 each way, depending on restrictions. Taxis and buses meet each flight in Catalina.

By Boat   The *Catalina Express* (tel. 310/519-1212, or toll free 800/540-4753 in California) operates almost 20 daily departures year round to Catalina from San Pedro and Long Beach. From mid-June to Labor Day there is additional service from Redondo Beach. The trip takes about an hour. One-way fares from San Pedro are $15 for adults, $14 for seniors, $11 for children 2 to 11, 75¢ for infants. Long Beach/Redondo fares are about $2 higher for all except infants, who are still charged 75¢. The *Catalina Express* departs from the Sea/Air Terminal at Berth 95, Port of L.A. in San Pedro; the *Catalina Express* port at the *Queen Mary* in Long Beach; and from the

Catalina Express port at 161 N. Harbor Dr. in Redondo. Call for information and reservations.

Note: There are specific baggage restrictions on the *Catalina Express.* Luggage is limited to 50 pounds per person; reservations are necessary for bicycles, surfboards, and dive tanks; and there are restrictions on transporting domestic pets—call for information.

ESSENTIALS Orientation The picturesque town of Avalon is the island's only city. Named for a passage in Tennyson's *Idylls of the King,* Avalon is also the port of entry for the island. From the ferry dock you can wander along Crescent Avenue, the main road along the beachfront, and easily explore adjacent side streets.

Visitors are not allowed to drive cars on the island. Walk around Avalon and take tours to points inland (see "What to See and Do," below). About 86% of the island remains undeveloped. It's owned by the Santa Catalina Island Conservancy, which endeavors to preserve the island's natural resources.

Information The Catalina Island Chamber of Commerce and Visitor's Bureau, Dept. DG, P.O. Box 217, Avalon, CA 90704 (tel. 310/510-1520), located on Green Pleasure Pier, distributes maps, brochures, and information on island activities. It also offers information on local airlines, hotels, boat transport, and sightseeing tours, as well as brochures on camping, hiking, fishing, and boating. Write ahead for an extremely useful free 88-page visitor's guide.

The Santa Catalina Island Company–run Visitor's Information Center, just a minute away from the Chamber of Commerce on Metropole Street, across from the Green Pleasure Pier (tel. 310/510-2000, or toll free 800/428-2566 in California), handles hotel reservations, sightseeing tours, and other island activities.

Located 22 miles west of Long Beach, Catalina is a small, cove-fringed island famous for its laid-back resorts, largely unspoiled landscape, and crystal-clear waters. Because of its relative isolation, tourists don't crowd Catalina as they do the mainland. Visitors who do show up have plenty of elbow room to boat, fish, swim, scuba dive, and snorkel. There are miles of hiking and biking trails; and golf, tennis, and horseback-riding facilities abound.

Catalina is so different from the mainland that it almost seems like a different country—remote and unspoiled. The island separated from the mainland more than 500,000 years ago and evolved to meet environmental challenges. Even today there is unique plant life here, and archeology has revealed traces of a stone-age culture. From the time of its discovery by Western explorers in the 1600s, until the turn of the 20th century, Catalina was primarily a place for pirates and smugglers. The island was purchased by William Wrigley, Jr., the chewing gum manufacturer, in 1915 in order to develop a fashionable pleasure resort. To publicize the new vacationland, Wrigley brought big-name bands to the Avalon Casino Ballroom, and he moved the Chicago Cubs baseball team, which he owned, to the island for spring training. His marketing efforts succeeded, and Catalina became a favorite vacation resort spot for wealthy mainlanders. It no longer takes spectacular marketing to entice visitors to Catalina; the island's hotels are often fully booked months in advance. But Catalina is still far from overrun with tourists; it is still a genuinely tranquil and charming retreat.

WHAT TO SEE & DO

AVALON CASINO and CATALINA ISLAND MUSEUM, at the end of Crescent Avenue. Tel. 310/510-2414.

The Avalon Casino is the most famous and one of the oldest structures on the island. Built in 1929 as a resort for vacationers from the mainland, its massive circular rotunda, topped with a red tile roof, is the building's most famous feature—it appears on posters and postcards in shops all around town. Avalon Casino is widely known for its beautiful art deco ballroom that once hosted such top bands as the Tommy Dorsey and Glen Miller orchestras. You can see the inside of the building by attending a ballroom event or a film (the Casino is Avalon's primary movie theater). Otherwise, admission is by guided tour only, operated daily by the Santa Catalina Island Company (see "Organized Tours," below).

The **Catalina Island Museum,** located on the ground floor of the Casino, features exhibits on island history, archeology, and natural history. The small museum also has an excellent relief map that details the island's interior.

Admission: $1 adults; children under 12, free.
Open: Daily 10:30am–4pm.

AVALON PLEASURE PIER, Crescent Avenue and Catalina Street, Avalon.

Jutting out into Crescent Cove, the wood plank pier offers excellent views of the town and surrounding mountains. Food stands and bait-and-tackle shops line the pier, selling fish to eat and cast.

UNDERWATER PARK, at the end of Crescent Avenue, Avalon.

One of Catalina's top draws is its crystal-clear waters and abundant sea life. Underwater Park is filled with colorful fish and rich kelp beds. Several Crescent Avenue companies rent scuba and snorkeling equipment. Santa Catalina Island Company, Avalon Harbor Pier (tel. 310/510-8000), offers glass-bottom boat tours of the area daily, leaving every half hour from 10am to 5pm. The trip takes about 40 minutes and costs $5 per person. The schedule is reduced somewhat in winter.

ORGANIZED TOURS

Since visitors are not allowed to drive cars around the island, it may be difficult to tour Catalina on your own; therefore, organized tours are recommended. The Santa Catalina Island Company's Discovery Tours, Avalon Harbor Pier (tel. 310/510-8000), operates several motorcoach excursions that depart from the tour plaza in the center of town on Sumner Avenue.

The Skyline Drive tour basically follows the perimeter of the island and takes about 1 hour and 45 minutes. Trips leave several times a day from 11am to 4pm and cost $11.50 for adults, $10.50 for seniors, and $8 for children 3 to 11.

The Inland Motor Tour is more comprehensive; it includes some of the 66 square miles of preserve owned by the Santa Catalina Island Conservancy. You'll see El Rancho Escondido—for an Arabian horse show and refreshments—and probably have a chance to view buffalo, deer, goats, and boars. Tours, which take about 3 hours and 45 minutes, leave at 9am. From June to October there are additional schedules. Tours cost $22 for adults, $19 for seniors, and $13 for children 3 to 11.

Other excursions offered by the company include a 40-minute Casino Tour, which explores Catalina's most famous landmark; a 40-minute Glass-Bottom Boat Trip to Catalina's undersea gardens; and a one-hour Flying Fish Boat Trip, during which an occasional flying fish lands right on the boat.

Check with the Catalina Island Company for other tour offerings, as well as various dining cruises.

WHERE TO STAY

Catalina's 30 or so hotels (none of which belongs to a chain) are beautifully situated and maintain an almost affected unpretentiousness. Somehow they seem to go out of their way not to be quaint or charming. Don't worry about your hotel's decor (or lack of it), since there's nary an eyesore on the entire island. If you do plan to stay overnight on Catalina, be sure to reserve a room in advance, since the hotels regularly reach 100% occupancy, especially on weekends.

MODERATE

CATALINA CANYON HOTEL, 888 Country Club Dr., Avalon, CA 90704. Tel. 310/510-0325, or toll free 800/253-9361. Fax 310/510-0325. 80 rms. No smoking rooms available. A/C TV TEL **Directions:** From Avalon Pleasure Pier, go up Catalina Avenue, turn right onto Tremont Street and then left onto Country Club Drive to the hotel.

$ Rates: $75–$135 single or double. Extra person $20. AE, DISC, MC, V.

The Catalina Canyon Hotel is set on beautifully landscaped grounds in the foothills of Avalon. The guest rooms are tastefully decorated and comfortably furnished; all have AM/FM radios and balconies overlooking the outdoor pool and Jacuzzi. The Canyon Restaurant serves breakfast, lunch, and a continental dinner. Room service is available. Cocktails may be enjoyed in the lounge or on the outdoor terrace overlooking the pool. The hotel is adjacent to a golf course and tennis courts. A courtesy van meets guests at the air and sea terminals.

HOTEL MACRAE, 409 Crescent Ave. (P.O. Box 1517),

Avalon, CA 90704. Tel. 310/510-0246, or toll free 800/698-2266. 23 rms and suites. TEL **Directions:** From the Avalon Pleasure Pier, walk north on Crescent Avenue.

$ Rates (including continental breakfast): $76–$125 single or double; from $100, suite. AE, CB, DC, MC, V.

This pleasant two-story hostelry is right across from the beach. It's decorated in bright, cheerful colors—parrot green, orange, yellow, red, and white. Rooms are individually equipped with heaters for chilly nights. Wine, cheese, and crackers are served in the evening. In the center of the hotel is a large, open courtyard, perfect for lounging or sunning. Kitchen units are available.

ISLAND INN, 125 Metropole, P.O. Box 467, Avalon, CA 90704. Tel. 310/510-1623. Fax 310/510-7218. 35 rms, 1 suite. TV **Directions:** From the Avalon Pleasure Pier, go up Catalina Street and turn right onto Beacon Street. After 4 blocks, turn right onto Metropole to the hotel.

$ Rates (including continental breakfast): May–Sept, hols, and weekends year round, $75–$160 single or double; $185 minisuite. Oct–May except hols and weekends, $45–$130 single or double; $155 minisuite. AE, DISC, MC, V.

Innkeepers Martin and Bernadine Curtin have created some of the most attractive accommodations in town. Pale blue-gray rooms are accented in peach and set off by blue carpeting and blue-and-peach bedspreads. Shuttered windows and stained-glass lighting fixtures add further charm. Most rooms have AM/FM radios, and all have color TVs. There are no telephones in the rooms, but the front desk will take phone messages. There are ice and soda machines in the hall. Free transportation is provided from the ferry dock.

ZANE GREY PUEBLO HOTEL, off Chimes Tower Rd. (P.O. Box 216), Avalon, CA 90704. Tel. 310/510-0966. 17 rms (all with bath). **Directions:** From the Avalon Pleasure Pier, go north on Crescent Avenue, turn left onto Hill Street and right onto Chimes Tower Road.

$ Rates (including continental breakfast): June–Sept $75–$125 single or double; Nov–Mar $55 single or double; rest of the year $65–$85 single or double. Weekends and hols may be slightly higher. Extra person $35. AE, MC, V.

The most superb views on the island are from the lofty Zane Grey Pueblo Hotel. This Shangri-la mountain retreat is the former home of novelist Zane Grey, who spent his last 20 years in Avalon enjoying isolation with an ocean view. He wrote many books here, including *Tales of Swordfish and Tuna,* which tells of his fishing adventures off Catalina Island.

The hotel has teak beams that the novelist brought from Tahiti on one of his fishing trips. Most of the rooms also have large windows and ocean or mountain views. They have all been renovated with new furniture, carpeting, and ceiling fans. An outdoor patio has an excellent view, while the original living room has a grand piano, a fireplace, and a TV. The hotel also offers a swimming pool/sun deck, with chairs overlooking Avalon and the ocean. Coffee is served all day, and there's a courtesy bus to town.

WHERE TO DINE

MODERATE

EL GALLEON, 411 Crescent Ave. Tel. 310/510-1188.
  Cuisine: AMERICAN. **Reservations:** Accepted.
$ **Prices:** Appetizers $4–$8; lunch main courses $6–$12; dinner
  main courses $10–$30. AE, DISC, MC, V.
  Open: Lunch, daily 11:30am–2:30pm; dinner, daily 5–10pm; bar,
  daily 10am–1:30am.

El Galleon is large, warm, and woody, complete with portholes, rigging, anchors, big wrought-iron chandeliers, oversize tufted-leather booths, and tables with red-leather captain's chairs. There's additional balcony seating, plus outdoor café tables overlooking the ocean harbor. Lunch choices include fresh seafood, burgers, steak, stews, salads, and sandwiches. The dinner menu features many seafood items, too, like cioppino, fresh swordfish steak, and broiled Catalina lobster tails in drawn butter. "Turf" main dishes range from country-fried chicken and beef Stroganoff to broiled rack of lamb with mint jelly.

THE BUSY BEE, 306 Crescent Ave. Tel. 310/510-1983.
  Cuisine: AMERICAN. **Reservations:** Not accepted. **Direc-
  tions:** From the Avalon Pleasure Pier, walk 2 blocks north on
  Crescent Avenue to the end of Metropole.
$ **Prices:** Appetizers $3–$6; main courses $7–$15. AE, CB, DC,
  DISC, MC, V.
  Open: Summer, Mon–Fri 8am–10pm, Sat–Sun 8am–10pm;
  winter, daily 8am–8pm.

The Busy Bee has been an Avalon institution since 1923. The restaurant is located on the beach directly over the water. You can eat in several locations, including a lovely wraparound outdoor patio.

The fare is light—deli style. Breakfast, lunch, and dinner are served at all times; the extensive menu includes omelets, various sandwiches and salads, and Buffalo burgers. The restaurant grinds its own beef and cuts its own potatoes for French fries. Salad dressings are also made on the premises. Even if you're not hungry, come here for a drink; it's Avalon's only bar with a harbor view.

INEXPENSIVE

SAND TRAP, Avalon Canyon Road. Tel. 310/510-1349.
  Cuisine: CALIFORNIA/MEXICAN. **Reservations:** Not ac-
  cepted. **Directions:** From the Avalon Pleasure Pier, go up
  Catalina Avenue and turn right onto Tremont. Take the next left
  onto Falls Canyon Road, which soon turns into Avalon Canyon
  Road.
$ **Prices:** Appetizers $2–$5; main courses $3–$7. No credit cards.
  Open: Daily 7:30am–3pm.

Long a local favorite, the Sand Trap is a great place to escape from the bayfront crowds. Enjoy breakfast, lunch, or snacks while looking out over the golf course. Specialties of the house include delectable omelets served till noon and soft tacos served all day. Either can be made with any number of fillings, including Cheddar cheese, mushrooms, turkey, homemade chorizo, spicy shredded beef, sour cream, and salsa. Burgers, sandwiches, salads, and chili are also served. Beer and wine are available.

2. ORANGE COUNTY: DISNEYLAND, KNOTT'S BERRY FARM & ENVIRONS

27 miles SE of downtown Los Angeles

GETTING THERE By Plane Most visitors who fly in to see Orange County theme parks arrive via Los Angeles International Airport (LAX), located about 30 miles west of Disneyland and Knott's Berry Farm.

John Wayne International Airport, in Irvine, is Orange County's largest airport. Located about 15 miles from Disneyland, and 20 miles from Knott's Berry Farm, the airport is served by Alaska Airlines, American Airlines, Continental, Delta, Northwest, TWA, and United.

By Train The nearest Amtrak (800/USA-RAIL) stations are located in San Clemente and San Juan Capistrano, near the coast in the southern part of the county. Trains travel both north and south between Los Angeles and San Diego. Call for fare and schedule information.

By Bus Greyhound/Trailways can get you here from anywhere. The company doesn't operate a nationwide toll-free telephone number, so check your local directory for the phone number and call for information.

By Car From Los Angeles, take I-5 south. Exit south onto Beach Boulevard for Knott's Berry Farm. Continue for another 5 miles to the Harbor Boulevard exit for Disneyland. The theme parks are about an hour's drive from downtown Los Angeles.

ESSENTIALS Orientation Located just blocks south of the Santa Ana Freeway (I-5), about 5 miles from each other, both Disneyland and Knott's Berry Farm are relatively compact theme parks completely surrounded by hotels, fast-food restaurants, and other tourist-oriented facilities. The surrounding communities of Anaheim and Buena Park, respectively, are primarily residential and not too exciting from a tourist's perspective.

Information For information relating specifically to Disneyland, call the park at 714/999-4565. The Anaheim Area Visitor and Convention Bureau, 800 W. Katella Ave. (P.O. Box 4270), Anaheim, CA 92803 (tel. 714/999-8999), can fill you in on other area attractions, beaches, and activities.

For information relating specifically to Knott's Berry Farm, call the park at 714/220-5200. The Buena Park Convention and Visitors Office, 6280 Manchester Blvd., Suite 103 (tel. 714/994-1511, or toll free 800/541-3953), has other area information.

Some people might say that the Orange County cities of Anaheim, Fullerton, Buena Park, and Irvine are among the most physically unprepossessing towns in California, but nevertheless they attract the most visitors. The natural surroundings may not be as inspiring as other parts of the state, but the specially created attractions are enchanting—transformed by the magic wand of Walt Disney into a wonderful world of make-believe. And Disneyland is just one of the spectacular sights in the area. There are also Knott's Berry Farm, the Movieland Wax Museum, and more. So take the kids—and if you don't have any kids, be a kid yourself for a while.

Tourist board protests to the contrary, Anaheim *is* Disneyland. Once a sleepy little town in the Valencia orange-grove belt, Anaheim has now become a playground of hotels, restaurants, and various other tourist-oriented attractions.

Knott's Berry Farm's Buena Park is just 5 miles west of Disneyland's Anaheim, but don't even think about conquering them both in the same day. Several hotel options are listed below so that you can stay a few days and do what appeals to you the most.

WHAT TO SEE & DO

DISNEYLAND, 1313 Harbor Blvd., Anaheim. Tel. 714/ 999-4565.

Even the most jaded nose can hardly turn up at Disneyland. It's that special—a world of charm and magic, an "open sesame" to one's lost childhood, an extravagant doorway to yesterday and tomorrow. Opened in 1955 and constantly expanding, Disneyland has steadily grown to become the top tourist attraction in California.

The entertainment complex is divided into several theme "lands," each containing tailored rides and attractions. Many visitors tackle the park systematically, beginning at the entrance, and working their way clockwise around the park. But a better plan of attack may be to arrive early and run to the most popular rides first—Space Mountain, Big Thunder Mountain Railroad, Splash Mountain, and Pirates of the Caribbean. Lines for these rides can last an hour or more in the middle of the day.

Main Street U.S.A., the main drag of a small turn-of-the-century American town, is at the entrance to the park. This is a good area to save for the end of the day—particularly the "Great Moments with Mr. Lincoln," a patriotic look at America's 16th president, where you can rest your weary feet. You can start by touring the entire park by train—a 19th-century steam train departs from the Main Street Depot and completely encircles the park. After sunset during summer, there's a Main Street Electrical Parade spectacular—with fabulous whirling lights followed by Fantasy in the Sky fireworks.

Adventureland is inspired by exotic regions of Asia, Africa, and the South Pacific. Electronically animated tropical birds, flowers, and "tiki gods" present a musical comedy in the Enchanted Tiki Room. On the Jungle Cruise, which is within a spear's throw, passengers are threatened by wild animals and hostile natives. New Orleans square offers the ghost-packed Haunted Mansion; Pirates of the Caribbean is a hydroflume ride down a plunging waterfall and through pirate caves; and Splash Mountain is one of the largest towering log-flume attractions in the world.

Frontierland, which gets its inspiration from 19th-century America, is full of dense forests and broad rivers inhabited by hearty pioneers. You can take a raft to Tom Sawyer's Island and board the Big Thunder Mountain Railroad, a roller coaster that races through a deserted 1870s mine.

Fantasyland's storybook theme is illustrated with several rides based on famous children's books, including *Through the Looking Glass* and *Peter Pan*. The seemingly unrelated Matterhorn Bobsleds, a roller-coaster ride through chilling caverns and drifting fog banks, is here, too; it's one of the park's most popular rides.

Tomorrowland explores the world of the future and offers some of the park's best attractions. Space Mountain, a pitch-black indoor roller coaster, is one of the best-known rides at Disneyland. Captain Eo, a 3-D motion picture musical, is a space adventure starring Michael Jackson. One of the newest attractions is Star Tours, a 40-passenger StarSpeeder that encounters a spaceload of misadventures on the way to the Moon of Endor.

The "lands" themselves are only half the adventure. Other attractions include Disney characters, penny arcades, restaurants and snack bars galore, fireworks (during summer only), mariachi bands, ragtime pianists, parades, shops, marching bands, and much more.

Admission (including unlimited rides and all entertainment): $27.50 adults and children over 12; $22.50 children 3–11; $22 seniors (60 and over). Parking: $5.

Open: Mid-Sept–May, Mon–Fri 10am–6pm, Sat–Sun 9am–midnight; Jun–mid-Sept plus Thanksgiving, Christmas, and Easter, daily 8–1am.

KNOTT'S BERRY FARM, 8039 Beach Blvd., Buena Park. Tel. 714/827-1776, or 714/220-5200 for a recording.

In 1920, Walter and Cordelia Knott arrived in Buena Park in their old Model T Ford and leased a small farm on 10 acres of land. Things got tough during the Great Depression, so Cordelia set up a roadside stand selling pies, preserves, and home-cooked chicken dinners. Within a year sales were up to about 90 meals a day. Lines became so long that Walter decided to create an Old West Ghost Town as a diversion for waiting customers, and that's how it all began. The Knott family now owns the farm that surrounds the world-famous Chicken Dinner Restaurant, an eatery that now serves over a million meals a year! And Knott's Berry Farm has emerged as the nation's third-best-attended family entertainment complex (after the two Disney facilities). The park still maintains its original Old West motif and is divided into five Old Time Adventures areas.

Old West Ghost Town, the original attraction, is a collection of authentic buildings that have been relocated from actual deserted Western towns and refurbished. Visitors can pan for gold, climb aboard the stagecoach, ride rickety train cars through the Calico

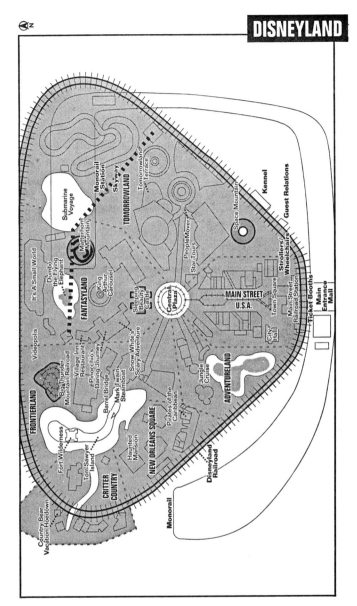

Mine, get held up aboard the Denver and Rio Grande Calico Railroad, and hiss at the villain during a melodrama in the Birdcage Theater.

Fiesta Village's south-of-the-border theme means festive markets, strolling mariachis, and wild rides like Montezooma's Revenge—a loop roller coaster that turns you upside down and goes backward.

Roaring '20s Amusement Area contains the thrilling Sky Tower, a parachute jump that drops riders into a 20-story free fall. Other white-knuckle rides include XK-1, the ultimate flight simulator "piloted" by the riders; the $7-million Kingdom of the Dinosaurs ride; and Boomerang, a state-of-the-art roller coaster that turns riders upside down six times in less than one minute.

Wild Water Wilderness is a $10-million, 3½-acre attraction styled like a turn-of-the-century California wilderness park. The top ride here is a white-water adventure called Bigfoot Rapids.

Camp Snoopy is meant to re-create the picturesque California High Sierra. Its 6 rustic acres are the playing grounds of Charles Schulz's beloved beagle, Snoopy, and his pals, Charlie Brown and Lucy, who greet guests and pose for pictures.

Admission (including unlimited access to all rides, shows, and attractions): $23 adults; $16 seniors over 60; $17 children 3–11; children under 3, free. Rates drop to $15 per person after 6pm.

Open: Summer, Mon–Thurs 9am–11pm, Fri–Sun 9am–midnight; the rest of the year, Mon–Thurs 10am–6pm, Fri–Sun 10am–10pm. Opening times vary, so call for the latest information. **Directions:** From I-5 or Calif. 91, exit south onto Beach Boulevard. The park is located about ½ mile south.

MEDIEVAL TIMES, 7662 Beach Blvd., Buena Park. Tel. 714/521-4740, or toll free 800/899-6600.

Basically, Medieval Times is a dinner show for those of us who were unlucky enough not to have been born into a royal family somewhere in 11th-century Europe. Guests crowd around long wooden tables and enjoy a four-course "banquet" of roast chicken, spare ribs, herbed potatoes, and pastries. More than 1,100 people can fit into the castle, where sword fights, jousting tournaments, and various feats of skill are performed by colorfully costumed actors, including knights on horseback.

It's kind of ridiculous, but kids love it, and Medieval Times is extremely popular year round.

Admission: Sun–Fri $30 adults, $20 children 12 and under; Sat $34 adults, $22 children.

Open: Shows Mon–Thurs 7:30pm; Fri 6:15pm and 9pm; Sat 4pm, 6:30pm, and 9:15pm; Sun 4:45pm and 7:30pm. Times can vary, so call for the latest information. **Directions:** From I-5 or Calif. 91, exit south onto Beach Boulevard. The attraction is located about ¼ mile south.

MOVIELAND WAX MUSEUM, 7711 Beach Blvd. (Calif. 39), Buena Park. Tel. 714/522-1155.

At the Movieland Wax Museum, located one block north of Knott's Berry Farm in Buena Park, you can see wax-molded reviews of past cinematic attractions—everything from Bela Lugosi as *Dracula* to Marilyn Monroe in *Gentlemen Prefer Blondes*.

Mary Pickford, "America's Sweetheart," dedicated the museum on May 4, 1962. It has risen steadily in popularity ever since, with new stars added yearly, taking their place next to the time-tested favorites. The museum was created by a film addict, Allen Parkinson, who saw to it that some of the most memorable scenes in motion pictures were re-created in exacting detail in wax, with such authentic touches as the ripped dress of Sophia Loren in *Two Women*.

Some of the most popular teams are featured in tableaux: Humphrey Bogart and Katharine Hepburn in *The African Queen,* Myrna Loy and William Powell in *The Thin Man,* Garbo and Gilbert in *Queen Christina,* Clark Gable and Vivien Leigh in *Gone with the Wind,* and Laurel and Hardy in *The Perfect Day.* Later sets include *Star Trek* and *Superman.*

Admission: $12.95 adults; $10.55 seniors; $6.95 children 4–11; children under 4, free. **Parking:** Free.

Open: Daily 9am–7pm. **Directions:** From either the Santa Ana Freeway (I-5) or the Riverside Freeway (Calif. 91), take the Beach Boulevard exit south straight to the museum.

WHERE TO STAY

EXPENSIVE

DISNEYLAND HOTEL, 1150 W. Cerritos Ave., Anaheim, CA 92802. Tel. 714/778-6600. Fax 714/965-6597. 1,131 rms, 62 suites. No smoking rooms available. A/C MINIBAR TV TEL **Directions:** From I-5, exit south onto Harbor Boulevard and turn right onto Katella Avenue. Pass the Disneyland parking lot and turn right onto West Street. The hotel is ahead on your left, at Cerritos Avenue.

$ Rates: $115–$195 single; $103–$240 double; from $400, suite. AE, MC, V. **Parking:** $7.

The "Official Hotel of the Magic Kingdom" offers its guests the most convenient transportation to the park via a monorail system that runs right through the hotel. Located on 60 attractively landscaped acres, the hotel offers six restaurants, five cocktail lounges, 20 shops and boutiques, every kind of service desk imaginable, a "wharfside" bazaar, a walk-under waterfall, three swimming pools, and 10 night-lit tennis courts. An artificial white sand beach is also adjacent to the hotel.

The rooms are not fancy, but they are comfortable and attractively furnished with king-size beds, table, and chairs. Many rooms feature framed reproductions of rare Disneyland conceptual art.

MODERATE

SHERATON-ANAHEIM HOTEL, 1015 W. Ball Rd., Anaheim, CA 92802. Tel. 714/778-1700, or toll free 800/325-3535. Fax 714/535-3889. 500 rms, 31 suites. No smoking rooms available. A/C MINIBAR TV TEL **Directions:** From I-5 north, exit onto Ball Road west, the hotel is on your right as you reach the top of the ramp.

$ Rates: $95–$135 single; $100–$145 double. Children 17 and under stay free in parents' room. AE, CB, DC, MC, V. **Parking:** Free.

Looking very much like an English Tudor castle, the Sheraton-Anaheim rises to the festive theme park occasion with an unusual architectural design and unique public facilities that include a 24-hour restaurant, lobby lounge and bar, a California-style delicatessen, and free shuttle service to and from Disneyland and the airport.

Rooms are completely modern and outfitted with separate dressing rooms, color TVs, and radios; some also have refrigerators. The hotel is adequate, but it is clear that guests are really paying for the location—just blocks from Disneyland.

HOWARD JOHNSON'S MOTOR LODGE, 1380 S. Harbor Blvd., Anaheim, CA 92802. Tel. 714/776-6120, or toll free 800/654-2000. Fax 714/533-3578. 313 rms, 6 suites. A/C TV TEL **Directions:** From I-5, exit onto Harbor Boulevard south.

$ Rates: $60–$80 single or double; $95 minisuite; $145 two-room suite. Children under 18 stay free in parents' room. AE, CB, DC, DISC, MC, V. **Parking:** Free.

In a 6-acre parklike setting, this relatively elegant building was designed in a contemporary style by award-winning architect W. L. Pereira. It's almost like a resort, and it's located just opposite Disneyland. Roofed balconies open onto a central garden with two heated swimming pools for adults, and one for children. Garden paths lead under eucalyptus and olive trees to a splashing circular fountain. During the summer, you can watch the nightly fireworks display at Disneyland from the upper balconies.

Rooms, some offering Disney views, are equipped with large color TVs with in-room movies, and coffee/tea-making facilities. Services and facilities include a game room, car-rental desk, room service, self-service laundry facilities, and babysitting for $8 per hour (four-hour minimum).

There's a Howard Johnson's restaurant on the premises, open around the clock and serving all the famous flavors. A bar/lounge adjoins.

INEXPENSIVE

ANAHEIM ALOHA TRAVELODGE, 505 Katella Ave., Anaheim, CA 92805. Tel. 714/774-8710, or toll free 800/255-3050. 50 rms. No smoking room available. A/C TV TEL **Directions:** From I-5, exit onto Harbor Boulevard south and turn left onto Katella Avenue to the hotel.

$ Rates (including continental breakfast): May–Sept $59 single, $68 double; Oct–Apr rates are lower. Children under 17 stay free in parents' room. AE, CB, DC, DISC, MC, V. **Parking:** Free.

Located just one block from Disneyland, these accommodations are highly recommended, not for their style, but for the simple comfort and close proximity to Disneyland. The rooms, which are pleasant, standard motel units, come equipped with free cable movies and in-room coffee-makers. There's a heated swimming pool with a slide.

FARM DE VILLE, 7800 and 7878 Crescent Ave., Buena Park, CA 90620. Tel. 714/527-2201. Fax 714/826-3826. 130 rms. A/C TV TEL **Directions:** From I-5, exit onto Beach Boulevard south. After about 2 miles turn right onto Crescent Avenue to the hotel.

$ Rates: $35 single; $40 double; extra person $4. Units for 4–6 $80. AE, MC, V. **Parking:** Free.

Although it's just a motel, the Farm de Ville has a lot to offer. It's located close to Knott's Berry Farm's south entrance and is convenient to all the nearby attractions, including Disneyland (just 10 minutes away).

The rooms are spacious, immaculate, and well furnished; each has a radio, dressing area, and individually controlled heat and air conditioning. Facilities include two swimming pools with slides and diving boards, two wading pools for kids, two saunas, and a coin-op laundry.

MOTEL 6, 921 S. Beach Blvd. Anaheim, CA 92804. Tel. 714/220-2866. 55 rms. A/C TV TEL **Directions:** From I-5 south, exit at Beach Boulevard and turn right. The motel is located about 5 miles ahead on your right, just before Ball Road.

$ Rates: $35 per room (up to 4 adults). AE, MC, V. **Parking:** Free.
Happily, this well-placed and priced Motel 6 is close to both Disneyland and Knott's Berry Farm, between Ball Road and Highway 91. It's easy on the budget, clean, efficient, and comfortable. There is a swimming pool and satellite TV.

FULLERTON HACIENDA AYH HOSTEL, 1700 N. Harbor Blvd., Fullerton, CA 92635. Tel. 714/738-3721. Fax 714/738-0925. 24 beds. **Directions:** From I-5 south, take Calif. 91 east and exit onto Harbor Boulevard north (the second Harbor Boulevard exit). Continue for 2½ miles past Brea Avenue. The hostel is located within the park on your right; look for the park entrance and the hostel sign.

$ Rates: $14 AYH/IYHF members; $17 nonmembers. MC, V. **Parking:** Free.
Just outside Anaheim is this ultimate in economy near Disneyland and Knott's Berry Farm. It's located on the site of an old dairy farm, surrounded by greenery (including lemon trees), rabbits, squirrels—and other country life. The sparse accommodations are comfortable, and the manager is congenial and helpful. The hostel provides complete kitchen and bathroom facilities. It operates under a cooperative arrangement: You're expected to clean up after yourself, leave the hostel tidy, and do some chores each morning as requested by the houseparents. The maximum stay is three consecutive days, smoking is not allowed, and the hostel observes an 11pm curfew.

WHERE TO DINE

Neither Anaheim nor Buena Park is famous for its restaurants. If you're visiting the area just for the day, you'll probably eat inside the theme parks; there are plenty of restaurants—in all price ranges—to choose from at both Disneyland and Knott's Berry Farm. For the most unusual dinner you've ever had with the kids, see Medieval Times, listed above under "What to See and Do."

MODERATE

MR. STOX, 1105 E. Katella Ave., Anaheim. Tel. 714/634-2994.

Cuisine: AMERICAN. **Reservations:** Accepted. **Directions:** From I-5, exit onto Harbor Boulevard south and turn left onto Katella Avenue to the restaurant.

$ Prices: Appetizers $5–$10; main courses $10–$25. AE, DC, MC, V.

Open: Lunch, Mon–Fri 11am–3pm; dinner, Mon–Sat 5:30–10pm, Sun 5–9pm.

Hearty steaks and fresh seafood are served in an early California setting. Hot main dish specialties include roast prime rib of beef au jus and mesquite-broiled fish, veal, and lamb; sandwiches and salads are also available. Homemade desserts such as chocolate-mousse cake are unexpectedly good. Mr. Stox has an enormous wine cellar, and there is live entertainment every night.

PEPPERS RESTAURANT, 12361 Chapman Ave., Garden Grove. Tel. 714/740-1333.

Cuisine: CALIFORNIA/MEXICAN. **Reservations:** Accepted. **Directions:** From I-5, exit south onto Harbor Boulevard and turn left onto Chapman Avenue to the restaurant.

$ Prices: Appetizers $3–$7; main courses $9–$14. AE, CB, DC, DISC, MC, V.

Open: Lunch, Mon–Fri 11am–3pm; dinner, Mon–Sat 5:30–10pm, Sun 5–9pm.

Located just south of Disneyland, this colorful California/Mexican-themed restaurant features mesquite-broiled "Norteno" cuisine and fresh seafood daily. Mexican specialties include all types of tacos and burritos, but the grilled meats and fish are best.

Dancing is available nightly to Top 40 hits, starting at 8pm, and there is a free shuttle to and from the area hotels.

---

3. NEWPORT BEACH

30 miles SE of downtown Los Angeles

GETTING THERE By Plane Los Angeles International Airport (LAX) is located approximately 35 miles northwest of Newport, along the Pacific Coast Highway (Calif. 1). John Wayne International Airport, in Irvine, is only about 1 mile from Newport Beach on the Newport Freeway (Calif. 55).

By Train The nearest Amtrak (800/USA-RAIL) station is located in San Juan Capistrano, at 26701 Verdugo St., about 15 miles from Newport Beach. Trains travel both north and south between Los Angeles and San Diego. Call for fare and schedule information.

By Bus Greyhound/Trailways can get you here from anywhere. The company doesn't operate a nationwide toll-free telephone number, so check your local directory for the phone number and call for information.

By Car From Los Angeles, take I-5 or I-405 south. Exit south onto the Newport Freeway (Calif. 55), and continue to the end in Newport Beach. It's about a one-hour drive from downtown Los Angeles.

ESSENTIALS Orientation Newport Beach encompasses several islands and peninsulas, as well as a good-sized swath of mainland. Balboa Island and Lido Isle are the two largest, though each is only 10 to 20 blocks long and only three or four blocks wide. The islands are situated in a gentle harbor, protected by the giant Lido Peninsula which reaches out from the mainland like a gnarled finger.

Information The Newport Beach Conference and Visitors Bureau, 3700 Newport Blvd., Ste. 107 (tel. 714/644-1190, or toll free 800/94-COAST), distributes the requisite maps, brochures, and information. Write for a free visitor's package.

Like a jigsaw puzzle of islands and peninsulas, Newport Beach is a major southern California recreational resort. Once a cattle ranch above an uncharted estuary, Newport is now a busy harbor that embraces the delightful peninsula/island town. The phenomenal growth of hotel and restaurant facilities in the last few years indicates that Newport Beach is fast becoming one of southern California's most popular coastal towns. It's an excellent vacation base from which to explore other coastal beaches, as well as sights in Anaheim and Buena Park.

WHAT TO SEE & DO

BALBOA PAVILION, 400 Main St., Balboa. Tel. 714/675-9444.

Designated as a California Historical Landmark, Balboa Pavilion was built in 1905 and originally served as a bathhouse. Today, the cupola-topped structure is a major focus of activity. Restored to its original "waterfront Victorian" splendor, the pavilion serves as the Newport terminal for Catalina Island Passenger Service boats, harbor cruises, and whale-watching trips. It's also home to several restaurants and shops. For cruise and charter information, call 714/673-5245; for sport-fishing information, call 714/673-1434.

You can also ferry from here to Balboa Island, across the small bay. Rides cost $1 for cars, and 50¢ for each adult passenger.

Directions: From Calif. 1, turn south onto Newport Boulevard, which becomes Balboa Boulevard on the peninsula. Continue straight to the pavilion.

HARBOR CRUISES, Catalina Passenger Service, Balboa Pavilion. Tel. 714/673-5245.

The best way to see Newport is from the bay. Several 45-minute narrated harbor cruises are offered daily. The boats pass the fancy homes that have made the area famous and the cruise guides provide passengers with good historical information on the area. Cruise times vary, so call for information.

Tickets: $6–$8 adults; $4 seniors; $1 children under 12; children under 5, free.

LIDO MARINA VILLAGE, Via Oporto. Tel. 714/675-8662.
One of the area's most upscale shopping complexes, the Lido's 40 restaurants and shops line a brick courtyard and adjacent boardwalk. Since this mall is located right on the marina, you will be able to see a big collection of super large yachts. Indeed, a unique feature of this mall is that it houses about eight establishments that sell yachts.

Directions: From Calif. 1, turn south onto Newport Boulevard, then turn left onto 32nd Street just after the bridge, and left again onto Via Oporto to the mall.

NEWPORT HARBOR ART MUSEUM, 850 San Clemente Rd. Tel. 714/759-1122.
The museum presents varying exhibitions of 20th-century works of art. The emphasis here is on California paintings, sculpture, installations, and photographs. Note that the galleries are closed between exhibitions; call for the current schedule before heading out.

Admission: $3 adults; $1 children 6–17; $2 students, seniors (aged 65 and over), and military with current I.D.

Open: Tues–Sun 10am–5pm. **Directions:** From Calif. 1, turn left onto Newport Center Drive and bear left around the oval to Santa Barbara Drive. Take the next right onto San Clemente Drive to the museum.

WHERE TO STAY

EXPENSIVE

NEWPORT BEACH MARRIOTT HOTEL AND TENNIS CLUB, 900 Newport Center Dr., Newport Beach, CA 92660. Tel. 714/640-4000, or toll free 800/228-9290. Fax 714/640-5055. 586 rms. A/C TV TEL **Directions:** From Calif. 1, turn left onto Newport Center Drive and continue straight to the hotel.

$ Rates: $139–$149 single; $139–$169 double. AE, CB, DC, DISC, MC, V **Parking:** $6

This 15-story hotel was built around a nine-story atrium—and a large 19th-century Italian Renaissance–style fountain; it's a clever design. Most of the guest rooms, all strikingly decorated with cheerful drapes and spreads, offer ocean views. In addition to the usual amenities, each room is equipped with a radio, individual climate controls, and an ironing board (irons furnished on request).

Two swimming and hydrotherapy pools are surrounded by a palm-lined sun deck. Eight tennis courts (all lit at night) are complemented by a well-stocked pro shop and snack bar. There's also a good health club, and golfing is available next door at the Newport Beach Country Club's 18-hole course.

Dining/Entertainment: J.W.'s Sea Grill is a pleasant and cheerful indoor/outdoor restaurant serving fresh seafood and American favorites.

Services: Room service, concierge, evening turndown.

Facilities: Two swimming pools, eight lighted tennis courts, health club, pro shop, off-premises golf course, tour desk, car rental.

HYATT NEWPORTER, 1107 Jamboree Rd., Newport

Beach, CA 92660. **Tel. 714/729-1234,** or toll free 800/233-1234. Fax 714/644-1552. 410 rms, 20 suites. A/C TV TEL **Directions:** From Calif. 1, exit north onto Jamboree Road. The hotel is just ahead on your right, near Backbay Drive.

$ Rates: $139–$170 single; $164–$195 double; from $300, suite. AE, CB, DC, DISC, MC, V. **Parking:** $6.

Located on 26 landscaped acres, the Hyatt Newporter is a resort complex par excellence, and an important hub of activity in this beach town. The John Wayne Tennis Club is on the premises—a top facility that includes 16 championship courts (all lit for night play), spa equipment, a steam/sauna, and a clubhouse. In addition, the hotel boasts a 9-hole, par-3 golf course, three heated Olympic-size swimming pools, three whirlpools, and a children's pool, as well as a fitness room and volleyball court; also available are shuffleboard, Ping-Pong, jogging trails, and much more.

The rooms, decorated in pastel tones, have contemporary furnishings, marble baths, and deluxe amenities. All have balconies or terraces with a view of the back bay, gardens, or golf course.

In addition to offering an attractive view of the back bay, the three-bedroom villas have a separate living and dining area, fireplace, and access to a private swimming pool.

Dining/Entertainment: Three meals a day are offered in the Jamboree Cafe, a casual California-style eatery. Dinner is served in both Ristorante Cantori, a northern Italian dining room, and in the award-winning gourmet room—The Wine Cellar—the hotel's flagship restaurant.

Services: Room service, concierge, evening turndown.

Facilities: 16 lighted tennis courts, a 9-hole golf course, three heated swimming pools, three whirlpools, health spa, tour desk, car rental, gift shop, beauty salon.

WHERE TO DINE

EXPENSIVE

CHANTECLAIR, 18912 MacArthur Blvd., Irvine. Tel. 714/752-8001.

Cuisine: CONTINENTAL. **Reservations:** Recommended. **Directions:** From Newport Beach, take the Newport Freeway (Calif. 55) north 1 mile to San Diego Freeway (I-405) east. Go just one exit to MacArthur Boulevard south. The restaurant is straight ahead opposite the Airport Terminal, between Campus and Douglas Drives.

$ Prices: Appetizers $8–$11; main courses $21–$37. AE, CB, DC, MC, V.

Open: Lunch, Sun–Fri 11:30am–2:30pm; dinner, daily 6–11pm.

Chanteclair is expensive, and a little difficult to reach, but it is included here because of its excellence. The restaurant is designed in the style of a provincial French inn. The rambling stucco structure, built around a central garden court, houses several dining and drinking areas: a grand and petit salon, a boudoir, a bibliothèque, a garden area with a skylight roof, and a hunting lodge–like lounge. Furnished in antiques, it has five fireplaces.

At lunch you might order double-ribbed lamb chops, creamed

chicken in pastry, or steak tartare. Dinner is a worthwhile splurge that might begin with a game bird and pistachio pâté, or beluga caviar with blinis. For a main dish I recommend the rack of lamb served with fresh vegetables and potatoes Dauphine. The captain will be happy to help you choose from the considerable selection of domestic and imported wines.

MARRAKESH, 1100 W. Coast Hwy. Tel. 714/645-8384.
  Cuisine: MOROCCAN. **Reservations:** Recommended. **Directions:** From Newport Boulevard turn east onto Pacific Coast Highway (Calif. 1). The restaurant is directly ahead, near Dover Drive.
$ Prices: Appetizers $6–$8; main courses $16–$22. AE, CB, DC, MC, V.
  Open: Dinner daily 5–11pm.

The decor is exotic, with dining areas divided into intimate tents furnished with Persian carpets, low cushioned sofas, and authentic Moroccan works of art.

Dinners here are something of a ritual feast that begins when a server comes around to wash your hands. Everyone in your party shares the same meal—an eight- or nine-course feast that is eaten with your hands. Meals start with Moroccan soup and a tangy salad that is scooped up with hunks of fresh bread. Next comes b'stila, a chicken-filled pastry topped with cinnamon; or kotban, a lamb shish kebab marinated in olive oil, coriander, cumin, and garlic. Main dish choices are squab with rice and almonds, chicken with lemon and olives, fish in a piquant sauce, and rabbit in garlic sauce. Leave room for the next course of lamb and vegetables with couscous, followed by fresh fruits, tea, and Moroccan pastries.

MODERATE

THE CANNERY, 3010 Lafayette Ave. Tel. 714/675-5777.
  Cuisine: SEAFOOD. **Reservations:** Recommended. **Directions:** From Calif. 1, turn south onto Newport Boulevard. After you cross the bridge, turn left onto 31st Street. The restaurant is directly ahead, at Lido Park Drive.
$ Prices: Appetizers $5–$7; main courses $12–$20; Sun brunch $9–$14. AE, CB, DC, MC, V.
  Open: Lunch, Mon–Sat 11:30am–3pm; dinner, Mon–Sat 4:30–9pm; brunch, Sun 10am–2:30pm.

The Cannery is housed in a remodeled 1934 fish cannery that used to turn out 5,000 cases of swordfish and mackerel a day. Now a historical landmark, the two-story restaurant is a favorite among locals and tourists alike—for good food, a colorful atmosphere, and friendly service. In the upper lounge, tables surround a corner platform where there's live entertainment every Thursday through Sunday evening.

Fresh fish and local abalone are specialties here. At dinner there's always a superfresh chef's catch of the day. Other good choices are eastern beef, chicken teriyaki, and rack of lamb. At lunch you might ask for shrimp and fries, or sandwiches and salads.

The restaurant also serves a champagne buffet brunch while you cruise Newport Harbor aboard the Cannery's *Isla Mujeres;* the cost is $25. Call for information and reservations.

4. PALM SPRINGS

103 miles E of Los Angeles, 135 miles NE of San Diego

GETTING THERE   By Plane   Several airlines service the Palm Springs Municipal Airport, 3400 E. Tahquitz-McCallum Way (tel. 619/323-8161), including Alaska Airlines, America West, American, Delta, TWA, and United. Flights from Los Angeles International Airport take about 40 minutes.

By Bus   Greyhound/Trailways can get you here from anywhere. The central terminal is located at 311 N. Indian Ave. (tel. 619/325-2053). The company doesn't operate a nationwide toll-free telephone number, so check your local directory for the phone number and call for information.

By Car   From I-10, take the Calif. 111 turnoff to Palm Springs. You drive into town on East Palm Canyon Drive, the main thoroughfare. The trip from downtown Los Angeles takes about 2½ hours.

ESSENTIALS   Orientation   Downtown   Palm   Springs stretches about half a mile along Palm Canyon Drive, a wide storefront-lined boulevard of restaurants, clothing stores, and hotels. The mountains lie directly west, while the rest of Palm Springs is laid out in a grid to the east. Tahquitz-McCallum Way, a street as wide as Palm Canyon Drive, creates the town's primary intersection and runs through the heart of downtown.

Information   The Palm Springs Desert Resorts Convention and Visitors Bureau, Atrium Design Centre, 69-930 Highway 111, Suite 201, Rancho Mirage, CA 92270 (tel. 619/770-9000), offers maps, brochures, and advice. It's open Monday through Friday from 8:30am to 5pm.

The Palm Springs Chamber of Commerce, 190 W. Amado Rd., at the corner of Belardo Road (tel. 619/325-1577, or toll free 800/65-HOTEL, 800/34-HOTEL in California), offers similar information, as well as hotel reservations. The office, located near the heart of town, is open Monday through Friday from 8am to 4:30pm and Saturday and Sunday from 10am to 2pm.

The self-proclaimed golf, tennis, and swimming pool capital of the world, Palm Springs is the traditional playground of the tasteless rich whose primary residences are often in Los Angeles. Famous residents include the Gabor sisters, Kirk Douglas, and Dean Martin. The honorary mayor is Bob Hope, and, until recently, the elected one was Sonny Bono (of Sonny and Cher fame).

The sun shines almost every day of the year here, which can make it extremely uncomfortable during summer, when temperatures regularly reach into the 100s. Palm Springs, designed with the rich in mind, was intended as a respite from L.A. winters. Hotel prices and availability are closely related to the seasons; in the middle of summer even the best accommodations can be had for a song.

A large number of golf tournaments are regularly held here, including the Bob Hope Desert Classic and the Nabisco Dinah Shore Invitational. The town has more than 300 tennis courts, 42 golf courses (although only seven 18-hole courses are public; the average greens fees are $50), and more than 7,000 swimming pools—one for every five residents!

WHAT TO SEE & DO

Palm Springs is a resort community, which means that there isn't much to do aside from sunning, swimming, dining, playing, and relaxing.

INDIAN CANYONS, S. Palm Canyon Dr., Palm Springs. Tel. 619/325-5673.

Located on Native American–owned lands, the canyons are full of hiking trails through Palm, Andreas, and Murray canyons. If you are able to do some light hiking, the canyons offer visitors some of the best natural sights in the area. You'll walk through palm groves, see desert plants and animals, encounter a trading post, and even visit a waterfall with picnic tables nearby. When writing for information, address your letters to M. A. Tribal Council Office, 960 E. Tahquitz Way, Palm Springs, CA 92262. The canyons are closed from June to September.

Admission: $3.50 adults; $2.50 students; $2 seniors (62 and over); $1 children.

Open: Daily 8am–5pm.

PALM SPRINGS AERIAL TRAMWAY, Tramway Road–Chino Canyon, Palm Springs. Tel. 619/325-1391.

To gain a bird's-eye perspective on the town, take a ride on the Aerial Tramway, which ascends 2½ miles up the slopes of Mount San Jacinto. You will travel from the desert floor to cool alpine heights in less than 20 minutes; in winter the change is dramatic, from warm desert to deep snowdrifts. There's a restaurant at the top, as well as a cocktail lounge, gift shop, and picnic area. It's also the starting point for 54 miles of hiking trails dotted with campgrounds. A special ride 'n' dine combination includes a sunset dinner at the Alpine Restaurant and costs only $4 more than the ride alone—a great bargain.

Admission: $15 adults, $10 children 5–12; ride 'n' dine $19 adults, $12.95 children.

Open: Mon–Fri 10am–8pm, Sat–Sun 8am–8pm; 1 hour later during Daylight Saving Time.

ORGANIZED TOURS

PALM SPRINGS CELEBRITY TOURS, 333 N. Palm Canyon Dr., Suite 113A, Palm Springs. Tel. 619/325-2682.

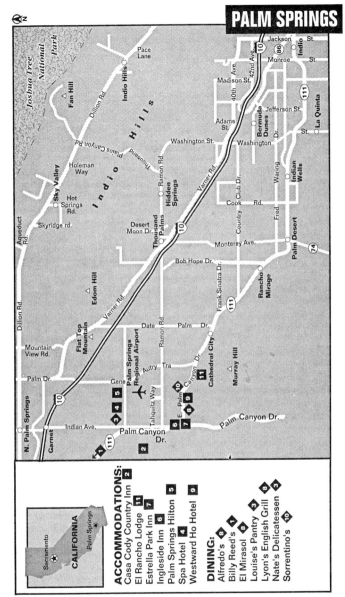

ACCOMMODATIONS:
Casa Cody Country Inn **2**
El Rancho Lodge **1**
Estrella Park Inn **7**
Ingleside Inn **6**
Palm Springs Hilton **5**
Spa Hotel **4**
Westward Ho Hotel **9**

DINING:
Alfredo's **6**
Billy Reed's **1**
El Mirasol **8**
Louise's Pantry **3**
Lyon's English Grill **2**
Nate's Delicatessen **8**
Sorrentino's **10**

Celebrity Tours has been around since 1963. Their professional guides know all the ins and outs of Palm Springs and specialize in personal tours and small groups; their air-conditioned deluxe coaches seat up to only 14.

The one- and two-hour tours provide a comprehensive look at Palm Springs, including the homes of certain movie stars and celebrities. The longer excursion includes everything you'd see during the shorter tour plus the estates of Frank Sinatra and businessman

Walter Annenberg, who has his own golf course. You'll also see the Tamarisk, Canyon, and Thunderbird country clubs, where the international elite meet to play. Then it's on to the Eisenhower Medical Center and beautiful date groves, with a brief stop for refreshments.

The one-hour tour meets at the office at the above address. For the two-hour excursion, Celebrity Tours will pick you up at any hotel in Palm Springs.

Reservations are required and should be made at least a day or two in advance. Tours are conducted daily; call for departure times.

Prices: One-hour tour: $10 adults, $9 seniors, $5 children under 12; two-hour tour: $14 adults, $12 seniors, $7 children under 12.

WHERE TO STAY

EXPENSIVE

INGLESIDE INN, 200 W. Ramon Rd., Palm Springs, CA 92262. Tel. 619/325-0046, or toll free 800/772-6655. Fax 619/325-0710. 29 rms, 16 suites. A/C TV TEL
$ Rates (including continental breakfast): Oct–May $85–$150 single, $95–$225 double, from $275, suite; Jun–Sept $65–$125 single, $75–$175 double, from $195, suite. AE, DISC, MC, V. **Parking:** Free.

Some of the most charming rooms in town can be found at this 65-year-old hideaway estate. Each room and suite is uniquely decorated with antiques—perhaps a canopied bed, or a 15th-century vestment chest. Many rooms have wood-burning fireplaces; all have in-room whirlpools, steambaths, and refrigerators stocked with complimentary light snacks and beverages. Once you pass the imposing wrought-iron gates, you leave the bustling world of the 20th century behind and enter an Old World era of luxurious relaxation and fine, unstuffy, remarkably friendly service.

If you decide to stay here, you'll join the ranks of Elizabeth Taylor, Howard Hughes, John Wayne, Bette Davis, Salvador Dali, and Gary Cooper, all of whom have enjoyed these luxurious facilities at one time or another.

A major renovation was completed in the summer of 1990. The redecorated accommodations include new drapes, spreads, and upholstery. Three rooms were gutted and rebuilt to include totally secluded patios blessed with a magnificent view of the mountains, and with wood-burning fireplaces.

Dining/Entertainment: Melvyn's, one of Palm Springs's most prestigious "in" spots, is located downstairs, and definitely worth a visit even if you're not staying here. Frank and Barbara Sinatra hosted a dinner here on the eve of their wedding. The food is excellent, the celebrity-watching first rate, and the decor lovely.

Services: Room service, concierge, massage, complimentary limousine service.

Facilities: Swimming pool, Jacuzzi, croquet, shuffleboard, sundry boutiques, business center, tour desk, car rental.

PALM SPRINGS HILTON, 400 E. Tahquitz Canyon Way,

Palm Springs, CA 92262. Tel. 619/320-6868, or toll free 800/522-6900. Fax 619/320-2126. 260 rms, 71 suites. A/C MINIBAR TV TEL

$ Rates: Jan–May $185–$215 single or double; mid-Sept–Dec, June–July $135–$165 single or double; Aug–mid-Sept $80–$100 single or double; $215–$695 year round for suite. Children under 17 stay free in parents' room. AE, CB, DC, DISC, MC, V. **Parking:** Self, free; valet, $4.

One of the town's most glittering resorts has the atmosphere of a busy country club. A large group-oriented hotel, the three-story Hilton blends into the natural environment and reflects the sand colors of the desert. The lobby, rooms, and restaurants are all contemporary and filled with original art, mostly contemporary serigraphs by David Weidman and sculptures by local artists.

Guest rooms—built around a central garden and swimming pool and decorated in soft earth tones—are large and residential in feel, with sitting areas and large window shutters. All rooms have patios or balconies, large baths with thermostatically regulated showers, brass fixtures, and individual temperature controls.

Dining/Entertainment: The Terrace Restaurant, overlooking the pool area, offers a continental cuisine; breakfast, lunch, and dinner daily. There's also a poolside dining facility for snacks, and Harvey's bar/lounge.

Services: Room service, concierge, complimentary airport transportation.

Facilities: Swimming pool, two Jacuzzis, six tennis courts, pro shop, exercise room, tour desk, car rental, beauty salon, video game room.

SPA HOTEL & MINERAL SPRINGS, 100 N. Indian Canyon Dr., Palm Springs, CA 92263. Tel. 619/325-1461, or toll free 800/854-1279. Fax 619/325-3344. 230 rms, 20 suites. A/C MINIBAR TV TEL

$ Rates (including continental breakfast): Jan–May $85–$115 single or double; June–Sept $45–$75 single or double, Oct–Dec $65–$85 single or double; from $125 year round for suite. Extra person $20. Various pampering packages are available. AE, CB, DC, MC, V. **Parking:** Free.

One of the unique choices in town is the only full-service "spa" resort. The site was formerly a shrine for Native American Cahuillas who claimed the springs had magical powers to cure illness. Modern Americans still make this claim and come here to pamper the body and soul by "taking the waters." There are three pools on the premises. One is a conventional outdoor swimming pool; the other two are filled from underground natural springs brimming with revitalizing minerals. There are an additional 30 indoor sunken Roman swirlpools, which are also fed from the springs.

The price of a guest room includes hot springs immersion, eucalyptus inhalation, sauna, cooling room, outdoor mineral pools, solarium, and gym. A variety of additional treatments are also available, including exercise classes, herbal wraps, herbal baths, loofah scrubs, salt glows, massages, and computerized body stretches.

Services: Evening turndown, massage, facials, manicures, pedicures, and other beauty treatments.

Facilities: Complete gym and spa, three lighted tennis courts.

MODERATE

CASA CODY COUNTRY INN, 175 S. Cahuilla Rd., Palm Springs, CA 92262. Tel. 619/320-9346, or toll free 800/231-2639. Fax 619/325-8610. 17 rms, 7 suites. A/C TV TEL **Directions:** From Palm Canyon Drive, turn west on Tahquitz Canyon Way and take the second left onto Cahuilla Road to the inn.

$ Rates: Mid-Dec–Apr $65–$160 single or double; May–Jun $60–$150 single or double; July–Sept $45–$105 single or double; Oct–mid-Dec $60–$150 single or double. Oct–Apr from $105 suite; May–Sept from $75 suite. Extra person $10. AE, MC, V. **Parking:** Free.

Originally built by Harriet Cody, a relative of Buffalo Bill Cody, the Casa Cody is a newly restored, very attractive inn peacefully nestled in the heart of Palm Springs at the base of the mountain. The hotel offers lovely, spacious, ground-level accommodations, most with wood-burning fireplaces and private patios. Elegant touches include saltillo tile floors, dhurri rugs, and original artwork; furnishings are in a comfortable Santa Fe style.

There are two swimming pools and a tree-shaded whirlpool spa. Services include complimentary poolside breakfasts and Saturday night wine-and-cheese parties. Arrangements can be made for nearby tennis and golf, and access to a private health spa. Complimentary bicycles are available, and the Carl Lyken mountain trailhead is located within walking distance.

ESTRELLA PARK INN, 415 S. Belardo Rd., Palm Springs, CA 92262. Tel. 619/320-4117. Fax 619/323-3303. 67 rms and cottages. A/C TV TEL **Directions:** From Palm Canyon Drive, turn west on Tahquitz Way, then left onto Belardo Road to the hotel.

$ Rates (including continental breakfast): Jan to mid-Apr $100 single or double, $140 one-bedroom cottage, $185 two-bedroom cottage; mid-Apr to May and Oct–Dec $75 single or double, $115 one-bedroom cottage, $150 two-bedroom cottage; Jun–Sept $55 single or double, $75 one-bedroom cottage, $95 two-bedroom cottage. Weekly and monthly rates available off-season, monthly rates in-season. AE, DC, DISC, MC, V. **Parking:** Free.

One of the best moderately priced establishments, Estrella Inn is located on a quiet, secluded street that seems to be miles from everywhere, even though it's just a block from the center of town. The rooms vary widely in size—from very small quarters to suites with decks, wet bars, full kitchens, and fireplaces.

There are two swimming pools and a children's pool, two Jacuzzis, and a lawn and court games area. There's no restaurant, but the inn serves a complimentary continental breakfast every morning in the lobby lounge.

INEXPENSIVE

WESTWARD HO HOTEL, 701 E. Palm Canyon Dr., Palm Springs, CA 92264. Tel. 619/320-2700, or toll free 800/854-4345 (800/472-4313 in California). Fax 619/322-5354. 208 rms. A/C TV TEL

$ Rates: Nov–May $42 single, $52 double; Jun–Oct $34 single, $46 double. AE, MC, V. **Parking:** Free.

Rooms at this pleasant, comfortable, and well-priced motel have a modified Western look. Most accommodations also have attractive Indian-print spreads, hanging cylinder lamps, upholstered chairs with casters, and dark-wood furnishings. A heated "therapy" pool for guests at the center of the complex is surrounded by comfortable lounges. There is also a small wading pool for children. During holiday periods and special events there is a two-night minimum stay, and rates are slightly higher.

One of the conveniences of the motel is that it adjoins Denny's, a coffee shop–style restaurant that's open 24 hours.

EL RANCHO LODGE, 1330 E. Palm Canyon Dr., Palm Springs, CA 92264. Tel. 619/327-1339. 19 rms. A/C TV TEL

$ Rates (including continental breakfast): June–Sept $40–$60 single or double; Oct–May $56–$80 single or double. Monthly discounts available. AE, DISC, MC, V. **Parking:** Free.

Relatively small in size, El Rancho is most popular with guests over 50, which gives it a congenial community feeling. The rooms are simple but pleasantly furnished, spacious, and nicely maintained. They are all situated around a large heated pool and spa.

Most of the rooms have one king-size bed or two twin beds. Some of the larger rooms also have full kitchens and some have two full baths—a luxury rarely found even in pricey hotels.

WHERE TO DINE

There are many attractive restaurants in Palm Springs and more in the offing, but frequently the food is not as smart as the surroundings. Some of the best restaurants in town are in hotels—notably Melvyn's at Ingleside Inn, and the Terrace Restaurant at the Hilton. Other good choices are listed below.

EXPENSIVE

ALFREDO'S, 292 E. Palm Canyon Dr. Tel. 619/320-1020. Cuisine: ITALIAN. **Reservations:** Accepted.

$ Prices: Appetizers $4–$7; main courses $15–$20. AE, DISC, MC, V.

Open: Daily 5–11pm.

The exterior of Alfredo's has always attracted me. It's simple, uncluttered, and inviting, with a forthright "Alfredo's" sign in neon script. The restaurant is just as handsome inside—dusty-rose and cream walls, with complementary maroon-and-cream furnishings, scenic lithographs, smoked mirrors, and frosted-glass art deco lamps overhead.

Appetizers include Mama's fava beans, a Sicilian-style artichoke, and mozzarella marinara—deep-fried cheese cooked with the chef's special sauce. Interesting salads range from the house's dandelion salad (yes, dandelion) to a cold seafood-and-linguine combination.

Main courses range from veal marsala or filet mignon "Alfredo style" to pizza. And the spicy chicken wings must be the best this side of Buffalo, N.Y. (Alfredo's hometown). They come in hot, medium, or mild, and are served authentically—with celery sticks and blue-cheese dip. If you thought that spaghetti and meatballs was not exactly an inspired choice for dinner, try this. Not to be ignored either is veal Alfredo—veal cutlets and eggplant in light batter, sautéed, separated with prosciutto, topped with mozzarella, then baked and finished with Alfredo's special sauce.

MODERATE

SORRENTINO'S, 1032 N. Palm Canyon Dr. Tel. 619/325-2944.

Cuisine: SEAFOOD. **Reservations:** Recommended.

$ Prices: Appetizers $3–$9; main courses $11–$30. AE, CB, DC, MC, V.

Open: Dinner, daily 5–10:30pm.

When you're in the mood for a truly fresh seafood dinner, visit Sorrentino's, undoubtedly the best seafood restaurant in town. Its Italian-American origins are reflected by the decor: green banquettes against orange walls decked with oil paintings and wrought-iron-encased fixtures.

Virtually all the fish is fresh, and when it's "fresh frozen"—more often than not the case in Palm Springs—Sorrentino's tells you so. Some of the great choices on the extensive menu include a hearty cioppino with lobster, shrimp, clams, crab, squid, and fish, served with rice; king crab legs; abalone steak; and fresh fish broiled, poached, baked, and grilled. Several Italian-style meat choices are also available, as is a special children's dinner which offers a choice of four main courses. The wine list, both domestic and imported, is limited but good. Sorrentino's has a huge bar adjacent to the main dining room, so you won't mind the inevitable wait for a table.

LYON'S ENGLISH GRILL, 233 E. Palm Canyon Dr. Tel. 619/327-1551.

Cuisine: ENGLISH/JEWISH. **Reservations:** Accepted.

$ Prices: Appetizers $3–$10; main courses $14–$20. AE, CB, DC, MC, V.

Open: Dinner, daily 4–11pm. **Closed:** July.

Lyon's English Grill has an almost theatrical woody English-pub ambience composed of stained-glass windows, old pub signs and maps, Tudor beamed walls, and heraldic banners suspended from the ceilings. Even the menus were made in England, originally for a restaurant in Hampton Court.

One of the Grill's most unusual menus combines English and Jewish specialties like steak and kidney pie, matzoh ball soup, prime rib, and chicken in the pot. Starters include shrimp scampi, sautéed mushrooms, and potato skins. Main courses run the gamut from filet mignon and barbecued ribs, to roast chicken and steak and kidney pie. Of course, since you are in California, cobb salad and fresh fish are also available.

BILLY REED'S, 1800 N. Palm Canyon Dr. Tel. 619/325-1946.

Cuisine: AMERICAN. **Reservations:** Accepted.
$ Prices: Appetizers $2–$4; main courses $8–$20. AE, CB, DC, DISC, MC, V.
Open: Daily 7am–11pm. **Closed:** Hols.

For hearty home cooking, a great selection, huge portions, and small-town ambience, you can't beat Billy Reed's. The entrance sports the characteristic Palm Springs hacienda look—small fountain, foliage, and cool patio—but the Spanish resemblance ends there. Wicker furniture graces the outer lobby, and the interior is American/Victorian, with lace curtains and Tiffany stained-glass lamp shades. Somehow it all works. And though the place is huge, the low ceilings and overhead pot-and-mug collections make it seem warm and friendly.

You can start your day here with a breakfast such as sausage and eggs served with hash browns, toast, and butter. At lunch you might order the shrimp Louis, served with garlic toast or cornbread; a delicious chicken pot pie; or a bowl of chili with cubed sirloin and beans. Among the main course options are jumbo prawns; top sirloin; fried chicken; prime rib; or broiled scallops and shrimp en brochette with bacon, mushroom caps, and onions.

INEXPENSIVE

NATE'S DELICATESSEN AND RESTAURANT, 100 S. Indian Ave. Tel. 619/325-3506.

Cuisine: JEWISH. **Reservations:** Accepted.
$ Prices: Appetizers $3–$7; main courses $6–$9. AE, CB, DC, DISC, MC, V.
Open: Daily 8am–8:30pm.

One of the really enjoyable eating experiences in Palm Springs is Nate's Delicatessen and Restaurant, also known as Mister Corned Beef of Palm Springs. Unlike its New York, Los Angeles, or San Francisco deli counterparts, Nate's looks like a well-bred restaurant, but not to worry—it has all the great aromas of a super deli.

For breakfast, there are omelets in every conceivable combination—with salami, pastrami, corned beef, chopped liver, and the like—as well as eggs with onions, lox, whitefish, and even grilled knockwurst. French toast and pancakes are also available.

At lunch, sandwich fillings are piled high onto homemade warm rye bread (or whatever bread or roll you prefer). Everything comes with a relish tray of kosher pickles and Old World sauerkraut. They have eight varieties of salad, blintzes, gefilte fish, potato pancakes, and knishes, too.

The restaurant's $11 nine-course dinner includes juice or homemade chopped liver; soup or salad; main dishes ranging from baked or fried chicken to corned beef brisket, or seafood catch of the day. An extensive à la carte menu is also available.

EL MIRASOL, 140 E. Palm Canyon Dr. Tel. 619/323-0721.
   Cuisine: MEXICAN REGIONAL. **Reservations:** Accepted.
$ **Prices:** Appetizers $4–$7; main courses $6–$11. MC, V.
   Open: Daily 11am–10pm.

A fine alternative to the better known Mexican eateries in Palm Springs, El Mirasol is a well-priced family restaurant, simply decorated with dark-wood furniture, a beautiful desert mural on one wall, and potted plants. Classic Mexican combinations include tacos, enchiladas, chiles rellenos, tostadas, and burritos; for the benefit of brunchers, egg dishes, including huevos rancheros or chorizo and eggs, are also served. But the excellence of the menu is in the many "especialidades de la casa"—whether you choose the pork chile verde cooked with green chiles and tomatillos, or opt for the well-seasoned shrimp rancheros, a special treat prepared with bell peppers, onions, olives, and tomatoes.

The chefs use only pure corn and olive oil, and prepare their guacamole without salt or mayonnaise.

LOUISE'S PANTRY, 124 S. Palm Canyon Dr. Tel. 619/ 325-5124.
   Cuisine: AMERICAN. **Reservations:** Not accepted.
$ **Prices:** Appetizers $3–$6; main courses $8–$10; lunch $5–$7. No credit cards.
   Open: Mid-Sept to mid–Jun daily 7am–9pm. **Closed:** Mid-Jun to mid-Sept.

Louise's Pantry is a real fixture on the Palm Springs eating scene. It's a small place—just 47 seats—but it packs 'em in every day and night, and with good reason. It's hard to match Louise's quality and even harder to beat the price.

This is like a real American diner; it offers burgers, sandwiches, triple-deckers, and salads. The restaurant squeezes fresh orange juice daily; grinds its own beef; and bakes the sweet rolls, cornbread, pies, and cakes on the premises. There are three to six specials each evening, plus choices from a regular list of eight entrées, such as roast beef, homemade meatloaf, grilled pork chops, New York steak, and fish and chips. Specials of the day may include lamb shanks, roast turkey, and pork tenderloin.

Louise's Pantry also serves breakfast, with all sorts of accompaniments. You can even create your own omelet from a lengthy mix-and-match list of goodies. No alcohol is served.

---

5. SANTA BARBARA

336 miles S of San Francisco; 96 miles N of Los Angeles

GETTING THERE   By Plane   Santa Barbara Municipal Airport (tel. 805/967-5608) is located in Goleta, about 10 minutes north of downtown Santa Barbara. Major airlines servicing Santa Barbara include American (tel. toll free 800/433-7300), Skywest/Delta (tel. toll free 800/453-9417), and United (tel. toll free 800/241-6522).

Walter's Limousine (tel. 805/964-7759), a share-ride taxi service, has a courtesy phone in the terminal and charges about $12 to a downtown hotel. Yellow Cab (tel. 805/965-5111) and other metered taxis line up outside the terminal and cost about $20 to a downtown hotel.

By Train Amtrak (800/USA-RAIL) offers daily service from both San Francisco and Los Angeles. Trains arrive and depart from the Santa Barbara Rail Station, 209 State St. (tel. 805/963-1015); fares can be as low as $30 to Los Angeles.

By Bus Greyhound/Trailways maintains a daily schedule into Santa Barbara from both the north and south. The central bus station is located right downtown at Carillo and Chapala Streets. America's largest long-distance coach line no longer operates a nationwide toll-free telephone number, so consult your local directory for the phone number and call for information.

By Car U.S. 101, one of the state's primary north-south roadways, which runs right through Santa Barbara, represents the fastest land route to here from anywhere. From the north, you can take Calif. 154, which meets U.S. 101 at Los Olivos and cuts across the San Marcos Pass, a scenic route into Santa Barbara.

ESSENTIALS Orientation State Street, the city's primary commercial thoroughfare, is in the geographic center of town. It ends at Stearns Wharf and Cabrillo Street; the latter runs along the ocean and separates the city's beaches from touristy hotels and restaurants.

Information The Santa Barbara Visitor Information Center, 1 Santa Barbara St., Santa Barbara, CA 93101 (tel. 805/966-9222, or toll free 800/927-4688), is on the ocean, at the corner of Cabrillo Street. This small but busy office distributes maps, literature, an events calendar, and excellent advice. Be sure to ask for their handy guide to places of interest and public parking. The office is open Monday through Saturday from 9am to 5pm, Sunday from 10am to 6pm; it closes one hour earlier in winter. A second Visitor Information Center, maintaining the same hours, is located in a storefront at 504 State St. in the heart of downtown.

Be sure to pick up a free copy of *The Independent,* a weekly listing of events, from one of the sidewalk racks around town.

Situated on a small, flat thumb of land nestled between the Santa Ynez Mountains and the Pacific Ocean, Santa Barbara's downtown area occupies a spectacular spot. Just as awesome is the town's homogeneous architecture, a Spanish-Mediterranean medley of styles, especially the ubiquitous red-tile roofs. But it wasn't always this way. Beginning in the 19th century, undistinguished buildings were erected, without any unified architectural plan, around the old Spanish mission. But then a powerful earthquake struck on June 29, 1925, virtually destroying the entire business district. Soon thereafter, an Architectural Board of Review was formed to guide the city's rebuilding. It decreed that all new buildings were to be constructed in a similar Mediterranean style—a California adobe look characterized by light-colored, sparkling stucco walls and low, sloping, terra-cotta-tile roofs.

With careful planning, Santa Barbara has become one of America's most beautiful cities; its unique beauty cannot be disguised, even on an overcast day.

WHAT TO SEE & DO

COUNTY COURTHOUSE, 1100 Anacapa St. Tel. 805/962-6464.

Occupying a full city block and set in a lush tropical garden, this courthouse is a supreme example of Santa Barbara nouveau-Spanish architecture—a tribute to bygone days when style and elegance outweighed more practical considerations. Few would guess that it was built as late as 1929. The architect, William Mooser, was assisted by his son who had lived in Spain for 17 years and was well versed in Spanish-Moorish design. Among its most impressive features are: the towers and a turret, graceful arches, unexpected windows, brilliant Tunisian tilework, a winding staircase, intricately stenciled ceilings, palatial tile floors, lacy iron grillwork, heavy wood doors, and Spanish lanterns resembling hammered iron. The magnificent historic murals by Dan Sayre Groesbeck depicting memorable episodes in Santa Barbara history are worth a visit in themselves. (The murals were done on canvas, which can be removed in case of a predicted earthquake.) A compact elevator takes visitors up to the 85-foot-high observation deck roof of the clock tower. From here visitors are treated to fine views of the ocean, mountains, and the red terra-cotta-tile roofs that cover the city.

A free guided tour is offered Wednesday and Friday at 10:30am, and Tuesday through Saturday at 2pm.

Admission: Free.

Open: Mon–Fri 8am–5pm; Sat–Sun and hols 9am–5pm.

MORETON BAY FIG TREE, Chapala Street and Montecito Street.

Famous for its massive size, Santa Barbara's best-known tree has a branch spread that would cover half a football field. It has been estimated that well over 10,000 people could stand in the tree's shade, while its roots run under more than an acre of ground. Planted in 1877, the *Figus macrophylla* is a native of Moreton Bay in eastern Australia. It is related to both the fig and rubber tree but produces neither figs nor rubber. The tree is hands-down the largest of its kind in the world. Once in danger of being leveled (for a proposed gas station) and later threatened by excavation for nearby U.S. 101, the revered tree is now the unofficial home of Santa Barbara's homeless community.

SANTA BARBARA MISSION, Laguna Street and Mission Street. Tel. 805/682-4173, or 682-4175.

Called the "Queen of the Missions" for its twin bell towers and graceful beauty, Santa Barbara's hilltop mission overlooks the town and the Channel Islands beyond. The structure's gleaming white buildings are surrounded by green lawns with

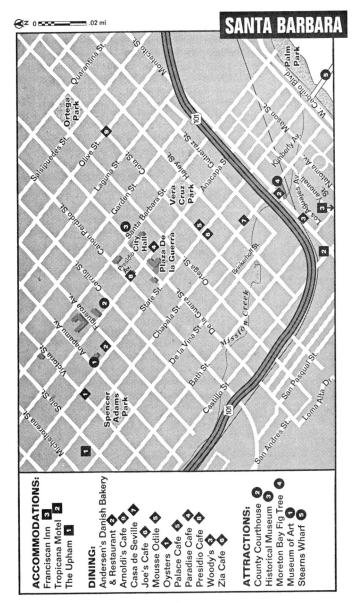

SANTA BARBARA

flowering trees and shrubs. The Santa Barbara Mission was established in 1786 and is still used by a local parish. Displayed inside are a typical missionary bedroom, 18th- and 19th-century furnishings, paintings and statues from Mexico, and period kitchen utensils, including grinding stones, baskets, and copper kettles. The museum also displays Native American tools, crafts, and artifacts.

Admission: $2 adults; children under 16, free.

Open: Daily 9am–5pm.

SANTA BARBARA MUSEUM OF NATURAL HISTORY, 2559 Puesta del Sol Rd. Tel. 805/682-4711.

Located just beyond the mission, this museum focuses on the display, study, and interpretation of Pacific Coast natural history: flora, fauna, and prehistoric life. The museum's architecture—typical Santa Barbara style—reflects early Spanish and Mexican influence, with ivy-colored stucco walls, graceful arches, arcades, and a central patio. Exhibits range from diagrams to dioramas. Native American history is emphasized, including basketry, textiles, and a full-size replica of a Chumash canoe. Other displays encompass everything from fossil ferns to the complete skeleton of a blue whale. An adjacent planetarium projects sky shows every Saturday and Sunday.

The museum store has a nice selection of books, jewelry, textiles, and handcrafted gifts.

Admission: $3 adults; $2 seniors and teens; $1 children.
Open: Mon–Sat 9am–5pm; Sun and hols 10am–5pm.

SANTA BARBARA MUSEUM OF ART, 1130 State St. Tel. 805/963-4364.

Considering the relatively small size of the community served by this museum, the Santa Barbara Museum of Art is extraordinary. From Egyptian reliefs to kinetic sculptures, there is something of interest for everyone. Top draws include Greek and Roman sculpture, representative works from the Italian Renaissance and Flemish schools; European impressionist paintings (including some by Monet and Pissarro), and works by such early-20th-century European modernists as Chagall, Hoffmann, and Kandinsky. If all that isn't enough, you'll also find a selection of American art by O'Keeffe, Eakins, Sargent, Hopper, and Grosz; as well as Asian sculpture, prints, ceramic ware, scrolls, screens, and paintings. The museum's photography collection boasts more than 1,500 items.

Most of the museum's 14,000-plus works are exhibited on a rotating basis in newly remodeled climate- and light-controlled galleries. Temporary shows usually have a local focus. Free docent-led tours are scheduled Tuesday through Sunday at 1pm. Focus tours are held on Wednesdays and Saturdays at noon.

Admission: $3 adults, $1.50 children 6–16, $2.50 seniors (over 65); free on Thurs and first Sun of each month.
Open: Tues–Wed, Fri–Sat 11am–5pm; Thurs 11am–9pm; Sun noon–5pm.

SANTA BARBARA HISTORICAL MUSEUM, 136 E. de la Guerra St. Tel. 805/966-1601.

Local lore exhibits include late-19th-century paintings of California missions by Edwin Deakin; a 16th-century carved Spanish coffer from Majorca, home of Padre Serra; and objects from the Chinese community that once flourished here, including a magnificent carved shrine from the turn of the century.

History buffs will appreciate some of the other displays, including early pieces of correspondence, antique dolls, period clothing, and assorted memorabilia. A knowledgeable docent leads a most interesting free tour every Wednesday, Saturday, and Sunday at 1:30pm.

Admission: Free, but donation requested.

Open: Tues–Fri 10am–4pm, Sat 10am–5pm, Sun noon–5pm.

SANTA BARBARA BOTANIC GARDEN, 1212 Mission Canyon Rd. Tel. 805/682-4726.

About 1½ miles north of the mission, the garden encompasses 65 acres of native trees, shrubs, cacti, and wildflowers, and more than 5 miles of trails. Docent tours are offered daily at 2pm, with additional tours on Thursday, Saturday, and Sunday at 10:30am.

Admission: $3 adults; $2 children 13–19 and seniors (over 64); $1 children 5–12; children under 5, free.

Open: Daily 8am–sunset.

STEARNS WHARF, at the end of State Street. Tel. 805/963-2633.

In addition to a small collection of shops, attractions, and restaurants, the city's 1872-vintage pier offers terrific views of the city and good drop-line fishing. The Dolphin Fountain at the foot of the wharf was created by Bud Bottoms for the city's 1982 bicentennial (copies are located in Puerto Vallarta, Mexico; Toba, Japan; and Yalta, Ukrainia).

SANTA BARBARA ZOOLOGICAL GARDENS, 500 Ninos Dr. Tel. 805/962-5339, or 962-6310 for a recording.

You can see the entire zoo, with its more than 500 animals displayed in open, naturalistic settings, in about 30 minutes. There is also a children's Discovery Area, a miniature train ride, a small carousel, a gift shop, a snack bar, and picnic areas with barbecue pits. Beautiful botanic displays augment the exhibits.

Admission: $5 adults; $3 seniors and children 2–12; children under 2, free.

Open: Jun–Aug 9am–6pm, Sept–May 10am–5pm; last admission is one hour prior to closing.

WHERE TO STAY

VERY EXPENSIVE

FOUR SEASONS BILTMORE, 1260 Channel Dr., Santa Barbara, CA 93108. Tel. 805/969-2261, or toll free 800/332-3442. Fax 805/969-4682. 234 rms, 24 suites. A/C MINIBAR TV TEL **Directions:** From U.S. 101, exit onto Olive Mill Road, which turns into Channel Drive, to the hotel.

$ Rates: $270–$350 single or double; from $555, suite; $605 cottage suite. Special midweek and package rates are available. AE, DC, MC, V. **Parking:** $10.

The most elegant hotel in town is also one of the most prestigious in California. Its beautiful 21 acres of gardens front a private ocean beach. When the Biltmore opened in 1927, a concert orchestra performed twice daily in the dining room, and separate quarters were provided for personal servants who accompanied guests. Although few people travel with servants these days, the hotel still emphasizes service.

Designed by Reginald Johnson, the hotel's award-winning Spanish architecture combines Portuguese, Basque, Iberian, and Moorish elements in a graceful blend of arcades, winding staircases, patios, and artistic walkways, with lovely hand-painted Mexican tiles and grillwork throughout. The beauty of the estate is further enhanced by imposing views of the Pacific Ocean, the Santa Ynez Mountains, and the hotel's own palm-studded formal gardens. Updated with a $16-million renovation in 1988, this refined resort hotel features deluxe accommodations with plush, Iberian-style furnishings. Many of the rooms have romantic Spanish balconies and/or fireplaces, and some have private patios. All have ceiling fans and individual climate controls, as well as terry-cloth robes and hairdryers. Cottage suites, which are set back on the property, are as private as they are elegant.

Dining/Entertainment: La Marina restaurant offers elegant dining and a select list of California-inspired specialties such as seared salmon with orzo pasta, and sweetbreads with yellow beans and crisp potato cakes. The Patio, a glass-enclosed atrium, is more casual, serving breakfast, lunch, dinner, and Sunday brunch. La Sala lounge is a beautifully plush room serving afternoon tea and evening cocktails. There's live piano music nightly.

Services: Concierge, 24-hour room service, evening turndown, overnight shoeshine, exercise classes, complimentary bicycle rental, video library, and special programs for children.

Facilities: Three lighted tennis courts, two swimming pools, putting green, shuffleboard and croquet courts, beachfront cabanas, sun deck, beauty salon, and gift shop.

SAN YSIDRO RANCH, 900 San Ysidro Lane (off U.S. 101), Montecito, CA 93108. Tel. 805/969-5046, or toll free 800/368-6788. Fax 805/565-1995. 45 cottages, 26 suites. MINIBAR TV TEL **Directions:** From U.S. 101, take the San Ysidro Lane exit and turn toward the mountains. Follow the road for about 2 miles to the ranch.

$ Rates: $195–$225 double; $300–$325 cottage room; from $350, suite. Extra person $15. AE, MC, V.

Santa Barbara's most famous hotel, nestled far from town in the Santa Ynez Mountains, San Ysidro was originally part of a Spanish land grant on which mission padres raised cattle. It opened as a guest ranch in 1893. Oranges from the orange groves still on the property are used for fresh-squeezed juice each morning. Over the years, Winston Churchill, Sinclair Lewis, Rex Harrison, Groucho Marx, and Sidney Poitier have signed the register at this quiet, beautifully landscaped 540-acre retreat. Robert and Ethel Kennedy honeymooned here.

The rooms are decorated with charming country-inn-style antique furnishings. All have fireplaces, and during the day a woodman makes the rounds with wood and kindling. Fresh-cut flowers from the garden enliven every room. Most accommodations have porches so guests can sit outside and enjoy the view. The cottages are secluded, hidden behind lush foliage and flowers. Thirteen units have Jacuzzis, and some suites have private hot tubs.

Dining/Entertainment: The Stonehouse restaurant, in the old citrus-packing house, is a charming candlelit dining room with a beamed ceiling, shuttered windows, antique furnishings, and paintings of local landmarks adorning the white sandstone walls. A delightful and airy glass-enclosed café area adjoins, its view of the grounds enhanced by many hanging plants inside. The Plow and Angel bar is a good place for drinks. It draws a local crowd and features live music on the weekends.

Services: Room service, concierge.

Facilities: Two tennis courts, swimming pool, riding stables, badminton, croquet, and hiking and riding trails.

EXPENSIVE

THE UPHAM, 1404 De La Vina St., Santa Barbara, CA 93101. Tel. 805/962-0058, or toll free 800/727-0876. Fax 805/963-2825. 49 rms, 3 suites. TV TEL **Directions:** From U.S. 101, exit at Mission Street and turn right onto De La Vina Street. The hotel is 6 blocks ahead at Sola Street.

$ Rates (including continental breakfast): $95–$185 single or double; from $200, suite. Additional person $10. AE, CB, DC, DISC, MC, V.

Established in 1871, The Upham, located right in the heart of town just two blocks from State Street, is one of the oldest and most charming hotels in Santa Barbara. Built by Amasa Lyman Lincoln, a Boston banker, The Upham's bed-and-breakfast design is reminiscent of an old-fashioned New England boarding house. A two-story clapboard structure, it has wide eaves and is topped by a glassed-in cupola and a widow's walk that faces the sea.

Fronted by a pair of immense ivy-entwined palms, the entrance is through a large colonnaded porch surrounded by a well-tended garden with neat flowerbeds. Refurbished in 1983, guest rooms are outfitted with antique armoires, brass or four-poster beds, and pretty pillow shams. Many rooms have private porches and fireplaces. The Master Suite features a fireplace, Jacuzzi, private yard, and king-size bed.

Complimentary wine, cheese, and crackers are served in the lobby and garden each afternoon. Louie's at The Upham, a cozy restaurant, is open for lunch and dinner.

MODERATE

BATH STREET INN, 1720 Bath St., Santa Barbara, CA 93101. Tel. 805/682-9680, or toll free 800/788-BATH (800/549-BATH in California). 8 rms. **Directions:** From U.S. 101, exit at Mission Street and turn right on De La Vina, then right on Valerio, and right again onto Bath Street.

$ Rates (including breakfast): $85–$115 single or double. AE, MC, V.

This handsome Victorian inn was built more than 100 years ago. The historic residence has two unusual features—a semicircular "eyelid" balcony and a hipped roof, unique even for Santa Barbara. The century-old trees, the flower-filled patio with white wicker furniture, the brick courtyard, and the graciousness of the innkeepers are all part of the inn's charm.

The living room is the hearth of this home, comfortable and inviting, with a fireplace, oriental rug, period prints, and fresh flowers. The dining area has a traditional blue-and-white floral-print wallpaper that complements the finely crafted woodwork and furnishings.

Each individually decorated room has its own special charm. One features a king-size canopied bed, from another under the eaves you can enjoy superb sunsets from a private balcony. Guests enjoy complimentary evening refreshments, and access to the inn's bicycles. Pets are not accepted, and no smoking is allowed in the house.

BEST WESTERN ENCINA LODGE, 2220 Bath St., Santa Barbara, CA 93105. Tel. 805/682-7277, or toll free 800/526-2262. Fax 805/563-9319. 121 rms, 38 suites. A/C TV TEL **Directions:** From U.S. 101, exit at Mission Street and turn left onto Bath Street. The hotel is 2 blocks ahead at Los Olivos Street.

$ Rates: $92–$94 single; $96–$126 double. AE, CB, DC, MC, V.
Set in a quiet residential area, this hotel is a short walk from the mission and a mere five-minute drive from the beach. All rooms are immaculate and tastefully decorated. Soft goods—furnishings, bedspreads, rugs—all look spanking new. Second-floor accommodations in the old building, outfitted with beamed raw-pine ceilings, are best. All rooms come with coffee-makers, hairdryers, fresh fruit, candies, and cookies. Old-wing rooms have showers only; the rest have tub/shower combinations and dressing rooms.

Facilities include a swimming pool, whirlpool, sauna, lobby shop, beauty parlor, and barbershop. There is also a complimentary limousine service to downtown locations. The ever changing menu in the hotel restaurant might feature sweet-and-sour chicken, barbecued ribs, and crab Mornay.

MIRAMAR HOTEL-RESORT, 1555 S. Jameson Lane (P.O. Box 429), Montecito, CA 93102. Tel. 805/969-2203. Fax 805/969-3163. 200 rms. A/C TV TEL **Directions:** From U.S. 101, take the San Ysidro exit and turn toward the ocean; Jameson Lane parallels the freeway right near the overpass.

$ Rates: $70–$135 single or double; from $130, cottage suite. AE, MC, V.
The Miramar's blue-roofed cottages, which can be seen from U.S. 101, have long been a famous Santa Barbara landmark. Actually located in Montecito, a ritzy area just south of Santa Barbara, the hotel dates from 1887, when the Doulton family began to augment their meager farm income by taking in paying guests. When a railroad was built, the property was split in two. The Miramar became an important rail station when affluent guests began arriving in their own private railroad cars. As the popularity of beach and ocean vacations grew, the hotel became a very chic place to stay.

The modern Miramar is set on 14 garden acres overlooking the Pacific Ocean. Guest room furnishings are indifferent at best, but accommodations are quite comfortable. The best rooms are those with peaked raw-wood ceilings facing the pool on the second floor. Some of the attractive, homey cottages have fully equipped kitchens.

Facilities include two swimming pools, four tennis courts, a paddle-tennis court, 500 feet of private sandy beach, saunas, exercise rooms, a Jacuzzi, bike rental, and table tennis. Golf and horseback riding can be arranged. The dated Terrace Dining Room, filled with potted palms, is open for breakfast, lunch, and dinner. Sandwiches, salads, steaks, and seafood are featured. There's live music Tuesday through Saturday nights in the adjoining Santa Fe-Amtrak Railcar Diner.

INEXPENSIVE

FRANCISCAN INN, 109 Bath St., Santa Barbara, CA 93101. Tel. 805/963-8845. Fax 805/564-3295. 53 rms, 25 suites. TV TEL **Directions:** From U.S. 101, take the Castillo Street exit and turn toward the water; turn left onto Mason Street and drive 1 block to the hotel.
$ Rates (including continental breakfast): $65–$80 single or double; from $100, suite. AE, CB, DC, MC, V.

This excellent choice is just off Cabrillo Boulevard, one short block from the marina and beach. Each individually decorated room is airy, comfortable, and spacious; most have ceiling fans. Bathrooms come stocked with thick, fluffy towels. Several rooms have fully equipped kitchenettes. Suites are split-level, complete with a living room, a separate kitchen, and sleeping quarters that can accommodate up to four adults. One suite also has a fireplace.

Breakfast is served in the comfortable lobby. The inn is just steps away from several restaurants for other meals. There's also a heated swimming pool, Jacuzzi, and coin-operated laundry; complimentary newspapers are distributed every morning. Reservations should be made well in advance, especially for the period May through September.

TROPICANA MOTEL, 223 Castillo St., Santa Barbara, CA 93101. Tel. 805/966-2219, or toll free 800/468-1988. Fax 805/962-9428. 31 rms, 16 suites. TV TEL **Directions:** From U.S. 101, exit at Castillo Street and turn toward the water. The hotel is 2 blocks ahead between Montecito and Yanonali Streets.
$ Rates (including continental breakfast): $65–$85 single; $65–$99 double; $95–$160 suite. Extra person $5. AE, DISC, MC, V.

This newly renovated pink stucco structure is just a short walk from the beach. The rooms are homey, attractive, and equipped with AM/FM radios and refrigerators. The suites, which have a large bedroom and living room, accommodate up to eight adults. They also have large eat-in kitchens that are fully equipped with ovens, full-size refrigerators, toasters, and even eggbeaters and potholders. Suites can be economical if you use them to do your own cooking. Facilities include a heated pool and Jacuzzi, both of which are away from the street and very private, with lots of room for sunning. No smoking is allowed in any of the rooms.

MOTEL 6, 443 Corona del Mar, Santa Barbara, CA 93103. Tel. 805/564-1392. 52 rms. TV TEL **Directions:** From U.S. 101, exit at Milpas Street and head toward the ocean. Turn left, drive 1 short block, then turn left again onto Corona del Mar.
$ Rates: $40 single; $46 double. Extra adult $7. AE, DISC, MC, V.
Inexpensive, clean accommodations near the beach are not easy to

find, but this basic motel fits the bill. There's a small, heated swimming pool and cable color TVs; local phone calls are free. Be sure to reserve far in advance since this motel books up quickly.

MOTEL 6, 3505 State St. Santa Barbara, CA 93105. Tel. 805/687-5400. 60 rms. TV TEL **Directions:** From U.S. 101, exit at Mission Street and turn left onto State Street. The motel is about 1 mile ahead, between Las Positas and Hitchcock Way.

$ Rates: $39 single; $45 double. Extra adult $6. AE, CB, DC, DISC, MC, V.

On "upper" State Street, this property's location is not as desirable as those by the beach. But it is nice, featuring a large pool, and there is plentiful shopping nearby.

MOUNTAIN VIEW INN, 3055 De La Vina St., Santa Barbara, CA 93105. Tel. 805/687-6636. 34 rms. TV TEL **Directions:** From U.S. 101, exit at Mission Street, turn toward the hills, and left onto State Street. The hotel is located about 10 blocks ahead, at the corner of State and De La Vina Streets.

$ Rates (including continental breakfast): Oct–May $40–$50 single, $46–$74 double; Jun–Aug $55–$65 single, $59–$87 double. AE, DISC, MC, V.

Although it occupies a busy street corner, close to shops, sights, and restaurants, this well-priced inn maintains a hometown bed-and-breakfast atmosphere. Each room is individually decorated—some with lace tablecloths and ruffled pillow shams and matching comforters. Accommodations are bright and cheery, and are outfitted with both niceties (fresh flowers) and necessities (small refrigerators). The inn surrounds a large, heated swimming pool, and is adjacent to a small park, complete with a children's playground.

Coffee, tea, fresh juice, and croissants are served each morning in the lobby.

SANDPIPER LODGE, 3525 State St., Santa Barbara, CA 93105. Tel. 805/687-5326. Fax 805/687-2271. 75 rms. TV TEL **Directions:** From U.S. 101, take the Las Positas exit and turn toward the mountains. Turn left onto State Street and look for the motel on your left.

$ Rates: Oct–Jun $48–$58 single or double, $53–$63 triple; July–Aug $58–$68 single or double, $63–$73 triple. Weekly and monthly rates available. AE, CB, DC, MC, V.

Modest accommodations at low rates make this small hotel one of Santa Barbara's best buys. Nothing's fancy here, but the rooms are clean and tastefully (if sparsely) decorated. The lodge's "upper" State Street location means you'll have to drive to the beach and downtown shopping areas, but both are just 10 minutes away.

Coffee and tea are available all day, and some rooms include small refrigerators. There is also a swimming pool on the premises.

WHERE TO DINE

MODERATE

ARNOLDI'S CAFE, 600 Olive St. Tel. 805/962-5394.
Cuisine: ITALIAN. **Reservations:** Accepted. **Directions:**

From Stearns Wharf, drive up State Street and turn right onto Cota Street, 3 blocks past the U.S. 101 underpass. The restaurant is 5 blocks ahead on Olive Street.

$ Prices: Main courses $8–$14. No credit cards.

Open: Dinner, Thurs–Tues 5–11pm.

Serving straightforward, authentic Italian cuisine for more than 40 years, Arnoldi's offers fresh-cut steaks, homemade soups, and pastas like ravioli, spaghetti, and lasagna. Portions are huge, and most dinners include soup, salad, spaghetti or potatoes, and coffee.

This is not a fancy place. Candlelit tables are covered with red-and-white-checked tablecloths, while three enclosed mahogany booths up front provide intimate dining. The jukebox is full of wonderful old Italian songs like Mario Lanza's "Be My Love"; a TV over the bar is always tuned to sporting events; and old-timers play boccie ball in the court out back. A mural in the back room depicts the mountains of Lake Como, the former home of Arnoldi's owners.

BROPHY BROS. CLAM BAR & RESTAURANT, yacht basin and marina. Tel. 805/966-4418.

Cuisine: SEAFOOD. **Reservations:** Not accepted. **Directions:** From Stearns Wharf, drive west on Cabrillo Boulevard past the Castillo Street traffic light. Turn left at the second light, which is Harbor Way. Brophy Bros. is a short walk along the yacht basin, on the second floor of the small light-gray building ahead on your right.

$ Prices: Appetizers $5.50–$9.50; main courses $12–$16. AE, MC, V.

Open: Sun–Thurs 11am–10pm; Fri–Sat 11am–11pm.

I am reluctant to tell even more people about one of my favorite restaurants in Santa Barbara. First-class seafood is served in beautiful surroundings that overlook the city's lovely marina from a second-floor location. The restaurant is a fun, friendly, noisy, convivial mix of locals and tourists almost every night of the week. Dress is casual; service is excellent; and it's hard to beat the view of fishing boats, sailboats, and power launches. There are fewer than 24 tables, and about 10 seats at an open oyster bar. Most of the chairs are usually occupied, and the wait on a weekend night can be up to two hours.

Portions are huge, and everything on the menu is good. Favorites include New England clam chowder, cioppino (California fish stew), and any one of an assortment of seafood salads. The scampi is consistently good, as are the tuna, shark, swordfish, salmon, and all fresh fish. A nice assortment of beers and wines is available.

CASA DE SEVILLA, 428 Chapala St. Tel. 805/966-4370.

Cuisine: SPANISH. **Reservations:** Accepted. **Directions:** From Stearns Wharf, drive up State Street and turn left on Gutierrez Street, 1 block past the U.S. 101 underpass. Turn right onto Chapala Street.

$ Prices: Appetizers $4–$12; main courses $14–$23. AE, CB, DC, MC, V.

Open: Lunch, Tues–Sat noon–2pm; dinner, Tues–Sat 6–10pm.

Reputedly the oldest restaurant in Santa Barbara, this has been a local favorite for more than half a century. The restaurant is divided into several dining areas; I particularly like the front room with its wood-burning fireplace and sloped beamed ceiling. The ambience is warm and intimate, with shuttered windows, brass candle lamps on every table, and graceful chandeliers. Liberal use of sienna (drapes, walls, and carpeting) and antique bullfight posters complete the Spanish look. Men must wear jackets in the evening.

The recipes used here are really "old family secrets," handed down through generations and brought here from Spain. The menu is the same at lunch and dinner. You might begin with an appetizer of chili con queso (cheese), guacamole, or lobster cocktail. There are many barbecued main dishes such as salmon, filet mignon, and spareribs. Besides the entrée, a full Casa dinner will include Castilian soup (garbanzo purée), salad, relishes, chili con queso, rice or potato, dessert, and beverage.

JOE'S CAFE, 536 State St. Tel. 805/966-4638.

Cuisine: AMERICAN. **Reservations:** Recommended, but not accepted Sat. **Directions:** From Stearns Wharf, drive up State Street; the restaurant is on your right at Cota Street.

$ Prices: Appetizers $2–$5; main courses $7–$15. AE, MC, V.
Open: Mon–Sat 11am–11:30pm, Sun 4–11:30pm.

One of downtown's longest lived institutions, Joe's has been offering good home-cooking since 1928. It's Thanksgiving every night here, as the kitchen turns out plate after plate of turkey, mashed potatoes, cranberry sauce, and stuffing. Rainbow trout, home-style fried chicken, and hefty 12-ounce charbroiled steaks are also available. The ravioli is terrible, but addicting. Meals are prepared by chefs in big white hats working in an open kitchen behind the long bar.

The decor is as down-home as the food; red-and-white-checked tablecloths, captain's chairs, mounted hunting trophies, and photos of old Santa Barbara on the walls. There are no desserts on the menu. "We give them enough starch without it," explains the owner.

MOUSSE ODILE, 18 E. Cota St. Tel. 805/962-5393.

Cuisine: FRENCH. **Reservations:** Accepted. **Directions:** From Stearns Wharf, drive up State Street and turn right onto Cota Street, 3 blocks past the U.S. 101 underpass.

$ Prices: Breakfast $4–$6; appetizers $4–$6.25; main courses $13.25–$17; lunch $4.25–$9.79. AE, MC, V.
Open: Breakfast, Mon–Sat 8–11:30am; lunch, Mon–Sat 11:30am–2:30pm; dinner, Mon–Thurs 5:30–9pm, Fri–Sat 5:30–9:30pm.

The restaurant's brasserie side, nicely outfitted with oak flooring, red-and-blue-checked tablecloths, and fresh flowers, is the setting for breakfast and lunch. It's not fancy, though it does have a pleasant, simple French provincial air. There's a bar along one wall, and a refrigerated case and counter to the rear.

Breakfast choices include: various quiches, waffles with crème anglaise (a delicious light custard sauce), and a variety of omelets served with French bread, applesauce, and potatoes au gratin. Most *specialités de la maison* are also served with fresh fruit—slices of banana, orange, and strawberries. Giant croissants can be ordered separately, along with one of the best cups of French roast coffee you've ever had. The lunch menu includes: cold pasta salad with smoked salmon and peas, and foot-long Parisian sandwiches of roast lamb or chicken and white veal sausage.

The simple, somewhat formal adjoining dining room opens in the evening for dinner. The wood-and-window interior is illuminated by art deco lamps and brightened with green plants, fresh flowers, and candles on every table. Leg of lamb, roasted with garlic and herbs, is especially recommended. Other offerings might include Norwegian salmon poached in champagne and port wine, or filet mignon with pepper sauce and cognac. Appetizers include julienned celery root in mustard sauce, and marinated mussels or warm smoked salmon with pasta, caviar, and chives. There is no bar, but a nice selection of California and French wines is available. By the way, save room for dessert; mousse is the restaurant's specialty.

OYSTERS, Victoria Court, 9 W. Victoria St. Tel. 805/962-9888.

Cuisine: CALIFORNIA. **Reservations:** Recommended. **Directions:** From Stearns Wharf, drive up State Street and turn left onto Victoria Street, 10 blocks past the U.S. 101 underpass; the restaurant is immediately on your left.

$ Prices: Appetizers $4–$8; main courses: dinner $8–$17, lunch $6–$10.

Open: Lunch, Mon–Sat 11:30am–2:30pm; dinner, daily 5–10pm.

Hidden behind lush bushes near the corner of State Street, Oysters' small, oddly shaped, window-wrapped dining room provides some of the best food in the city. Despite its name, the restaurant is not a shellfish bar; it's a select sampling of California cuisine offered by Jerry and Laurie Wilson, a brother and sister team. Still, oyster appetizers are on the menu: grilled with cilantro butter, chopped into corn fritters, and stewed with spinach and shallots. Pasta, chicken, and veal entrées are also available, but the best ones are usually the daily fresh market specials like poached trout with salmon mousse, or saffron rice with Cajun sausage, lobster, and scallops. Desserts here are predictably decadent, but even the richest looking chocolate torte should be passed up for the restaurant's home-churned ice cream.

PALACE CAFE, 8 E. Cota St. Tel. 805/966-3133.

Cuisine: CAJUN/CREOLE/CARIBBEAN. **Reservations:** Recommended. **Directions:** From Stearns Wharf, drive up State Street and turn right onto Cota Street, 3 blocks past the U.S. 101 underpass.

$ Prices: Appetizers $3.50–$8.50; main courses $12–$22. AE, MC, V.

Open: Dinner, Sun–Thurs 5:30–10pm, Fri–Sat 5:30–11pm.

One of the best Cajun restaurants in southern California, Palace Cafe enlarged its reputation when it became a regular stop for the press corps that followed President Reagan to his nearby ranch. Busy, relaxed, and fun, this is no place for a couple looking for a quiet, romantic hideaway. The café is divided into two rooms: hot pink on the left and cool cream on the right. High ceilings, overhead fans, wood tables, bentwood chairs, posters, paintings, and murals create a Cajun look, while wine racks and street lamps provide a French accent. The tables are furnished with a huge bottle of McIlhenny Company Tabasco sauce and topped with an assortment of hot muffins, including molasses-jalapeño. Favorite starters: Cajun popcorn (Louisiana crayfish tails dipped in a cornmeal-buttermilk batter and flash-fried), and the Bahamian conch chowder, served with a pony of sherry. Main courses emphasize seafood. Louisiana barbecue shrimp are sautéed with three-pepper butter and served with white rice. An assortment of blackened fish and filet mignon are served with a side of browned garlic butter. Rabbit is sometimes available, as is veal flambéed with sherry and finished with an oyster-sherry cream sauce. Although it's not on the menu, vegetarians should ask for the vegetable platter; it's terrific. For dessert, the tart, tasty Key Lime pie is unusualy good. There is a decent choice of beer and wine, but the Cajun martinis are the house specialty—an icy concoction of vodka and vermouth marinated with jalepeño peppers (limit: one per customer).

PIATTI'S RISTORANTE, 516 San Ysidro Rd. Tel. 805/ 969-7520.
Cuisine: ITALIAN. **Reservations:** Recommended. **Directions:** From Stearns Wharf, take Cabrillo Boulevard east to U.S. 101. Exit at San Ysidro Road and follow it toward the mountains about half a mile to the restaurant.
$ Prices: Appetizers $4–$8; main courses $8–$18. AE, MC, V.
Open: Mon–Thurs 11:30am–10pm, Fri 11:30am–11pm, Sat noon–11pm, Sun 10am–10pm.

One of the area's best Italian restaurants is located 10 minutes south of downtown Santa Barbara, in the exclusive residential hideaway of Montecito. During warm weather, the best seats are at the faux-marble-topped tables set under handsome cream-colored umbrellas on the outdoor patio.

The spacious interior is airy, comfortable, and relaxed. Everything is attractive here, from the small bar to the exhibition kitchen, to the upscale good-looking clientele. The dining room has a polished country look, complete with pine sideboards, wall murals, and terra-cotta tile floors.

Exceptional appetizers include eggplant rolled with goat cheese, fresh sweetbreads with porcini mushrooms, and homemade truffle and eggplant ravioli. Featured main dishes include pasta dumplings with cabbage, pancetta, Fontina cheese, garlic, and butter; and lasagna al pesto—with layers of fresh tomato pasta, pesto, grilled zucchini, sun-dried tomatoes, pinenuts, and cheeses. Both are rich but delicious. A specialty of the house is zuppa di pesce, seasonal fresh fish and shellfish cooked in a light tomato broth and served with garlic toast.

There is an excellent selection of California wines, with a few Italian labels sprinkled about. Many are available by the glass. There's also a full bar.

PARADISE CAFE, 702 Anacapa St. Tel. 805/962-4416.
Cuisine: AMERICAN. **Reservations:** Accepted for large

parties. **Directions:** From Stearns Wharf, drive up State Street
and turn right onto Ortega Street, 5 blocks past the U.S. 101
underpass. The restaurant is located 1 block from State Street on
the corner of Ortega and Anacapa Streets.

$ Prices: Breakfast $4–$6; appetizers $4–$7; main courses $6–
$17; lunch $5–$8; AE, MC, V.

Open: Mon–Sat 11am–11pm, Sun 8:30am–11pm.

White linen tablecloths and blond wood floors give this converted
home a relaxed elegance that seems like quintessential Santa Barbara.
The most coveted seats, however, are outside, on the open brick patio
behind tall hedges and colorful wildflowers.

Excellent salmon, swordfish, half-pound burgers, and 22-ounce
T-bone steaks are prepared on an open oak grill. Devoid of heavy
sauces, meals here are consistently fresh and simple. Paradise Pie, an
extremely decadent chocolate dessert is an absolute must.

The downstairs bar, well known for strong drinks, is especially
popular with the local thirty-something crowd.

PRESIDIO CAFE, 812 Anacapa St. Tel. 805/966-2428.

Cuisine: CALIFORNIA. **Reservations:** Recommended at lunch
and dinner. **Directions:** From Stearns Wharf, drive up State
Street and turn right onto Canon Perdido Street, 6 blocks past the
U.S. 101 underpass. Turn right onto Anacapa Street; the restaurant is located immediately on your right.

$ Prices: Breakfast $6–$8; appetizers $4–$8; main courses $8–
$14; lunch $6–$8. MC, V.

Open: Daily 8am–3pm; dinner Tues–Sat 5–9pm.

Presidio Cafe actually occupies a portion of Santa Barbara's old
fortress, or presidio. Breakfast or lunch on a sunny day is best, when
you can dine out on the patio, under an umbrella, around the pretty,
splashing fountain. Inside it is more elegant—white-clothed tables
overlook the garden terrace through a wall of windows.

Unfortunately, the food here does not match the wonderful
atmosphere. The breakfast menu offers mostly omelets, muffins, and
croissants, while leisurely lunches include quiches, crepes, salads,
sandwiches, and the Presidio's specialty—tortilla soup. Dinner
choices include bacon-wrapped shrimp and Spanish chicken—a
sautéed breast seasoned with garlic, cilantro, tomatoes, green onions,
and white wine. Main dishes are served with sautéed vegetables, rice
pilaf, and the Presidio's own special French bread. There's a full bar.

YOUR PLACE, 22A N. Milpas St. Tel. 805/966-5151.

Cuisine: THAI. **Reservations:** Recommended. **Directions:**
From Stearns Wharf, take Cabrillo Boulevard east and turn left
onto Milpas Street. The restaurant is about 1 mile ahead on your
right at Mason Street.

$ Prices: Appetizers $3–$7; main courses $5–$13. AE, DC, MC,
V.

Open: Tues–Thurs, Sun 11am–10pm, Fri–Sat 11am–11pm.

There are an unusually large number of Thai restaurants in Santa
Barbara, but when locals argue about which one is best, Your Place
invariably ranks high on the list. In addition to a tank of exotic fish,
carved screens, and a serene Buddha, the restaurant's decor includes
an impressive array of framed blowups of restaurant reviews.

Traditional dishes are prepared with absolutely fresh ingredients and represent a veritable cross-section of Thai cuisine. There are more than 100 menu listings, including lemongrass soups, spicy salads, coconut curries, meat and seafood main dishes, and a variety of noodles. It's best to begin with soup, ladled out of a hotpot tableside, and enough for two or more. Tom kah kai, a hot-and-sour chicken soup with coconut milk and mushrooms, is excellent. Siamese duckling, a top main dish, is prepared with sautéed vegetables, mushrooms, and ginger sauce. Like other dishes, it can be made mild, medium, hot, or very hot, according to your preference. The restaurant serves wine, sake, beer, and a variety of nonalcoholic drinks, including hot ginger tea.

ZIA CAFE, 532 State St. Tel. 805/962-5391.
   Cuisine: AMERICAN SOUTHWEST. **Reservations:** Not accepted. **Directions:** From Stearns Wharf, continue 5 blocks straight up State Street.
$ **Prices:** Main courses $6–$10. MC, V.
   Open: Mon–Thurs 11am–10pm, Fri 11am–1am, Sat 8am–1am.
   New Mexican–style Zia Cafe is the culinary child of Santa Fe natives Douglas and Jane Scott. It's a great place, and one of the few eateries in town serving late weekend dinners. Sand-colored walls, light-wood chairs, desert prints, and the requisite hang-dried chilies adorn the dining rooms, which occupy two levels overlooking the city's main shopping street.
   Zia's enchiladas, burritos, and tamales may sound familiar, but there's nothing commonplace about any of these house specialties. Served with red or green chile, enchiladas are layered with chicken and sour cream and served with blue-corn tortillas and guacamole. The chiles rellenos are a pair of green-chile peppers stuffed with cheese and piñon nuts, dipped in batter, and deep fried. Every chicken dish comes with a large portion of hot breast meat, enough to satisfy the appetite of the most voracious diner.
   For an excellent and unusual breakfast, try huevos rancheros—blue-corn tortillas topped with two fried eggs and your choice of red or green chile. I always opt for the green chile myself—Zia Cafe serves the best kind, which is found along the southern Rio Grande. Beer and wine are available by the glass or the pitcher.

INEXPENSIVE

ANDERSEN'S DANISH BAKERY AND RESTAURANT, 1106 State St. Tel. 805/962-5085.
   Cuisine: DANISH. **Reservations:** Accepted. **Directions:** From Stearns Wharf, drive up State Street. The restaurant is on your right, near Figueroa Street.
$ **Prices:** Breakfast $4–$9; lunch $5–$10. No credit cards.
   Open: Mon–Sat 8am–6pm; Sun 9am–6pm.
Only tourists eat here, but this small place is eminently suited to people-watching or reading the day's paper. You'll spot it by the red-and-white Amstel umbrellas protecting the outside diners seated on wrought-iron garden chairs. Even mid-November can be warm enough to eat outdoors at 9am.

The food is both good and well presented. Portions are substantial and the coffee is outstanding. A set breakfast includes eggs, bacon, cheese, fruit, homemade jam, and fresh baked bread. Fresh fruit is also available.

For lunch, try soup and a sandwich, or liver pâté and quiche. Vegetarians can opt for an omelet with Danish Havarti cheese, a vegetable sandwich, or a cheese plate with fruit. Fresh fish and smoked Scottish salmon are also usually available. A daily changing selection of European dishes may include Hungarian goulash, frikadeller (Danish meatballs), schnitzel, duckling, chicken with caper sauce, Danish meatloaf, and roast turkey with caramel sautéed potatoes. But if you yearn for smörgåsbord, Andersen's is a first-rate choice. Wine is available by the bottle or glass; beer is also served.

LA SUPER-RICA TAQUERIA, 622 N. Milpas St. Tel. 805/963-4940.

Cuisine: MEXICAN. **Reservations:** Not accepted. **Directions:** From Stearns Wharf, take Cabrillo Boulevard east and turn left onto Milpas Street. The restaurant is about 2 miles ahead on your right between Cota and Ortega Streets.

$ Prices: Main courses $3–$6. No credit cards.

Open: Daily 11am–9pm.

Following celebrity chef Julia Child's lead, several south coast aficionados have deemed this place the best Mexican restaurant in California. The food is good but somewhat overrated. Excellent soft tacos are the restaurant's real forte; filled with any combination of chicken, beef, cheese, cilantro, and spices, they make a good meal. My primary complaint about this restaurant is that the portions are quite small; you have to order two or even three items in order to satisfy average hunger.

There's nothing grand about La Super-Rica except the food. The plates are paper, the cups Styrofoam, and the forks plastic. Unadorned wooden tables and plastic chairs are arranged under an unappealing tent; you might want to order your food "to go" and then have your meal on a pretty beachside bench.

WOODY'S, 229 W. Montecito St. Tel. 805/963-9326.

Cuisine: AMERICAN BARBECUE. **Reservations:** Not accepted. **Directions:** From Stearns Wharf, go 1 block west on Cabrillo Boulevard, turn right onto Chapala Street, then left onto Montecito Street.

$ Prices: Appetizers $2–$5; main courses $4–$12. MC, V.

Open: Mon–Sat 11am–11pm, Sun 11am–10pm.

This place is woody, all right—sort of "early cowpoke," with real wood paneling, post-and-beam construction, wood booths, and wood-plank floors. Order at the counter just inside the door, have a seat, and wait for your number to be called. Barbecued chicken and ribs head the short menu. A variety of burgers, chili by the bowl, and French fries round out the offerings. Woody's home-smoked meats smothered in sauce might not be the best barbecue in the world, but it is easily the best in town. Children's portions are also available. Popular with fraternity types, Woody's sells beer by the glass, jug, bucket, or bottle.

A second Woody's is located in nearby Goleta, at 5112 Hollister Ave. (tel. 805/967-3775).

SPORTS & RECREATION

One of the best things about Santa Barbara is the accessibility of almost every sport known to humankind, from mountain hiking to ocean kayaking. This is the southern California of the movies, where windsurfing and bunjee jumping are everyday activities. Pick up a free copy of "Things to See and Do" at the Santa Barbara Visitor Information Center, 1 Santa Barbara St., Santa Barbara, CA 93101 (tel. 805/966-9222, or toll free 800/927-4688).

BICYCLING

A relatively flat, 4-mile palm-lined coastal pathway runs along the beach and is perfect for biking. More adventurous riders can peddle through town, up to the mission, or to Montecito, the next town over. Beach rentals, 8 W. Cabrillo Blvd. (tel. 805/963-2524), at State Street, rents well-maintained one- and ten-speeds. They also have tandem bikes and surrey cycles that can hold as many as four adults and two children. Rates vary depending on equipment. Bring an I.D. (driver's license or passport) to expedite your rental. They are open daily from 8am to dusk.

GOLF

SANTA BARBARA GOLF CLUB, 3500 McCaw Ave., at Las Positas Road. Tel. 805/687-7087.

The 18-hole course is 6,009 yards and encompasses a driving range. The golf shop and other nonplaying facilities were reconstructed and refurbished early in 1989. Unlike many municipal courses, the Santa Barbara Community Course is well maintained and has been designed to present a moderate challenge for the average golfer. Greens fees are $17 Monday through Friday, $19 Saturday and Sunday; seniors pay $12 weekdays, $16 weekends. Optional carts cost $18.

SANDPIPER, 7925 Hollister Ave. Tel. 805/968-1541.

An 18-hole, 7,000-yard course, the Sandpiper, a pretty nice course, has a pro shop and driving range, plus a pleasant coffee shop. Greens fees are $45 Monday through Friday, $65 Saturday and Sunday. Carts cost $22.

HIKING

The hills and mountains surrounding Santa Barbara have excellent hiking trails. One of my favorites begins at the end of Mission Canyon Drive. Take Mission Canyon Road past the mission, turn right onto Foothill Road, and take the first left onto Mission Canyon Drive. Park at the end (where all the other cars are) and hike up. At the Santa

Barbara Visitor Information Center purchase a trail map for other trail information.

HORSEBACK RIDING

Several area stables rent horses, including San Ysidro Ranch Stables, 900 San Ysidro Lane (tel. 805/969-5046, ext. 307). They charge $35 for a one-hour guided trail ride; reservations are essential.

POWER BOATING & SAILING

Sailing Center of Santa Barbara, at the Santa Barbara Breakwater (tel. 805/962-2826), rents 40 horsepower boats and sailboats ranging from 13 to 50 feet. Both crewed and bare-boat charters are available by the day or hour. The center also offers sailing instruction for all levels of experience.

ROLLER SKATING

Beach Rentals, 8 W. Cabrillo Blvd. (tel. 805/963-2524), rents conventional roller skates as well as Rollerblade in-line skates. The charge of $5 per hour includes wrist and knee pads.

SPORT FISHING, DIVING & WHALE WATCHING

Sea Landing, at the foot of Bath Street and Cabrillo Boulevard (tel. 805/963-3564), makes regular sport fishing runs from specialized boats. They also offer a wide variety of other fishing and diving cruises. All boats are equipped with a stocked galley (food and drink served on board), and rental rods and tackle are available. Rates vary according to excursion, and reservations are recommended.

Whale-watching cruises are offered from February to the end of April, when the California Gray Whale makes its migratory journey from Baja, Mexico, to Alaska. Whale tours cost $20 for adults, $10 for children, and sightings of large marine mammals are guaranteed.

SHOPPING

State Street from the beach to Victoria Street is the city's chief commercial thoroughfare, and has the largest concentration of shops. Although many of the stores here specialize in T-shirts and postcards, there are a number of boutiques as well. The best way to become familiar with the area is to walk; the entire stretch is less than 1 mile. If you get tired, hop on one of the city's free electric shuttle buses that run up and down State Street at regular intervals.

PASEO NUEVO, State Street and Canon Perdido Street.
Opened in mid-1990, this Spanish-style shopping mall in the heart of downtown is anchored by Nordstrom and The Broadway, two West Coast–based department stores. Between these giant stores are smaller chain shops like The Sharper Image, Brentano's bookshop, and Express clothing store.

EL PASEO, 814 State St.
A picturesque shopping arcade, El Paseo is lined with stone

walkways reminiscent of an old street in Spain. Built around the 1827 original adobe home of Spanish-born Presidio Commandante José de la Guerra, the mall is lined with charming shops and art galleries, each of which is worth a look.

BRINKERHOFF AVENUE, off Cota Street, between Chapala and De La Vina Streets.

Santa Barbara's "antique alley" is packed with Victorian antique shops selling quilts, antique china, Early American furnishings, jewelry, orientalia, unusual memorabilia, bric-a-brac, and interesting junk. Most shops are open Tuesday through Sunday from 11am to 5pm.

EVENING ENTERTAINMENT

THEATERS

CENTER STAGE THEATER, Chapala Street and De La Guerra Street, upstairs at Paseo Nuevo. Tel. 805/963-0408.

The city's newest stage is a "black box" theater that can transform seating and sets into innumerable configurations. It's an intimate space that is often booked by local talent for plays, musical performances, and comedy. Call to see what's scheduled while you're in town. Ticket prices range from $6 to $12. The box office is open Tuesday through Sunday from noon to 5:30pm and one hour before showtime.

LOBERO THEATER, 33 E. Canon Perdido St. Tel. 805/963-0761.

Built by Italian immigrant Giuseppi Lobero in 1872, Santa Barbara's largest playhouse bankrupted its owner and quickly fell into disrepair. Rebuilt in 1924, the beautiful Lobero has struggled from season to season, boasting a spotty career at best. Many famous actors and actresses have performed here, including Lionel Barrymore, Edward G. Robinson, Clark Gable, Robert Young, Boris Karloff, and Betty Grable as well as such concert luminaries as Andrés Segovia, Arthur Rubinstein, Igor Stravinsky, and Leopold Stokowski. More recent productions have included the Martha Graham Dance Company.

The theater is home to the Santa Barbara Civic Light Opera, an excellent musical theater troupe that usually stages a repertoire of four plays from September to June. A wide variety of other productions are also offered throughout the year. Call the theater to find out what's on during your stay. Tickets usually cost about $25. The box office is open during the summer Monday through Saturday from noon to 5pm; during the winter it is open Monday through Friday from 10am to 5:30pm and Saturday from 10am to 5pm.

ARLINGTON THEATER, 1317 State St. Tel. 805/963-4408.

Now primarily a movie theater, the Arlington regularly augments its film schedule with big-name theater and musical performances. The theater's interior is designed to look like an outdoor Spanish plaza, complete with trompe l'oeil artwork and a shimmering ceiling that winks like thousands of stars. The ornate theater, opened in 1931 at the birth of the talking-picture era, quickly became Hollywood's testing ground for unreleased movies; big stars flocked to Santa Barbara to monitor audience reaction at sneak previews. Tickets cost from $7 to $40. The box office is open Monday through Friday from 11am to 5:30pm and Saturday and Sunday from 9am to 4pm.

EARL WARREN SHOWGROUNDS, Las Positas Road and U.S. 101. Tel. 805/687-0766.

Whether it be a rodeo, circus, or factory outlet sale, something's always happening at this indoor/outdoor convention center. Banquets, antiques shows, barbecues, rummage sales, flower shows, music festivals, horse shows, dances, and cat shows are just some of the regular annual offerings. Call to find out what's planned while you're in town. Entry fees range from free to $20, and opening times vary for each event.

INDEX

GENERAL INFORMATION

SIGHTS & ATTRACTIONS

LOS ANGELES

EXCURSION AREAS

NOTE: An asterisk (*) after an attraction indicates that the attraction is an author's personal favorite.

ACCOMMODATIONS

LOS ANGELES

KEY TO ABBREVIATIONS: *E* = Expensive; *I* = Inexpensive; *M* = Moderately priced; *VE* = Very Expensive; *$* = Super-Special Value; * = An Author's Personal Favorite.

EXCURSION AREAS

RESTAURANTS

LOS ANGELES

KEY TO ABBREVIATIONS: *E* = Expensive; *I* = Inexpensive; *M* = Moderately priced; *VE* = Very Expensive; *$* = Super-Special Value; * = An Author's Personal Favorite.

EXCURSION AREAS

Now Save Money on All Your Travels by Joining
FROMMER'S ™ TRAVEL BOOK CLUB
The World's Best Travel Guides at Membership Prices

FROMMER'S TRAVEL BOOK CLUB is your ticket to successful travel! Open up a world of travel information and simplify your travel planning when you join ranks with thousands of value-conscious travelers who are members of the FROMMER'S TRAVEL BOOK CLUB. Join today and you'll be entitled to all the privileges that come from belonging to the club that offers you travel guides for less to more than 100 destinations worldwide. Annual membership is only $25 (U.S.) or $35 (Canada and all foreign).

The Advantages of Membership

1. Your choice of three free FROMMER'S TRAVEL GUIDES. You can pick two from our FROMMER'S COUNTRY and REGIONAL GUIDES (listed under Comprehensive, $-A-Day, and Family) and one from our FROMMER'S CITY GUIDES (listed under City and City $-A-Day).
2. Your own subscription to **TRIPS & TRAVEL** quarterly newsletter.
3. You're entitled to a **30% discount** on your order of any additional books offered by FROMMER'S TRAVEL BOOK CLUB.
4. You're offered (at a small additional fee) our **Domestic Trip Routing Kits.**

Our quarterly newsletter **TRIPS & TRAVEL** offers practical information on the best buys in travel, the "hottest" vacation spots, the latest travel trends, world-class events and much, much more.

Our **Domestic Trip Routing Kits** are available for any North American destination. We'll send you a detailed map highlighting the best route to take to your destination—you can request direct or scenic routes.

Here's all you have to do to join:
Send in your membership fee of $25 ($35 Canada and foreign) with your name and address on the form below along with your selections as part of your membership package to FROMMER'S TRAVEL BOOK CLUB, P.O. Box 473, Mt. Morris, IL 61054-0473. Remember to check off 2 FROMMER'S COUNTRY and REGIONAL GUIDES and 1 FROMMER'S CITY GUIDE on the pages following.

If you would like to order additional books, please select the books you would like and send a check for the total amount (please add sales tax in the states noted below), plus $2 per book for shipping and handling ($3 per book for all foreign orders) to:

FROMMER'S TRAVEL BOOK CLUB
P.O. Box 473
Mt. Morris, IL 61054-0473
1-815-734-1104

[ ] YES. I want to take advantage of this opportunity to join FROM-MER'S TRAVEL BOOK CLUB.
[ ] My check is enclosed. Dollar amount enclosed_____*
                (all payments in U.S. funds only)

Name_____

Address_____

City_____ State_____ Zip_____

To ensure that all orders are processed efficiently, please apply sales tax in the following areas: CA, CT, FL, IL, NJ, NY, TN, WA, and CANADA.

*With membership, shipping and handling will be paid by FROMMER'S TRAVEL BOOK CLUB for the three free books you select as part of your membership. Please add $2 per book for shipping and handling for any additional books purchased ($3 per book for all foreign orders).

Allow 4-6 weeks for delivery. Prices of books, membership fee, and publication dates are subject to change without notice.

Please Send Me the Books Checked Below

FROMMER'S COMPREHENSIVE GUIDES
(Guides listing facilities from budget to deluxe, with emphasis on the medium-priced)

	Retail Price	Code		Retail Price	Code
☐ Acapulco/Ixtapa/Taxco 1993–94	$15.00	C120	☐ Jamaica/Barbados 1993–94	$15.00	C105
☐ Alaska 1990–91	$15.00	C001	☐ Japan 1992–93	$19.00	C020
☐ Arizona 1993–94	$18.00	C101	☐ Morocco 1992–93	$18.00	C021
☐ Australia 1992–93	$18.00	C002	☐ Nepal 1992–93	$18.00	C038
☐ Austria 1993–94	$19.00	C119	☐ New England 1993	$17.00	C114
☐ Austria/Hungary 1991–92	$15.00	C003	☐ New Mexico 1993–94	$15.00	C117
☐ Belgium/Holland/ Luxembourg 1993–94	$18.00	C106	☐ New York State 1992–93	$19.00	C025
☐ Bermuda/Bahamas 1992–93	$17.00	C005	☐ Northwest 1991–92	$17.00	C026
☐ Brazil, 3rd Edition	$20.00	C111	☐ Portugal 1992–93	$16.00	C027
☐ California 1993	$18.00	C112	☐ Puerto Rico 1993–94	$15.00	C103
☐ Canada 1992–93	$18.00	C009	☐ Puerto Vallarta/ Manzanillo/ Guadalajara 1992–93	$14.00	C028
☐ Caribbean 1993	$18.00	C102	☐ Scandinavia 1993–94	$19.00	C118
☐ Carolinas/Georgia 1992–93	$17.00	C034	☐ Scotland 1992–93	$16.00	C040
☐ Colorado 1993–94	$16.00	C100	☐ Skiing Europe 1989–90	$15.00	C030
☐ Cruises 1993–94	$19.00	C107	☐ South Pacific 1992–93	$20.00	C031
☐ DE/MD/PA & NJ Shore 1992–93	$19.00	C012	☐ Spain 1993–94	$19.00	C115
☐ Egypt 1990–91	$15.00	C013	☐ Switzerland/ Liechtenstein 1992–93	$19.00	C032
☐ England 1993	$18.00	C109	☐ Thailand 1992–93	$20.00	C033
☐ Florida 1993	$18.00	C104	☐ U.S.A. 1993–94	$19.00	C116
☐ France 1992–93	$20.00	C017	☐ Virgin Islands 1992–93	$13.00	C036
☐ Germany 1993	$19.00	C108	☐ Virginia 1992–93	$14.00	C037
☐ Italy 1993	$19.00	C113	☐ Yucatán 1993–94	$18.00	C110

FROMMER'S $-A-DAY GUIDES
(Guides to low-cost tourist accommodations and facilities)

	Retail Price	Code		Retail Price	Code
☐ Australia on $45 1993–94	$18.00	D102	☐ Israel on $45 1993–94	$18.00	D101
☐ Costa Rica/ Guatemala/Belize on $35 1993–94	$17.00	D108	☐ Mexico on $50 1993	$19.00	D105
			☐ New York on $70 1992–93	$16.00	D016
☐ Eastern Europe on $25 1991–92	$17.00	D005	☐ New Zealand on $45 1993–94	$18.00	D103
☐ England on $60 1993	$18.00	D107	☐ Scotland/Wales on $50 1992–93	$18.00	D019
☐ Europe on $45 1993	$19.00	D106	☐ South America on $40 1993–94	$19.00	D109
☐ Greece on $45 1993–94	$19.00	D100			
☐ Hawaii on $75 1993	$19.00	D104	☐ Turkey on $40 1992–93	$22.00	D023
☐ India on $40 1992–93	$20.00	D010	☐ Washington, D.C. on $40 1992–93	$17.00	D024
☐ Ireland on $40 1992–93	$17.00	D011			

FROMMER'S CITY $-A-DAY GUIDES
(Pocket-size guides with an emphasis on low-cost tourist accommodations and facilities)

	Retail Price	Code		Retail Price	Code
☐ Berlin on $40 1992–93	$12.00	D002	☐ Madrid on $50 1992–93	$13.00	D014
☐ Copenhagen on $50 1992–93	$12.00	D003	☐ Paris on $45 1992–93	$12.00	D018
☐ London on $45 1992–93	$12.00	D013	☐ Stockholm on $50 1992–93	$13.00	D022

FROMMER'S TOURING GUIDES
(Color-illustrated guides that include walking tours, cultural and historic sights, and practical information)

	Retail Price	Code		Retail Price	Code
☐ Amsterdam	$11.00	T001	☐ New York	$11.00	T008
☐ Barcelona	$14.00	T015	☐ Rome	$11.00	T010
☐ Brazil	$11.00	T003	☐ Scotland	$10.00	T011
☐ Florence	$ 9.00	T005	☐ Sicily	$15.00	T017
☐ Hong Kong/Singapore/ Macau	$11.00	T006	☐ Thailand	$13.00	T012
			☐ Tokyo	$15.00	T016
☐ Kenya	$14.00	T018	☐ Venice	$ 9.00	T014
☐ London	$13.00	T007			

FROMMER'S FAMILY GUIDES

	Retail Price	Code		Retail Price	Code
☐ California with Kids	$17.00	F001	☐ San Francisco with Kids	$17.00	F004
☐ Los Angeles with Kids	$17.00	F002			
☐ New York City with Kids	$18.00	F003	☐ Washington, D.C. with Kids	$17.00	F005

FROMMER'S CITY GUIDES
(Pocket-size guides to sightseeing and tourist accommodations and facilities in all price ranges)

	Retail Price	Code		Retail Price	Code
☐ Amsterdam 1993–94	$13.00	S110	☐ Minneapolis/St. Paul, 3rd Edition	$13.00	S119
☐ Athens, 9th Edition	$13.00	S114			
☐ Atlanta 1993–94	$13.00	S112	☐ Montréal/Québec City 1993–94	$13.00	S125
☐ Atlantic City/Cape May 1991–92	$ 9.00	S004	☐ New Orleans 1993–94	$13.00	S103
☐ Bangkok 1992–93	$13.00	S005	☐ New York 1993	$13.00	S120
☐ Barcelona/Majorca/ Minorca/Ibiza 1993–94	$13.00	S115	☐ Orlando 1993	$13.00	S101
			☐ Paris 1993–94	$13.00	S109
☐ Berlin 1993–94	$13.00	S116	☐ Philadelphia 1993–94	$13.00	S113
☐ Boston 1993–94	$13.00	S117	☐ Rio 1991–92	$ 9.00	S029
☐ Cancún/Cozumel/ Yucatán 1991–92	$ 9.00	S010	☐ Rome 1993–94	$13.00	S111
			☐ Salt Lake City 1991–92	$ 9.00	S031
☐ Chicago 1993–94	$13.00	S122			
☐ Denver/Boulder/ Colorado Springs 1990–91	$ 8.00	S012	☐ San Diego 1993–94	$13.00	S107
			☐ San Francisco 1993	$13.00	S104
			☐ Santa Fe/Taos/ Albuquerque 1993–94	$13.00	S108
☐ Dublin 1993–94	$13.00	S128	☐ Seattle/Portland 1992– 93	$12.00	S035
☐ Hawaii 1992	$12.00	S014			
☐ Hong Kong 1992–93	$12.00	S015	☐ St. Louis/Kansas City 1993–94	$13.00	S127
☐ Honolulu/Oahu 1993	$13.00	S106			
☐ Las Vegas 1993–94	$13.00	S121	☐ Sydney 1993–94	$13.00	S129
☐ Lisbon/Madrid/Costa del Sol 1991–92	$ 9.00	S017	☐ Tampa/St. Petersburg 1993–94	$13.00	S105
☐ London 1993	$13.00	S100	☐ Tokyo 1992–93	$13.00	S039
☐ Los Angeles 1993–94	$13.00	S123	☐ Toronto 1993–94	$13.00	S126
☐ Madrid/Costa del Sol 1993–94	$13.00	S124	☐ Vancouver/Victoria 1990–91	$ 8.00	S041
☐ Mexico City/Acapulco 1991–92	$ 9.00	S020	☐ Washington, D.C. 1993	$13.00	S102
☐ Miami 1993–94	$13.00	S118			

Other Titles Available at Membership Prices

SPECIAL EDITIONS

	Retail Price	Code		Retail Price	Code
☐ Bed & Breakfast North America	$15.00	P002	☐ Where to Stay U.S.A.	$14.00	P015
☐ Caribbean Hideaways	$16.00	P005			
☐ Marilyn Wood's Wonderful Weekends (within a 250-mile radius of NYC)	$12.00	P017			

GAULT MILLAU'S "BEST OF" GUIDES
(The only guides that distinguish the truly superlative from the merely overrated)

	Retail Price	Code		Retail Price	Code
☐ Chicago	$16.00	G002	☐ New England	$16.00	G010
☐ Florida	$17.00	G003	☐ New Orleans	$17.00	G011
☐ France	$17.00	G004	☐ New York	$17.00	G012
☐ Germany	$18.00	G018	☐ Paris	$17.00	G013
☐ Hawaii	$17.00	G006	☐ San Francisco	$17.00	G014
☐ Hong Kong	$17.00	G007	☐ Thailand	$18.00	G019
☐ London	$17.00	G009	☐ Toronto	$17.00	G020
☐ Los Angeles	$17.00	G005	☐ Washington, D.C.	$17.00	G017

THE REAL GUIDES
(Opinionated, politically aware guides for youthful budget-minded travelers)

	Retail Price	Code		Retail Price	Code
☐ Able to Travel	$20.00	R112	☐ Kenya	$12.95	R015
☐ Amsterdam	$13.00	R100	☐ Mexico	$11.95	R016
☐ Barcelona	$13.00	R101	☐ Morocco	$14.00	R017
☐ Belgium/Holland/ Luxembourg	$16.00	R031	☐ Nepal	$14.00	R018
			☐ New York	$13.00	R019
☐ Berlin	$11.95	R002	☐ Paris	$13.00	R020
☐ Brazil	$13.95	R003	☐ Peru	$12.95	R021
☐ California & the West Coast	$17.00	R121	☐ Poland	$13.95	R022
			☐ Portugal	$15.00	R023
☐ Canada	$15.00	R103	☐ Prague	$15.00	R113
☐ Czechoslovakia	$14.00	R005	☐ San Francisco & the Bay Area	$11.95	R024
☐ Egypt	$19.00	R105			
☐ Europe	$18.00	R122	☐ Scandinavia	$14.95	R025
☐ Florida	$14.00	R006	☐ Spain	$16.00	R026
☐ France	$18.00	R106	☐ Thailand	$17.00	R119
☐ Germany	$18.00	R107	☐ Tunisia	$17.00	R115
☐ Greece	$18.00	R108	☐ Turkey	$13.95	R027
☐ Guatemala/Belize	$14.00	R010	☐ U.S.A.	$18.00	R117
☐ Hong Kong/Macau	$11.95	R011	☐ Venice	$11.95	R028
☐ Hungary	$14.00	R118	☐ Women Travel	$12.95	R029
☐ Ireland	$17.00	R120	☐ Yugoslavia	$12.95	R030
☐ Italy	$13.95	R014			